生态文明教育中学校本课程
Middle-school Based Curriculum on Ecological Civilization Education

中 国 湿 地
Wetlands in China

中 国 绿 色 碳 汇 基 金 会
北京第二外国语学院附属中学 编写

Compiled by China Green Carbon Foundation
The High School Affiliated to Beijing International Studies University

科学普及出版社
·北 京·

图书在版编目（CIP）数据

中国湿地：汉、英 / 中国绿色碳汇基金会，北京第二外国语学院
附属中学编写． — 北京：科学普及出版社．　2016.1
生态文明教育中学校本课程
ISBN 978-7-110-09188-3

Ⅰ．①中… Ⅱ．①中… ②北… Ⅲ．①沼泽化地－中国－中学－
教材－汉、英 Ⅳ．① G634.931

中国版本图书馆 CIP 数据核字（2015）第 151813 号

策划编辑	徐扬科
责任编辑	林　然
责任校对	何士如
责任印制	马宇晨
装帧设计	北京市青少年音像出版社设计部

出版发行	科学普及出版社
地　　址	北京市海淀区中关村南大街 16 号
邮　　编	100081
发行电话	010-62103130
传　　真	010-62179148
投稿电话	010-62176522
网　　址	http://www.cspbooks.com.cn

开　　本	787mm×1092mm　1/16
字　　数	300 千字
印　　张	14
版　　次	2016 年 1 月第 1 版
印　　次	2016 年 1 月第 1 次印刷
印　　刷	廊坊飞腾印刷包装有限公司

书　　号	ISBN 978-7-110-09188-3/G·3852
定　　价	45.00 元

编 委 会
Editorial Board

序　言
Foreword

为普及和宣传湿地知识，启发广大中学生对自然和生态保护的兴趣，培养广大中学生生态保护意识，由中国绿色碳汇基金会、北京第二外国语学院附属中学和中国林业科学研究院湿地研究所合作组织编写了《中国湿地》一书。

The book *Wetlands in China* was compiled as a joint effort by the China Green Carbon Foundation, the High School Affiliated to Beijing International Studies University and the Institute of Wetland Research of the Chinese Academy of Forestry. Its aim is to spread and publicize knowledge about wetlands throughout high schools in China, inspire high school students to become interested in nature and ecological protection, and enhance their awareness of ecological protection.

《中国湿地》详尽且生动地介绍了湿地的相关知识，可以激发青少年爱护湿地、保护湿地的积极性和主动性，同时也对其他读者具有普适性。该书有助于提高青少年乃至全民的湿地保护意识，更好地促进中国湿地保护工作的健康发展。该书展示了湿地的丰富多样、秀美壮丽，也介绍了湿地的生态功能及不合理利用给湿地带来的伤害，最后提出了可行的湿保护管理措施。

Thanks to its vivid presentation of information on wetlands, *Wetlands in China* will not only inspire teenagers to be curious about wetlands and care about their protection, but will also be a good book for ordinary readers as well. It will help efforts to improve awareness of wetland protection amongst teenagers and common readers alike; and, it will make a contribution to the broad effort to protect wetlands in China. Not only does this book reveal to teenagers the diversity and beauty of wetlands, but it also describes the problems caused by their irrational use by human beings. In the end, the book calls on teenagers to join in the protection of wetlands through various protective and managerial measures.

《中国湿地》文字深入浅出，活泼生动，并辅助以漫画、照片等形象化的语言使湿地知识更直观、更吸引人。如书中将湿地的供水功能和调节小气候的功能形象地比作"饮水机"和"空调器"，将湿地水资源匮乏和富营养化等问题比作"贫血"和"高血脂"等，可以更好地被读者理解，进而引发思考。书中的"想一想""试一试"，引导读者思考、践行，使读者不仅"读到"湿地，更"看到""走进"湿地，真正地"了解湿地"。

Wetlands in China explains difficult concepts in a simple language and through wise use of cartoons and pictures, thereby making wetland knowledge easily accessible and interesting for high school students. For example, wetland functions such as supplying water and regulating the climate are vividly compared to those fulfilled by a water dispenser and air conditioner. Problems related to water resource deficiencies and eutrophication suffered by wetlands are likened to anemia and hyperlipidemia. Such vivid expressions are not only easy for readers to understand, but are likely to provoke them to contemplation. What's more, columns like *Give This Some Thought* and *Give It A Try* are designed to encourage teenagers to not only read, but experience wetlands first-hand.

本书选材科学严谨，图文并茂，形象生动，集科学性、知识性和趣味性于一体，符合中学生认知规律，是一部很好的对中学生进行湿地知识普及的教学用书，对帮助中学生认识了解自然、热爱保护自然，引导中学生关注生态、保护环境，积极参与力所能及的保护地球家园的活动具有重要的指导意义。

Featuring easy-to-understand language and vivid and intuitive pictures, *Wetlands in China* successfully turns its scientifically rigorous contents into a well-organized collection of information specially tailored to the reading and cognitive habits of high school students. It is widely believed that this excellent textbook on wetland education will play an important role in helping high school students to understand, love, and protect nature; and, leading them to care about ecological civilization, protect our shared environment, and take part in activities beneficial to the protection of our Earth Mother.

中国科学院院士
Academician of the Chinese Academy of Sciences

中国林科院研究员
Professor of the Chinese Academy of Forestry

2014 年 10 月 21 日

Jiang Youxu
October 21, 2014

前　言
Preface

　　湿地与森林、海洋一起被称为全球三大生态系统，在供水、防洪、净化和调节气候、能源供给等方面发挥不可替代作用，同时也遭受着严重的破坏与威胁。与发达国家相比，我国的湿地保护工作起步较晚，知识的普及不够广泛深入，许多公众尚不清楚什么是湿地，以及为什么要保护湿地。为培养青少年生态文明意识，树立生态文明理念，在中学生中普及和宣传湿地保护知识，中国绿色碳汇基金会、北京第二外国语学院附属中学和中国林业科学研究院湿地研究所合作编写了《中国湿地》一书，作为中学生生态文明教育校本课程教材。

Wetlands, together with forests and oceans constitute the three major ecosystems of the Earth, and play an indispensible role in performing some of our planet's most important functions. These include supplying water, preventing floods, purifying water, adjusting the climate, and supplying energy, but now wetlands are being seriously damaged and confronted with many kinds of threats. Not only does China fall behind advanced countries in terms of wetland protection, but it has a long way to go in providing mass education in related knowledge. Many people in the nation still have no idea what wetlands are and why we should protect them. To enhance awareness of ecological civilization among Chinese youth and spread knowledge about wetland protection across high schools in China, the China Green Carbon Foundation, the High School Affiliated to Beijing International Studies University, and the Institute of Wetland Research of the Chinese Academy of Forestry have jointly compiled *Wetlands in China* as a high school textbook for education in ecological civilization.

　　本书分为4章，较为详尽地介绍了湿地的定义、类型、组成、分布、功能、湿地面临的危机、湿地保护管理等多方面相关知识，阐述了湿地对人类生存环境的重要性，湿地面临的各种威胁和保护湿地的主要措施，以及我们作出的积极努力。对中学生学习湿地科学和树立湿地保护理念具有十分积极的现实意义。为便于课堂教学和学生研讨，本书章节编写结构紧紧围绕教学主题，设计了学习日志、学海拾贝、拓展阅读、想一想、试一试等多个栏目，每个课题可根据需要随机选用这些栏目。本书的内容只是为中学生认识湿地开启了一扇门，以期学生们能够对湿地科学与管理有较为全面的认识，树立良好的生态文明理念，以更多的自觉性去认识探究自然。

Composed of four chapters, this book aims to give students a fairly comprehensive knowledge of what there is to know about wetlands as a kind of natural resource, including the definition, types, composition, distribution, the various functions they play, the crisis they are now facing, and wetland protection management. Furthermore, the book aims to bring home to students, important ideas about wetlands such as their significance to man's living environment, the various kinds of threats they are now confronted with, the major protective measures currently in use, and what has already been done in protecting wetlands. This book is expected to be of great assistance to high school students as they seek to learn knowledge about wetlands and enhance their wetland protection awareness. To facilitate classroom teaching and discussions, various columns such as *Notebook, Pearls of Knowledge, Extra Reading Material, Give This Some Thought,* and *Give It A Try* have been incorporated to give prominence to highlights in each section. Teachers can select columns at will to suit their own teaching needs. The book is meant to be a resource that introduces high school students to wetlands as a science, with the aim of letting them gain a comprehensive, but very superficial, knowledge of wetlands and their management. This book is expected to inspire these students to hold a positive attitude toward ecological civilization and explore nature with greater enthusiasm.

因时间仓促，加之水平有限，书中难免有不当之处，敬请批评指正。

Because it was compiled within a rather short period of time, and we are not as capable as we would want ourselves to be as editors, this book is bound to contain some errors. Your suggestion and comments will be highly appreciated.

编 者

Editors

2014 年 7 月 20 日

July 20, 2014

目　　录
Table of Contents

第一章 生命的摇篮 ⋯⋯⋯⋯⋯⋯⋯⋯⋯⋯⋯⋯⋯⋯⋯⋯⋯⋯⋯⋯⋯⋯⋯ **1**
Chapter Ⅰ　The Cradle of Life ⋯⋯⋯⋯⋯⋯⋯⋯⋯⋯⋯⋯⋯⋯⋯ 1

第一节　什么是湿地 ⋯⋯⋯⋯⋯⋯⋯⋯⋯⋯⋯⋯⋯⋯⋯⋯⋯⋯⋯⋯ 1
Section I　What are Wetlands? ⋯⋯⋯⋯⋯⋯⋯⋯⋯⋯⋯⋯⋯⋯⋯ 1

第二节　湿地的类型 ⋯⋯⋯⋯⋯⋯⋯⋯⋯⋯⋯⋯⋯⋯⋯⋯⋯⋯⋯⋯ 13
Section II　Type of Wetlands ⋯⋯⋯⋯⋯⋯⋯⋯⋯⋯⋯⋯⋯⋯⋯ 13

第三节　湿地的生态功能 ⋯⋯⋯⋯⋯⋯⋯⋯⋯⋯⋯⋯⋯⋯⋯⋯⋯ 31
Section III　Ecological Services of Wetlands ⋯⋯⋯⋯⋯⋯⋯ 31

参考文献 ⋯⋯⋯⋯⋯⋯⋯⋯⋯⋯⋯⋯⋯⋯⋯⋯⋯⋯⋯⋯⋯⋯⋯⋯ 47
References ⋯⋯⋯⋯⋯⋯⋯⋯⋯⋯⋯⋯⋯⋯⋯⋯⋯⋯⋯⋯⋯⋯⋯ 47

第二章 旅行者日志 ⋯⋯⋯⋯⋯⋯⋯⋯⋯⋯⋯⋯⋯⋯⋯⋯⋯⋯⋯⋯⋯ **49**
Chapte Ⅱ　Diary of Backpacker ⋯⋯⋯⋯⋯⋯⋯⋯⋯⋯⋯⋯⋯ 49

第一节　中国湿地概览 ⋯⋯⋯⋯⋯⋯⋯⋯⋯⋯⋯⋯⋯⋯⋯⋯⋯⋯ 49
Section I　Overview of Wetlands in China ⋯⋯⋯⋯⋯⋯⋯⋯ 49

第二节　绚烂多彩的湿地植物 ⋯⋯⋯⋯⋯⋯⋯⋯⋯⋯⋯⋯⋯⋯ 65
Section II　Colorful Wetland Plant ⋯⋯⋯⋯⋯⋯⋯⋯⋯⋯⋯ 65

第三节　种类繁多的湿地动物 ⋯⋯⋯⋯⋯⋯⋯⋯⋯⋯⋯⋯⋯⋯ 99
Section III　Diversified Wetland Animals ⋯⋯⋯⋯⋯⋯⋯⋯ 99

参考文献 ⋯⋯⋯⋯⋯⋯⋯⋯⋯⋯⋯⋯⋯⋯⋯⋯⋯⋯⋯⋯⋯⋯⋯ 115
References ⋯⋯⋯⋯⋯⋯⋯⋯⋯⋯⋯⋯⋯⋯⋯⋯⋯⋯⋯⋯⋯⋯ 115

第三章 湿地的倾诉 ⋯⋯⋯⋯⋯⋯⋯⋯⋯⋯⋯⋯⋯⋯⋯⋯⋯⋯⋯⋯ **116**
Chapter Ⅲ　Wetlands' Sadness ⋯⋯⋯⋯⋯⋯⋯⋯⋯⋯⋯⋯⋯ 116

第一节　数据告诉我们中国湿地的现状 ⋯⋯⋯⋯⋯⋯⋯⋯ 116
Section I　Data Tell Us The Status Quo of China's Wetlands ⋯⋯ 116

第二节　现状背后的原因 ⋯⋯⋯⋯⋯⋯⋯⋯⋯⋯⋯⋯⋯⋯⋯ 127
Section II　Potential Damage-causing Factors ⋯⋯⋯⋯⋯⋯ 127

第三节 病症的表象 ························· 139
Section III Symptoms ························· 139

参考文献 ····································· 152
References ··································· 152

第四章 保护湿地 我们在行动 ··········· **155**
Chapter Ⅳ Wetland Protection: We Are in Action ··········· **155**

第一节 湿地保护公约及相关内容 ········· 155
Section I International Conventions on Wetland Protection and Related Information ···· 155

第二节 湿地保护措施 ··················· 176
Section II Measures for Wetland Protection ··········· 176

第三节 中学生：我为湿地添光彩 ········· 183
Section III Middle School Students: Let's Make Due Contributions to Wetland Protection ··········· 183

参考文献 ····································· 193
References ··································· 193

附录 1 ································· 194
Appendix 1 ······························· 194

附录 2 ································· 199
Appendix 2 ······························· 199

附录 3 ································· 210
Appendix 3 ······························· 210

第一章　生命的摇篮
Chapter Ⅰ　The Cradle of Life

　　说起湿地，我们会不由得想起"出淤泥而不染"的荷花、烟波浩渺的芦苇荡、优雅长寿的丹顶鹤等。湿地不仅有美丽壮观的景象和种类繁多的生物，还有诸如"地球之肾""生命的摇篮""物种基因库"等美誉。那么究竟什么是湿地呢？滚滚而逝的江河、潺潺流过的小溪、神秘幽静的沼泽、明媚灿烂的沙滩、奇秀坚挺的红树林、郁郁葱葱的水稻田……你知道其实这些都是湿地景观吗？

When it comes to wetlands, the view of pure lotus, mist-covered reed marsh, and long-lived red-crowned cranes spring to mind. As home to splendid scenery and various living creatures, wetlands are acclaimed as "the Kidneys of the Earth", "the Cradle of Life", and "the Gene Bank of Species". Then, what are wetlands? Do you know that all the beautiful sceneries such as billowing rivers, murmuring creeks, mysteriously tranquil marshes, bright sandy beaches, towering mangrove forests, and lush paddy fields are all wetlands?

第一节　什么是湿地
Section Ⅰ　What are Wetlands?

学习日志
Notebook

　　中国湿地种类繁多，覆盖范围广泛，无论是在寒带、温带、热带，还是平原、山地、高原，都能看到多种多样的湿地。请观察图片完成以下问题。

Various categories of wetlands can be seen across China. No matter if you are in the frigid zone, temperate zone, tropical zone, or on plains, mountains or highlands, you will come across highly diversified wetlands. Please answer the following questions after careful observation of the pictures shown below.

请你完成以下问题吧!

Now, please answer the following questions.

1. 请观察这几幅图后，完成下面的湿地信息表。

1. Please observe the above pictures carefully, and fill in the form.

(张曼胤摄)

图 1.1 河流
Picture 1.1 River
(Photo by Zhang Manyin)

(李伟摄)

图 1.2 湖泊
Picture 1.2 Lake (Photo by Li Wei)

(李伟摄)

图 1.3 沼泽
Picture 1.3 Marsh (Photo by Li Wei)

(俞肖剑摄)

图 1.4 滨海
Picture 1.4 Seaside
(Photo by Yu Xiaojian)

(李伟摄)

图 1.5 水稻田
Picture 1.5 Paddy Field
(Photo by Li Wei)

湿地信息表

Information Form of Wetlands

图序号 Serial number	各自的特点 Features of each type of body of water	共同点 Common features
1 河流 1 River		
2 湖泊 2 Lake		
3 沼泽 3 Marsh		
4 滨海 4 Costal		
5 水稻田 5 Paddy field		

2. 根据湿地图片的观察和上表的填写，试着用一句话来表述什么是湿地。

2. Please describe wetlands in one sentence based on your observation of such pictures and the form above filled up by you.

学海拾贝
Pearls of Knowledge

一、湿地的概念
I. Concept of Wetlands

湿地（wetlands），在我国古代就已经有了相关的描述，那时候我们称湿地为"薮（sǒu）""泽"或"海"，专指水草茂密的湖泽。早在春秋时期，我们的祖先就开始通过围湖造田来利用湿地资源。

Wetlands were already recorded by our ancestors in ancient times. Back then, wetlands were termed simply as "lake", "pond" or "sea"; and specially referred to lakes covered with dense water plants. Our ancestors started to make good use of wetlands by turning lakes into agricultural fields, as early as the Spring and Autumn Period.

关于湿地的概念，不同的科学家，比如水文学家、地质学家、土壤学家和植物学家，从各自学科的角度出发提出过大约 100 种定义。在这里，我们主要简单了解一下从狭义与广义角度出发对湿地的定义。

With respect to the concept of wetlands, there have been about 100 definitions given to them by different hydrologists, geologists, pedologists, and botanists from different academic angles. Now, we would like to introduce you the concept of wetlands from both the narrow and the broad sense.

狭义的湿地定义认为湿地是一类生态系统，这一生态系统需要具备 3 个主要要素：湿地生物、土壤和水文。此定义强调 3 个要素的相互作用，并要求其共同存在。也就是说，不管是天落龙涎、与银河争流的千尺悬瀑，还是浩浩汤汤、横无际涯的洞庭一湖，抑或光影徘徊、澄如明镜的半亩方塘，皆为湿地。除此外，那承载着长征历史的漫漫沼泽，孕育过古国文明的滚滚江河，以及那植根海滨的红树林，色彩缤纷的珊瑚礁，洒碧水上的稻田也都是湿地。

In their narrowest sense, wetlands are one kind of ecosystem, constituted by three major elements: wetland creatures, soil and hydrology. These three major elements, as emphasized by the definition, are co-existent and highly interactive. That is to say, all water bodies ranging from cascading waterfalls, and the boundless Dongting Lake, to mirror-like ponds, are all wetlands. In addition, the marshes which witnessed the history of the Long March; the billowing rivers which gave birth to our ancient civilization; the mangrove forests which spread along our southern seashores; the colorful coral reefs; and, rice fields, are all wetlands too.

广义的湿地定义源起于 20 世纪 50 年代，美国鱼类和野生动物保护协会在 1956 年提出："湿地是指被浅水和有时被暂时性或间歇性积水所覆盖的低地，包括沼泽、泥炭地、湿草甸、滨河泛滥地等。"后来于 1971 年 2 月 2 日在伊朗拉姆萨尔签订的《关于特别是作为水禽栖息地的国际重要湿地公约》（*Convention on Wetlands of International Importance Especially as Waterfowl Habitat*），简称《湿地公约》（*The Ramsar Convention on Wetlands*）中，学者们进一步确定了湿地的边界，提出："湿地是指，不问其为天然或人工、长久或暂时的沼泽地、泥炭地或水域地带，带有静止或流动的淡水、半咸水或咸水水体，包括低潮时水深不超过 6 米的水域。"如今，这一概念得到了人们的普遍认可。根据这个定义，湖泊、河流、沼泽、滩地、盐湖、盐沼和海岸带区域的珊瑚礁、海草区、红树林、河口以及水库、鱼塘等都属于湿地，其中，水库、鱼塘属于人工湿地，其余属于天然湿地。

In a much broader sense, originating as a definition in 1950s, wetlands were defined by the United States Fish and Wildlife Conservation Commission in 1956 as "lowland covered by shallow water, and temporary or intermittent hydrops, including marsh, peatland, wet meadow, riverside floodplains, etc." In the Convention on Wetlands of International Importance Especially as Waterfowl Habitat (or the Ramsar Convention on Wetlands for short), which was concluded in the city of Ramsar, Iran on Feb 2, 1971, scholars further defined wetlands as "areas of marsh, fen, peatland or water, whether natural or artificial, permanent or temporary, with water that is static or flowing, fresh, brackish or salt, including areas of marine water the depth of which at low tide does not exceed six metres". Nowadays, this definition is widely recognized throughout the world. Accordingly, lakes, rivers, marshes, bottomlands, salt lakes, salt marshes, coral reefs along the coast, sea grass beds, mangrove forests, estuaries, reservoirs, and fishponds are all considered to be wetlands. Of these, reservoirs and fishponds are constructed, or man-made wetlands, and the others are natural wetlands.

二、湿地的特点
II. Features of Wetlands

湿地生态过程包括湿地土壤—生物—大气中的水循环和水平衡、养分循环、能量流动、微量气体产生、输送和转化、有机物的分解、积累、传输等过程。对这些生态过程的研究需要对湿地的特点有一定的了解。湿地作为一种生态系统，有着森林、海洋生态系统不具有的多种特点，具体体现在以下 4 个方面。

Ecological processes occurring in wetlands include such sub-processes as water circulation, water balance, nutrient circulation, energy flow, generation and transfer and transition of trace gases, decomposition, accumulation and transfer of organic compounds in the wetland physical-biological and chemical system. To conduct sound research into such ecological processes requires a good command of knowledge about the features of wetlands. As a unique ecosystem, wetlands have many features that are not observed in forest and marine ecosystems. Specifically, wetland systems are characterized by the following four features.

1. 生物多样性

1. Biodiversity

湿地是陆地生态系统与海洋生态系统的过渡地带，因此它同时兼具丰富的陆生和水生动植物资源，形成了其他任何单一生态系统都无法比拟的天然基因库和独特的生境。同时，湿地拥有特殊的水文、土壤状况等，这些因素使湿地具备了复杂且完备的动植物群落，对于保护物种、维持生物多样性都具有难以替代的生态价值。

As the transitional zone between terrestrial and marine ecosystems, wetlands are home to a rich variety of terrestrial/aquatic animals and plants alike, forming a natural gene pool and unique eco-environment unparalleled by any other single bio-system. At the same time, wetlands are endowed with unique hydrology and soil conditions, making them home to complex and complete flora and fauna communities – an ecosystem with irreplaceable ecological value in terms of species protection and maintenance of biodiversity.

2. 生态系统脆弱性

2. Eco-vulnerability

湿地水文、土壤、气候相互作用，形成了湿地生态系统的主要因素。每一因素的改变，或多或少的添加都会导致湿地生态系统的变化。此外，湿地生态系统处于陆地和海洋的过渡地带，各种要素之间相互作用强烈，也使湿地生态系统对外力的阻抗作用相对较低。

Wetland ecosystems are the result of complex interactions between hydrology, soil, and climate, and an alteration to any of these constituting elements will lead, more or less, to ecosystem change. In addition, these strong interactions between the constituting elements of wetlands – being in the transitional zone between terrestrial and marine ecosystems – also leave them vulnerable to external forces.

易变性是湿地生态系统脆弱性的特殊表现形态之一，其与湿地水文因素有密切的联系。湿地中水量的变化，使得生态系统在陆地与湿地之间交替变化，这在某种程度上也体现了湿地生态系统的脆弱性。

Volatility is one of the trademarks of vulnerable wetland ecosystems, and is strongly related to hydrological factors in the wetland. Fluctuating water volumes and levels within wetlands determines that wetland ecosystems may irregularly alternate between a terrestrial and an aquatic state. This unique feature of wetlands reflects, to a certain degree, the overall vulnerability of wetland ecosystems.

3. 生产力高效性
3. High Productivity

相对于其他生态系统，湿地生态系统具有较高的初级生产力。1997年美国的 Robert Constanza 等人对全球生态系统的功能和自然资本的价值进行了估算，结果显示，湿地生态系统提供的生态服务功能相当于 49 万亿美元，约占全球生态系统的 14.7%，占全球自然资源总价值的 45%，而值得一提的是，全世界所有湿地面积之和仅占地球陆地面积的 6%。此外，有学者研究指出，湿地生态系统每年平均生产蛋白质 $9g/m^2$，是陆地生态系统的 3.5 倍。

Compared to other ecosystems, wetland systems support high primary productivity. It has been estimated by an American scientist named Robert Constanza, and other scientists, in 1997 that wetland ecosystems contribute the equivalent of USD 49 trillion in eco-services towards the overall value of global ecosystems. This accounted for 45% of the total value of global natural resources. This is all the more remarkable as the total area of all wetlands across the world only comprises 6% of the total global terrestrial area. In addition, it has been pointed out by some scholars, that wetland ecosystem can generate $9g/m^2$ of protein on a yearly basis, a 3.5 times higher volume than that of terrestrial ecosystems.

4. 效益的综合性
4. Comprehensive Benefits

湿地生态系统不仅仅能产生生态效益，如调节气候、净化水质、保存物种等，它还具有一定的经济效益和社会效益。由于湿地生态系统具有丰富的物质资源，使得它可以为工业、农业、能源、医疗业等提供大量生产原料，从而产生巨大的经济效益。同时湿地生态系统拥有丰富的物种和特殊的环境因素，使得它还可以作为物种研究和教育基地以及旅游资源，从而提供极大的社会效益。

In addition to providing such rich ecological benefits as climate regulation, water purification, species maintenance, wetland ecosystem also boasts high economic and social benefits. Thanks to its abundance in various material resources, wetland ecosystem could provide production raw material in great quantity to industry, agriculture, energy, medicineand other sectors, thus bringing about substantial economic benefits to the society. Meanwhile, wetland ecosystem is endowed with rich species and peculiar environmental conditions. It thus can work as premier research and education base on species and precious tourism destination with high social benefits.

图 1.6　湿地生态特征
Picture 1.6　Eco-features of Wetland (Illustration by Sun Baodi)

（孙宝娣绘）

拓展阅读
Extra Reading Material

《湿地公约》
The Ramsar Convention on Wetlands

　　我们都知道候鸟迁徙的现象，迁徙候鸟的停歇地、繁殖地都在湿地里，随着人口的增加、经济的发展，很多湿地遭到破坏并影响到候鸟的生存。为了保护候鸟的栖息地，1971 年 2 月 2 日，在伊朗的拉姆萨尔由各国政府签订了《关于特别是作为水禽栖息地的国际重要湿地公约》（ *Convention on Wetlands of International Importance Especially as Waterfowl Habitat* ），简称《湿地公约》）。在这个公约中给湿地作了这样的定义，即 "湿地是指，不问其为天然或人工、长久或暂时的沼泽地、泥炭地或水域地带，带有静止或流动的淡水、半咸水或咸水水体，包括低潮时水深不超过 6 米的水域。"因此，所有季节性或常年积水地带，包括沼泽、泥炭地、湿草甸、湖泊、河流、洪泛平原、河口三角洲、滩涂、珊瑚礁、红树林、盐沼、低潮时水深不超过 6 米的海岸带以及水稻田、鱼塘、盐田、水库和运河等，均属于湿地范畴。

We all know the phenomenon of bird migration. Wetlands provide important habitats where many migrant birds stop for rest, food and reproduction. The survival of many species of migratory birds has been compromised due to damage to wetlands, along with increasing human populations and the pressures of development of the economy. To protect the habitats of migratory birds, the Convention on Wetlands of International Importance Especially as Waterfowl Habitat (The Ramsar Convention on Wetlands for short) was developed and agreed in the city of Ramsar, Iran on Feb 2, 1971 by governments of many different countries. As defined by the Convention, wetlands refer to "areas of marsh, fen, peatland or water, whether natural or artificial, permanent or temporary, with water that is static or flowing, fresh, brackish or salt, including areas of marine water the depth of which at low tide does not exceed six metres" This includes all areas with seasonal or permanent hydrops, including marshes, peatlands, wet meadows, lakes, rivers, floodplains, fan deltas, the intertidal zone, coral reefs, mangrove forests, salt marshes, the coastal zone with water depths no deeper than 6m at the time of low tide, paddy fields, fishponds, salt pans, reservoirs, canals, etc.

《湿地公约》是全球第一个环境公约，也是世界上当时唯一针对单一生态系统保护缔结的国际性政府间公约。当时仅把湿地作为水鸟栖息地来保护，现在已发展到将"湿地保护与合理利用"的理念作为《湿地公约》的宗旨，这是随着人们对湿地重要性的不断深入认识而转变的。截止 2014 年 10 月，湿地公约已经有 168 个缔约方，中国在1992 年加入《湿地公约》。

The Ramsar Convention on Wetlands is not only the first global environmental convention, but the sole global inter-government convention targeted at protecting one single ecosystem. Back then when the convention was concluded, wetlands were protected only as the habitat of water birds. Now, along with the deepened understanding of the public about the significant role of wetlands, the mission to "protect and reasonably use wetlands" has become the tenet of the Ramsar Convention on Wetlands. As of October 2014, there are 168 contracting parties to the Ramsar Convention on Wetlands, including China, which joined the convention in 1992.

湿地与人类文明
Wetlands and Human Civilization

包括人类在内的任何有机生命形式的产生和发展都源于水，水以各种形式出现，由最初的海洋到河流、湖泊、沼泽等，这些都是湿地的表现形式。

The birth and evolution of all living creatures in the world, including human being, are indispensible from water. Water is stored in various forms like sea, river, lake, marsh, etc. And all these water bodies are wetlands in nature.

　　人类文明的起源和发展也依托于湿地，例如四大文明古国，古代埃及、古代中国、古代巴比伦、古代印度的发源地具有一个共同的特点：文化起源以及人类聚集地都建立在河流的周边或者交汇处，这些地方为人们提供了种植粮食作物所需的肥沃土壤。中国文明的摇篮是黄河与长江，它们共同滋养了中华民族，我们的祖先依傍两条河流创造了灿烂而古老的中华文明。河流充足的水资源和两岸肥沃的土地为农牧业的发展提供了便利条件。古埃及尼罗河每年泛滥后形成的淤泥型河谷湿地，在尼罗河沿岸留下了独特的标记，不但造就了尼罗河沿岸农业的发展，还孕育并铸就古埃及天文学、数学、医学、哲学、建筑学等方面的辉煌。幼发拉底河和底格里斯河共同冲击形成了美索不达米亚平原，该平原是世界上最著名的湿地之一，孕育了无比辉煌的古巴比伦文化。古印度文明主要集中在印度河和恒河流域，恒河被印度人尊称为"圣河"和"印度的母亲"，两大河流用丰沛的河水哺育着两岸的土地，用肥沃的土泥冲击成辽阔的平原和三角洲，勤劳的人们世世代代在这里劳动生息，创造了古印度文明。

The origin and evolution of human civilizations are also indispensably linked to wetlands. For example, the birth place of ancient human culture and settlement, comprising the four ancient civilized countries – namely Egypt, China, Babylon, and India all shared one commonality – they were all located around or at the deltas of the major rivers of the world, which provided the fertile earth desirable for crop cultivation. The Yellow River and Yangtze River, the cradles of Chinese civilization, have nourished the Chinese people and given birth to the brilliant and time-honored Chinese culture. The abundant water resources and fertile soils along the banks of the two Mother Rivers provided a solid foundation for the development of China's husbandry. The riverine floodplain wetlands, created by annual inundation of the River Nile, have left a unique mark along both banks of the Nile. These wetlands have not only driven agricultural development in the Nile region, but also given birth to the brilliant achievements of ancient Egypt in astronomy, math, medicine, philosophy, architecture, etc. The Mesopotamian Plain, as one of the most famous wetlands in the world, came into being under the joint alluvial force of the Euphrates and Tigris rivers. In return, it gave birth to the gorgeous ancient Babylon culture. Ancient Indian civilization centered mainly on the basin of the Indus River and on that of the Ganges, revered as "India's Sacred River" and emotionally referred to as "Mother Ganges" by the Hindus. The two rivers nurtured the land through which they flowed, forming vast areas of flatlands and deltas from fertile soil. Generation after generation of industrious people lived there and multiplied, creating the so-called ancient Indian civilization.

（李惠绘）

图 1.7　美丽富饶的长江
Picture 1.7　The Beautiful and Affluent Yangtze
River (Illustration by Li Hui)

（李惠绘）

图 1.8　母亲河——黄河
Picture 1.8　The Mother River-Yellow River
(Illustration by Li Hui)

　　人类文明的发展与湿地存在着相互影响的关系，在不同时期，人类形态的差异也直接或间接地导致人类生产、生活环境与湿地关系的改变。人类文明依次会经历原始文明时代、农业文明时代、工业文明时代以及生态文明时代。原始时代，人类选择的居所附近往往具备的特点是，靠近水源便于生活取水、适于狩猎、捕鱼等生产活动或者处于河流阶地上避免受洪水侵袭等。可见这时的人们开始了能动地选择居住在湿地的周围。农业文明时代，人类往往偏向于选择优良的地形地质条件，可以较好地预防各种自然灾害，良好的生态环境背山面水。面山背北的良好朝向，充分体现了人们追求安全舒适、人与自然共生共存、"天人合一"的和谐人居建设观。在工业文明时期，人类开始走向了另一个忽视自然的极端。崇拜机械化以及物质享受，使得人们与湿地渐行渐远。人类将工业污水排入湿地中，植物等受到污染进而死去，日积月累，最终严重影响了人们的生产生活，一个新的文明形态亟待出现，来结束目前"消费自然"的错误观念，迎来绿色、生态的文明理念。

Wetlands and human civilization have always mutually interacted with each other. The continued evolution of human society continues to lead to changes in the relationship between human production activities, the living environment, and wetlands – both directly or indirectly. Human civilization has progressively evolved from a primitive society, an agricultural society, an industrial society, and an ecological society. In the primitive society, human beings were inclined to live adjacent to water resources for the convenience of fetching water, hunting, catching fish, etc. or lived on river berms to avoid floods. People were already wise enough at that time to choose living around wetlands for better survival. As the agricultural and industrial societies developed, human beings began to go ignore the need to cherish and respect nature, and blindly worshiped mechanization and indulged in material consumption. Wetlands became the victim of arbitrarily discharged agricultural and industrial pollutants, leading to the death of plants living in wetlands. As human development has resulted in increased environmental degradation, human beings have found it difficult to sustain their production activities and life styles. A brand-new model for human society has emerged that aims to put an end to the unsustainable ideas and practices of blindly consuming nature, and to embrace green living and the concepts of eco-civilization.

　　从社会发展以及变迁来看人类文明的建立与发展都以湿地为基础，湿地是人类最重要的生存环境，是人类最重要的环境资本之一，也是自然界富有生物多样性和较高生产力的生态系统，所以走向自然生态的湿地是我们的最优选择。从四大文明发展形态中可以看出，湿地与人类关系经历着不断亲近和偏离的变化发展关系。虽然在人类文明发展的过程中，工业文明时期，人类抛弃了和谐自然的发展导向，走向了较为极端的错误发展道路，但终究，人类的趋向是亲近自然。湿地，将生态特性作为新人类文明时代追求的目标。我们也期待着生态文明会在正确选择的方向上越走越好、趋于完善。

From the perspective of social development and change, both the origin and evolution of human civilization are based around wetlands. Wetlands continue to be the most important living environment for human beings, and provide some of the most significant environmental capital for our continued development, as well as an ecosystem with great biodiversity and high productivity. Therefore, to restore ecologically functioning wetlands is the best choice we can make for future growth and development. In retrospect, we can see that the relationship between wetlands and human beings has moved away from the intimate relationship enjoyed by primitive societies, towards alienation during today's industrial society. Although we have deviated from the course of harmonious co-existence with the nature, and have headed along a development path of extreme error, human beings are now more enlightened of the need to return to a respect for the nature, and restore and rehabilitate wetlands. These can be the objectives of a new society, with the hope that an eco-friendly, new civilization can evolve along the right path permanently and soundly.

（于菁菁绘）

图 1.9 尼罗河
Picture1. 9 The Nile
(Illustration by Yu Jingjing)

（李惠绘）

图 1.10 幼发拉底河
Picture 1.10 The Euphrates River
(Illustration by Li Hui)

想一想
Give This Some Thought

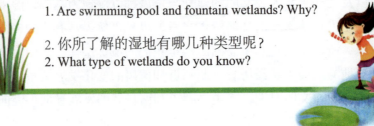

1. 游泳池和喷泉是湿地吗？为什么？
1. Are swimming pool and fountain wetlands? Why?

2. 你所了解的湿地有哪几种类型呢？
2. What type of wetlands do you know?

试一试
Give This A Try

　　请试着说出你最熟悉的一个湿地名称，并给这个湿地拍张照片吧！

Could you tell us the name of the wetland you are most familiar with? Please take a photo and show it to us.

第二节 湿地的类型
Section II Type of Wetlands

湿地与森林、海洋并称全球三大生态系统，也是价值最高的生态系统。湿地生态系统可以分成若干类型，如瀑布、河流、湖泊、鱼塘、沼泽、稻田、珊瑚礁、红树林都是湿地生态系统，那怎么样对这些湿地进行分类呢？

Wetlands, forest and sea are the three biggest and most valuable ecosystems in the world. Wetland ecosystems can be divided into many types. Do you know how to classify wetlands like waterfall, river, lake, fishpond, marsh, paddy field, coral reef, mangrove forest into different types?

学习日志
Notebook

生活在任何一个自然区域的生物都有着象征这一区域环境特点的痕迹，也就是说在任何一种类型的湿地生态系统中，都有着属于这一湿地生态系统的生物类群和生命模式，请观察图片完成以下问题。

Creatures living in any natural region will reveal traces relevant to the environmental characters of the certain region. This is to say in every type of wetland ecosystem, we can find biological groups and life patterns pertaining to the very type of wetland ecosystem. Please answer the following questions after careful observation of the pictures shown below.

(俞肖剑摄)

图 1.11 杭州湾滩涂
Picture 1.11 Hangzhou Bay Intertidal Zone
(Photo by Yu Xiaojian)

(李惠摄)

图 1.12 四川若尔盖湿地
Picture 1.12 Sichuan Ruoergai Marsh
(Photo by Li Hui)

（俞肖剑摄）

图 1.13 四川九寨沟湿地
Picture 1.13 Sichuan Jiuzhaigou Valley Wetland
(Photo by Yu Xiaojian)

（李惠摄）

图 1.14 杭州西溪湿地
Picture 1.14 Hangzhou Xixi Wetland
(Photo by Li Hui)

（孙宝娣摄）

图 1.15 北京汉石桥湿地
Picture 1.15 Beijing Hanshiqiao Wetland
(Photo by Sun Baodi)

（孙宝娣摄）

图 1.16 银川鸣翠湖湿地
Picture1. 16 Yinchuan Mingcui Lake Wetland
(Photo by Sun Baodi)

请在你的学习日志中完成下面的问题吧！
Please answer the following questions in your notebook.

1.上面几幅图是我国著名湿地景观，请根据你自己的分类角度，将它们进行归类。

1. The wetlands shown above are famous wetlands in China. Please classify them into different types based on your own judgement.

2. 如果你是一位导演，要拍摄一部有关我国湿地类型的小型纪录片，你会选择湿地中的哪些因素来进行比较？我们知道电影的表现形式主要是图像和语言，你会如何选择这几种因素的图片，并用怎样的语言对它们进行描述？

2. If you are a director and plan to produce a small documentary film about Chinese wetlands, what wetland elements will you choose for comparison of different wetland types? We know picture and language are the major expression means of film. What kind of language (or a keyword) you will use to describe pictures you choose for different wetland types?

学海拾贝
Pearls of Knowledge

一、《湿地公约》的湿地分类
I. Wetland types classified by *the Ramsar Convention on Wetlands*

《湿地公约》即拉姆萨尔公约。这里列出的类别仅仅为了提供一个宽泛的框架，以便迅速地确定每个湿地代表的主要湿地栖息地。

The Ramsar Convention on Wetlands has made a detailed classification of wetland types to enable categorization and description of different wetland sites. Below is a broad classification framework for you to quickly understand the major wetland habitats represented by each type of wetlands.

《湿地公约》的湿地分类

Wetland Types Classified by the *Ramsar Convention on Wetlanls*

1 级 Level 1	2 级 Level 2	3 级 Level 3	代码 Code	分类依据 Classification Criterions
天然湿地 Natural wetlands	海洋／海岸湿地 Ocean and coastal wetlands	永久性浅海水域 Permanent shallow marine waters	A	多数情况下低潮时水位小于 6 米，包括海湾和海峡 Permanent shallow marine waters in most cases less than six metres deep at low tide; includes sea bays and straits
		海草层 Marine subtidal aquatic beds	B	潮下藻类、海草、热带海草植物生长区 Kelp beds, sea-grass beds, tropical marine meadows
		珊瑚礁 Coral reefs	C	珊瑚礁及其邻近水域 Coral reefs and their adjacent waters
		岩石性海岸 Rocky marine shores	D	近海岩石性岛屿、海边峭壁 Rocky offshore islands, sea cliffs
		沙滩、砾石与卵石滩 Sand, shingle or pebble shores	E	滨海沙州、海岬以及沙岛；沙丘及丘间沼泽 Sand bars, spits and sandy islets; includes dune systems and humid dune slacks
		河口水域 Estuarine waters	F	河口水域和河口三角洲水域 Permanent water of estuaries and estuarine systems of deltas
		滩涂 Intertidal zone	G	潮间带泥滩、沙滩和海岸其他咸水沼泽 Intertidal belt mud flat, sand beach, coast and other salt water marshes
		盐沼 Intertidal marshes	H	滨海盐沼、盐化草甸 Mangrove marsh and coast freshwater marsh forest
		潮间带森林湿地 Intertidal forested wetlands	I	红树林沼泽和海岸淡水沼泽森林 Mangrove swamps, nipah swamps and tidal freshwater swamp forests
		咸水、碱水泻湖 Coastal brackish/saline lagoons	J	有通道与海水相连的咸水、碱水潟湖 Brackish to saline lagoons with at least one relatively narrow connection to the sea
		海岸淡水湖 Coastal freshwater lagoons	K	淡水三角洲潟湖 Freshwater delta lagoons
		海滨岩溶洞穴水系 Karst and other Subterranean hydrological systems	Zk(a)	滨海岩溶洞穴 Zittoral karst cave
	内陆湿地 Inland wetlands	永久性内陆三角洲 Permanent inland deltas	L	永久性内陆三角洲 Permanent inland deltas
		永久性的河流 Permanent rivers	M	包括河流及其支流、溪流、瀑布 Permanent rivers/streams/creeks waterfalls
		时令河 Seasonal streams	N	季节性、间歇性、定期性的河流、溪流、小河 Seasonal/intermittent/irregular rivers/streams/creeks
		湖泊 Lakes	O	面积大于 8 公顷永久性淡水湖，包括大的牛轭湖 Permanent freshwater lakes (over 8 ha); includes large oxbow lakes

续表

1级 Level 1	2级 Level 2	3级 Level 3	代码 Code	分类依据 Classification Criterions
天然湿地 Natural wetlands	内陆湿地 Inland wetlands	时令湖 Seasonal lakes	P	大于8公顷的季节性、间歇性的淡水湖，漫滩湖泊 Seasonal/intermittent freshwater lakes (over 8 ha); includes floodplain lakes
		盐湖 Salt lakes	Q	永久性的咸水、半咸水、碱水湖 Permanent saline/brackish/alkaline lakes
		时令盐湖 Seasonal salt lakes	R	季节性、间歇性的咸水、半咸水、碱水湖及其浅滩 Seasonal/intermittent saline/brackish/alkaline lakes and flats
		永久性的淡水草本沼泽、泡沼 Permanent freshwater marshes and swamps	Sp	永久性的咸水、半咸水、碱水沼泽与泡沼 Permanent saline/brackish/alkaline marshes/pools
		时令碱、咸水盐沼 Seasonal alkali, salt water marshes	Ss	季节性、间歇性的咸水、半咸水、碱性沼泽 Seasonal/intermittent saline/brackish/alkaline marshes/pools
		永久性的淡水草本沼泽、泡沼 Permanent freshwater marshes and swamps	Tp	草本沼泽及面积小于8公顷，无泥炭积累，大部分生长季节伴生浮水植物 Pools; ponds (below 8 ha), marshes and swamps on inorganic soils; with emergent vegetation water-logged for at least most of the growing season
		泛滥地 Seasonal freshwater marshes	Ts	季节性、间歇性洪泛地，湿草甸和面积小于8公顷的泡沼 Seasonal/intermittent freshwater marshes/pools on inorganic soils includes sloughs, potholes, seasonally flooded meadows, sedge marshes
		无林泥炭地 Non-forested peatlands	U	藓类泥炭地和草本泥炭地 Shrub or open bogs, swamps, fens
		高山湿地 Alpine wetlands	Va	高山草甸、融雪形成的暂时性水域 Alpine meadows, temporary waters from snowmelt
		苔原湿地 Tundra wetlands	Vt	高山苔原、融雪形成的暂时性水域 Tundra pools, temporary waters from snowmelt
		灌丛湿地 Shrub-dominated wetlands	W	灌丛沼泽、灌丛为主的淡水沼泽，无泥炭积累 Shrub swamps, shrub-dominated freshwater marshes, shrub carr, alder thicket on inorganic soils
		淡水森林沼泽 Freshwater, tree-dominated wetlands	Xf	淡水森林沼泽、季节泛滥森林沼泽、无泥炭积累的森林沼泽 Freshwater swamp forests, seasonally flooded forests, wooded swamps on inorganic soils
		森林泥炭地 Forested peatlands	Xp	泥炭森林沼泽 Peatswamp forests
		淡水泉及绿洲 Freshwater springs and oases	Y	

1 级 Level 1	2 级 Level 2	3 级 Level 3	代码 Code	分类依据 Classification Criterions
天然湿地 Natural wetlands	内陆湿地 Inland wetlands	地热湿地 Geothermal wetlands	Zg	温泉 Hot spring
		内陆岩溶洞穴水系 Karst and other subterranean hydrological systems, inland	Zk(b)	地下溶洞水系 Karst and other subterranean hydrological systems, inland
人工湿地 Human-made wetlands	水产池塘 Aquaculture ponds		1	例如鱼、虾养殖池塘 Aquaculture (e.g., fish/shrimp) ponds
	水塘 Ponds		2	农用池塘、储水池塘，一般面积小于 8 公顷 Farm ponds, stock ponds, small tanks; (generally below 8 ha)
	灌溉地 Irrigated land		3	灌溉渠系和稻田 Irrigation channels and rice fields
	农用泛洪湿地 Seasonally flooded agricultural land		4	季节性泛滥的农用地，包括集约管理或放牧的草地 Seasonally flooded agricultural land (including intensively managed or grazed wet meadow or pasture)
	盐田 Salt pans		5	晒盐池、采盐场等 Salt exploitation sites; salt pans, salines, etc
	蓄水区 Water storage areas		6	水库、拦河坝、堤坝形成的一般大于 8 公顷的储水区 Water storage areas; reservoirs/barrages/dams/impoundments (generally over 8 ha)
	采掘区 Excavations		7	积水取土坑、采矿地 Excavations; gravel/brick/clay pits; borrow pits, mining pools
	废水处理场所 Wastewater treatment areas		8	污水场、处理池、氧化池等 Wastewater treatment areas; sewage farms, settling ponds, oxidation basins, etc
	运河、排水渠 Canals and drainage channels		9	输水渠系 Canals and drainage channels, ditches
	地下输水系统 Karst and other subterranean hydrological systems		Zk(c)	人工管护的岩溶洞穴水系等 Karst and other subterranean hydrological systems, human-made

二、中国的湿地分类
II. Classification of Wetlands in China

参照中华人民共和国国家标准（GB/T24708—2009 湿地分类），综合考虑湿地成因、地貌类型、水文特征、植被类型将湿地分为三级。第一级将全国湿地生态系统分为自然湿地和人工湿地两大类。自然湿地往下依次分为第二级（4 类）、第三级（30）类。人工湿地相对比较简单，往下仅划分第 2 级，共有 12 个类。整个分类系统共包括 42 类。各级分类依据如下。

Wetlands in China have been classified using a different system to the Ramsar Convention on Wetlands. In light of the national standard of the People's Republic of China GB/T24708—2009 Wetland Classification Criterion, and taking into consideration factors relating to wetland formation, geomorphology, hydrology and vegetation types, wetlands in China have been classified into three levels. On the first level, wetlands in China are classified into natural wetlands and constructed wetlands. Natural wetlands are further classified into a second level (4 categories) and a third level (30 categories). Constructed wetlands all are classified as the second level of wetlands only (12 categories). In total, wetlands are classified into 42 categories. The table below lists detailed classification criterion:

中国的湿地分类

Classification of Wetlands in China

1级 Level 1	2级 Level 2	3级 Level 3	分类依据 Classification Criterions
自然湿地 Natural wetlands	近海与海岸湿地 Offshore and coastal wetlands	浅海水域 Permanent shallow marine water	湿地底部基质为无机部分组成，植被盖度＜30% 的区域。包括海滨、海峡 Areas with plant coverage of less than 30% and bottom sediments constituted by inorganic materials, including coasts and straits
		潮下水生层 Marine subtidal aquatic beds	海洋潮下，湿地底部基质为有机部分组成，植被盖度≥30% 的区域，包括海草层、热带海洋草地 Area below sea tide, whose plant coverage rate is no less than 30% and bottom base material is of organic material, including marine grass layer and tropical marine grass land
		珊瑚礁 Coral reefs	基质由珊瑚聚集生长而成的浅海区域 Neritic region whose base material is of aggregated corals
		岩石海岸 Rocky marine shore	底部基质 75% 以上是石头和砾石，包括岩石性沿海岛屿、海岩峭壁 Coast area whose bottom base material is comprised by more than 75% stones and gravel, including rock coast island and sea rock stiff
		沙石海滩 Sand, shingle or pebble marine shores	由砂质或沙石组成的，植被盖度＜30% 的疏松海滩 Loose sea beach comprised by sand or shingles, with plant coverage rate less than 30%
		淤泥质海滩 Intertidal mud; sand flats	由淤泥质组成的植被盖度＜30% 的泥 / 沙海滩 Sludge sea beach comprised by sludge, with plant coverage rate less than 30%

1 级 Level 1	2 级 Level 2	3 级 Level 3	分类依据 Classification Criterions
自然湿地 Natural wetlands	近海与海岸湿地 Offshore and coastal wetlands	潮间盐水沼泽 Intertidal marshes	潮间地带形成的植被盖度 ≥ 30% 的潮间区域。包括盐碱沼泽、盐水草地和海滩盐泽、高位盐水沼泽 Intertidal zone with plant coverage rate no less than 30% formed among intertidal belt, including saline and alkaline marsh, salt water grassland, sea beach salt marsh and salt water marsh in high altitude
		红树林 Mangrove	以红树植物为主的潮间沼泽 Intertidal marsh dominated by mangrove plants
		河口水域 Permanent estuarine water	从近口段的潮区界（潮差为零）至口外河海滨段的淡水舌峰缘之间的永久性水域 Permanent water area from tidal zone near estuary (tidal range is zero) to freshwater plume peak edge along coast outside estuary
		河口三角洲 / 沙洲 / 沙岛 Estuarine systems of deltas	河口系统四周冲积的泥 / 沙滩、沙洲、沙岛（包括水下部分）。植被盖度 < 30% Alluvial soil/sand beach, shoal, sand island (including underwater segment) around estuary, with plant rate less than 30%
		海岸性咸水湖 Coastal brackish; saline lagoons	地处海滨区域。有一个或多个狭窄水道与海相通的湖泊，也称为潟湖。包括海岸性微咸水、咸水或盐水湖 Lake (also termed as lagoon) located in coastal area and connected to sea by one or multiple shallow water channels, including coastal brackish lagoon, saline lagoon, or salt lagoon
		海岸性淡水湖 Coastal freshwater lagoons	起源于潟湖，但已经与海隔离后演化而成的淡水湖泊 Lake which was originated from lagoon and gradually evolved into freshwater lake after separation from sea
	河流湿地 River wetlands	永久性河流 Permanent river	常年有河水径流的河流，仅包括河床部分 River with permanent running water (only including river bed)
		季节性或间歇性河流 Seasonal or intermittently rivers	一年中只有季节性（雨季）或间歇性有水径流的河流 River only with seasonal (at rainy season) or intermittently running water
		洪泛湿地 Flooding wetlands	在丰水季节由洪水泛滥的河滩、河谷，季节性泛滥的草地，以及保持了常年或季节性被水浸润内陆三角洲的统称 General term for rive shoal and river valley formed by floods at rainy seasons, seasonal flooding grassland, permanent or seasonal inland delta soaked by water
		喀斯特溶洞湿地 Karst subterranean hydrological systems	喀斯特地貌下形成的溶洞集水区或地下河 / 溪 Cave water gathering area or underground river/brook formed under karst landform
	湖泊湿地 Lake wetlands	永久性淡水湖 Permanent freshwater lake	面积大于 8 公顷，由淡水组成的具有常年积水的湖泊 Lake comprised by permanent freshwater hydrops with an area large than 8hm²
		永久性咸水湖 Permanent brackish; alkaline lakes	由微咸水或咸水组成的具有常年积水的湖泊 Lake with permanent hydrops of brackish or salt water
		永久性内陆盐湖 Inland saline lake	由含盐量很高的卤水（矿化度 > 50g/L）组成的永久性湖泊 Permanent lake comprised by brine of very high salinity (degree of mineralization > 50g/L)

1级 Level 1	2级 Level 2	3级 Level 3	分类依据 Classification Criterions
自然湿地 Natural wetlands	湖泊湿地 Lake wetlands	季节性淡水湖 Seasonal freshwater lake	由淡水组成的季节性或间歇性湖泊 Seasonal or intermittent lake comprised by freshwater
		季节性咸水湖 Seasonal brackish; alkaline/saline lakes	由微咸水/咸水/盐水组成的季节性或间歇性湖泊 Seasonal or intermittent lake comprised by brackish water/salt water/saline water
	沼泽湿地 Marsh wetlands	苔藓沼泽 Bog	发育在有机土壤的、具有泥炭层的以苔藓植物为优势群落的沼泽 Marsh dominated by mosses, growing in turf bed layer, and nourished by organic soil
		草本沼泽 Herbage-dominated marsh	由水生和沼生的草本植物组成优势群落的淡水沼泽，包括无泥炭草本沼泽和泥炭沼泽 Freshwater marsh dominated by aquatic and marsh-based herbage, including free peat herbage-dominated marsh and peat marsh
		灌丛沼泽 Shrub-dominated marsh	以灌丛植物为优势群落的淡水沼泽，包括无泥炭灌丛沼泽和泥炭灌丛沼泽 Freshwater marsh dominated by bush plants, including free peat bush marsh and peat bush marsh
		森林沼泽 Forest-dominated freshwater marsh	以乔木植物为优势群落的淡水沼泽，包括无泥炭森林沼泽和泥炭森林沼泽 Freshwater marsh dominated by magaphanerophytes, including free peat forest-dominated freshwater marsh and peat forest-dominated freshwater marsh
		内陆盐沼 Inland saline marsh	受盐水影响，生长盐生植被的沼泽 Marsh affected by salt water and thus covered by halophytic plants
		季节性咸水沼泽 Seasonal brackish; alkaline marshes	受微咸水或咸水影响，只在部分季节维持浸湿或潮湿状况的沼泽 Seasonally soaked or damped marsh under the influence of brackish water or salt water
		沼泽化草甸 Marshy meadow	为典型草甸向沼泽植被的过渡类型，是在地势低洼、排水不畅、土壤过分潮湿、通透性不良等环境条件下发育起来的，包括分布在平原地区的沼泽化草甸以及高山和高原地区具有高寒性质的沼泽化草甸 Transitional belt from typical meadow to marsh plants, which grows in a low-lying place comprised by excessive humid soil and characterized by poor drainage and ventilation, including marshy meadow grown in plain area and in high mountain and high plateau areas of extreme frigidity
		地热湿地 Geothermal wetlands	由地热矿泉水补给为主的沼泽 Marsh mainly nourished by geothermal mineral water
		淡水泉或绿洲湿地 Freshwater springs; oases wetlands	由露头地下泉水补给为主的沼泽 Marsh mainly nourished by outcrop underground spring water

1 级 Level 1	2 级 Level 2	3 级 Level 3	分类依据 Classification Criterions
人工湿地 Constructed wetlands	水库 Reservoirs		以蓄水和发电为主要功能而建造的，面积大于 8 公顷的人工湿地 Constructed wetlands mainly for the purpose of water storage and power generation, with an area large than 8hm²
	运河、输水河 Canals and drainage channels		为输水或水运为主要功能而建造的人工河流湿地 Constructed river wetlands mainly for the purpose of drainage or water conveyance
	淡水养殖场 Freshwater aquaculture area		以淡水养殖为主要目的修建的人工湿地 Constructed wetlands mainly for the purpose of freshwater aquaculture
	海水养殖场 Marine aquaculture area		以海水养殖为主要目的的修建的人工湿地 Constructed wetlands mainly for the purpose of marine aquaculture
	农用池塘 Farm ponds		以农业灌溉、农村生活为主要目的修建的蓄水池塘 Water storage ponds mainly for the purpose of agricultural irrigation and rural life
	灌溉用沟、渠 Irrigation channels		以灌溉为主要目的修建的沟、渠 Channels mainly for the purpose of irrigation
	稻田 / 冬水田 Paddy fields		能种植水稻或者是冬季蓄水或浸湿状的农田 Farmland suitable for paddy cultivation or winter water storage; or moistened farmland
	季节性洪泛农业用地 Seasonally irrigated land		在丰水季节依靠泛滥能保持浸湿状态进行耕作的农地，集中管理或放牧的湿草场或牧场 Farmland moistened by floods in rainy seasons and suitable for agricultural cultivation, moistened grassland or pasture under centralized management for the purpose of graze
	盐田 Salt fields		为获取盐业资源而修建的晒盐场所或盐池 Salt drying field or salt pond built for the acquisition of salt material
	采矿挖掘区和塌陷积水区 Excavated or sunk water area		由于开采矿产资源而形成矿坑、挖掘场所蓄水或塌陷积水后形成的湿地。包括砂 / 砖 / 土坑；采矿地 Wetlands formed by water ponding areas on the existing or collapsed mine pits and excavated areas built for mining purpose, including sand/brick/soil pit, mining field
	废水处理场所 Wastewater treatment area		为污水处理而建设的污水处理场所。包括污水处理厂和以水净化功能为主的湿地 Wastewater treatment area, including wastewater treatment factory and wetlands for the purpose of water purification
	城市人工湿地景观水面和娱乐水面 Human-made recreational water area		在城镇、公园，为环境美化、景观需要、居民休闲、娱乐而建造的各类人工湖、池、河等人工湿地 Constructed wetlands like lake, pond, river built in city and park to beatify environment and landscape, and provide leisure and entertainment to local residents

拓展阅读
Extra Reading Material

绚丽多姿的中国湿地
Colorful Chinese Wetlands

1. 近海及海岸湿地
1.Offshore and Coastal Wetlands

中国有 579.59 万公顷的近海及海岸湿地，主要分布于沿海地区。杭州湾北部除山东半岛、辽东半岛的部分地区为岩石性海滩外，多为淤泥质海滩，由环渤海滨海和江苏近海及海岸湿地组成；杭州湾南部以岩石性海滩为主，主要河口及海湾有钱塘江—杭州湾、晋江口—泉州湾、珠江口—河口湾和北部湾等。

China has 5,795,900 hectares of offshore and coastal wetlands, commonly found in its coastal areas. Except for the rock beaches in regions like Shandong Peninsula and Liaodong Peninsula, north of the Hangzhou Bay are mainly beaches comprised of sand and sludge, which include the coastal wetlands along the coast of the Bohai Bay, and the wetlands in waters off, and on the coast of, Jiangsu. Beaches south of Hangzhou Bay are mainly comprised of rocks. The major estuaries and associated bays south of Hangzhou Bay include the Qiantang River Estuary and Hangzhou Bay, the Jin River Estuary and Quanzhou Bay, and the Pearl River Estuary and Hekou Bay and Beibu Bay.

辽宁双台河口国家级自然保护区地处辽东湾辽河入海口处，是由淡水携带大量营养物质的沉积并与海水互相浸淹混合而形成的适宜多种生物繁衍的河口湾湿地，形成大面积的淡水沼泽、咸水沼泽、沙滩和潮汐间泥滩。保护区生物资源极其丰富，从河口东部到大凌河西部，生长着大片芦苇，常见的还有香蒲、苔草、苦草等湿地植物；鸟类有 191 种，其中属国家重点保护动物有丹顶鹤、白鹤、白鹳、黑鹳等 28 种，是多种水禽的繁殖地、越冬地和众多迁徙鸟类的驿站。

Situated in the area where the Liao River empties into Liaodong Bay, Shuangtai Estuary National Nature Reserve is a vast expanse of the wetland near an estuary formed over time through the sedimentation of large amounts of nutrients carried off by the river water and the mixing of the river water and the sea water, where good conditions exist for the multiplication of many biological species. The nature reserve includes large areas of freshwater marshland, saltwater marshland, sands, and mudflats affected by tidal water, thereby enjoying enormous biological resources. Large tracts of reeds can be seen from the east of the estuary to the west part of the Daling River, and wetland plants like the bulrush, the sedges, and the eelgrass are frequently seen; there are 191 bird species, 28 of which, including the red-crown crane, the white crane, the white stork, and the black stork, are rare species protected at national level. In short, the nature reserve is a place where many aquatic birds multiply and winter and some birds stop on their migratory paths.

2. 河流湿地

2. River Wetlands

中国的河流湿地面积达 1055.21 万公顷，这些湿地主要集中在长江、黄河、珠江、松花江和辽河等流域内，有的河流属于外流型河流：向东注入太平洋的河流，主要有长江、黄河、黑龙江、辽河、海河、淮河、钱塘江、珠江、澜沧江；向南注入印度洋的有怒江和雅鲁藏布江；向西流入哈萨克斯坦境内的额尔齐斯河，再向北经俄罗斯流入北冰洋。有的河流属于内陆性河流：主要有 4 个地区：甘新地区、藏北与藏南地区、内蒙古地区、柴达木与青海地区，主要有塔里木河、黑河、伊犁河、泉吉河等，均属欧亚大陆内陆流域的一部分。

River wetlands make up 10,552,100 hectares in area in China. These wetlands are mainly found in the basins of major rivers like the Yangtze River, the Yellow River, the Pearl River, the Songhua River, and the Liao River. Some of China's rivers empty into the sea or foreign land, including those flowing east into the Pacific Ocean, like the Yangtze River, the Yellow River, the Amur River (pinyin: Hei Long Jiang), the Liao River, the Hai River, the Huai River, the Qiantang River, the Pearl River, and the Upper Mekong River (pinyin: Lan Cang Jiang); those flowing south into the Indian Ocean, like the Salween River (pinyin: Nu Jiang) and the Brahmaputra River (or the Yalu Tsangpo River); and those flowing into foreign land like the IrtySh River, which flows west into Kazakhstan territory and then turns north to flow through Russia before emptying into the Arctic Ocean. Some of China's rivers are inland, mostly distributed in four regions, namely the Gansu and Xinjiang region, the Tibetan region, the Inner Mongolian region, and the Qaidam Basin and Qinghai region. Such rivers include the Tarim River, the Black River, the Ili River, and the Quanji River, normally belonging to the inland drainage area of Eurasia.

在人们的印象中，凡是河流，都应算作河流湿地。而作为河流中的一类——"运河"，其实是不属于河流湿地的。运河是用以沟通地区或水域间水运的人工水道，通常与自然水道或其他运河相连。除航运外，运河还可用于灌溉、分洪、排涝、给水等。还有一些我们熟知的运河，包括京杭大运河、巴拿马运河都具有很大的规模，根据《湿地公约》的湿地分类，运河属于人工湿地，它和排水渠一样，都属于输水渠系的人工湿地。

As we know, rivers are counted as riverine wetlands, but what about "canals"? As one genre of rivers, should canals be classified as riverine wetlands? The answer is "no". Canals are artificial watercourses dug to link two areas of land or bodies of water not linked to each other previously. A canal is commonly linked to a natural watercourse or another canal. Aside from being used as waterways, canals can be used for irrigation, flood diversion, waterlogged field drainage, water supply, and other purposes. Although we are familiar with large canals like the Beijing-Hangzhou Grand Canal and the Panama Canal, they are indeed constructed wetlands in accordance with the wetland classification criterions of the Ramsar Convention on Wetlands. In the same way, drainage channels, are also constructed wetlands, built for the purpose of water conveyance.

3. 湖泊湿地

3. Lake Wetlands

中国湖泊湿地的面积有 859.38 万公顷，其分布广且不均匀。按湖群地理分布和形成特点，可将全国划分 5 个主要湖群：青藏高原湖群、东部平原湖群、蒙新高原湖群、东北平原及山地湖群和云贵高原湖群。这些湖泊各具特色，有世界上海拔最高的湖泊——西藏的纳木错，也有位于海平面以下的湖泊——吐鲁番盆地内的艾丁湖；有浅水湖如鄱阳湖，也有深水湖如喀纳斯湖、滇池等；有淡水湖如洞庭湖、太湖、微山湖、洪泽湖、巢湖等，有咸水湖如青海湖、罗布泊等，也有盐湖如察尔汗盐湖、运城盐湖、巴里坤盐湖等。

Lake wetlands cover about 8,593,800 hectares in China, which are distributed unevenly across a vast country. According to the geographic distribution of a particular group of lakes and how that group was formed, China's lakes may be roughly divided into 5 major groups, namely the one in the Tibetan Plateau, the one in the East China Plains, the one in the Inner Mongolia and Xinjiang Plateau, the one amid the Northeast China Plains and Mountains, and the one in the Yunnan-Guizhou Plateau. The lakes in these five groups vary greatly from each other: in the Tibet Autonomous Region there is Namtso, the lake with the highest elevation above sea level in the world; in the Turpan Basin there is Aydingkol Lake, a lake below sea level; there are shallow lakes like Poyang Lake and deep lakes like Kanas Lake and Lake Dian; there are freshwater lakes like Dongting Lake, Lake Tai, Weishan Lake, Hongze Lake, and Chao Lake; there are saltwater lakes like Qinghai Lake and Lop Nur; and there are salt lakes like Chaerhan Salt Lake, Yuncheng Salt Lake, and Balikun Salt Lake.

中国最大的湖泊湿地——青海湖。它位于青海省西北部的青海湖盆地内，既是中国最大的内陆湖泊，也是中国最大的咸水湖。由祁连山的大通山、日月山与青海南山之间的断层陷落形成。它浩瀚缥缈，波澜壮阔，是大自然赐予青海高原的一面巨大的宝镜。古代称其为"西海"，又称"鲜水"或"鲜海"。藏语叫做"错温波"，意思是"青色的湖"；蒙古语称它为"库库诺尔"，即"蓝色的海洋"。

China's largest area of wetlands is seen around Qinghai Lake. Situated in a depression to which it has given a name, in northwestern Qinghai Province, Qinghai Lake is not only China's largest inland lake, but it is also its largest saltwater lake. The lake formed due to the sinking of the fault among Mount Datong, Mount Riyue, and Qinghai South Mountain. It looks spectacular thanks to its vast area and great waters, like a huge mirror dropped from heaven on the Qinghai part of the Tibetan Plateau by nature. Qinghai Lake was referred to as the "West Sea," the "Fresh Waters," or the "Fresh Sea" in ancient times. The lake is known as the "Blue Lake" in Tibetan and as the "Blue Sea" in Mongolian.

4. 沼泽湿地

4. Marsh Wetlands

中国的沼泽有 2173.29 万公顷，在全国各省（自治区、直辖市）均有分布，但是在寒温带、温带湿润地区，沼泽湿地分布比较集中。大小兴安岭、长白山地、三江平原、辽河三角洲、青藏高原的南部和其东部的若尔盖高原、长江与黄河的河源区，河湖泛洪区，入海河流三角洲及沙质或淤泥质海岸地带沼泽湿地十分常见。山区和平原沼泽植被类型是不同的，在山区，沼泽植物多是木本的，而平原地区的沼泽植物以草本为主。

Marshes cover about 21,732,900 hectares in China, which are scattered in every province, autonomous region, and municipality directly under the Central Government, with most of the land appearing in wet regions in the temperate and cold temperate zones. Marshlands can be easily seen in the Greater Khingan, the Lesser Khingan, the Changbai Mountains, the Sanjiang Plain, the Liao River Delta, the southern part of the Tibetan Plateau and the Zoige Plateau located to the east, the regions where the Yangtze River or Yellow River starts, areas that get flooded due to a swelling river or lake nearby, estuarial deltas, and sandy or sludgy coastal areas. Mountain marshlands are different from plain marshlands. While plants growing in marshlands are mainly woody, those growing in plains are mainly herbaceous.

大家熟悉的中国工农红军在 1934—1935 年的二万五千里长征中，走过的漫漫草地就是沼泽地。沼泽下面是柔软的泥潭，看上去好像毛绒绒的绿色地毯，人一旦踏上去就会陷进去。当年许多红军战士就是这样牺牲在沼泽地里的，因此，人们称它为"绿色陷阱"。

The grassland trudged by Chinese Red Army back in 1934-1935 during Long March was exactly the marsh. What's hidden behind the lush-carpet-like marsh is abysmal mire, which will swallow anyone who steps upon it. Back then, many soldiers of Red Army lost their life to the marsh, the so-called Green Trap.

5. 人工湿地

5. Constructed wetlands

人工湿地，就是人工构筑而成的湿地。凡是满足湿地定义中所描述的各种特征，同时又以人为因素作为先决条件的湿地都可归入到人工湿地的范畴。如水稻田、库塘都属于人工湿地，这种湿地主要分布在我国水利资源比较丰富的地区。人为控制是人工湿地区别于天然湿地的决定性因素。

In a broad sense, constructed wetlands refer to man-made wetlands. Man-made wetlands which satisfy all definitions about wetlands can be classified into constructed wetlands. For instance, paddy field and water storage pond are of constructed wetlands mainly located in areas with abundant water resources. Artificial control is the judging factor for us to separate constructed wetlands from natural ones.

库塘湿地属于人工湿地，是指为灌溉、水电、防洪等目的而建造的人工蓄水设施，如密云水库、官厅水库等。密云水库，位于北京市密云县城北 13 千米处，位于燕山群山丘陵之中，建成于 1960 年 9 月。面积 180 平方千米，环密云水库有 200 千米。密云水库库容 40 亿立方米，平均水深 30 米，是首都北京最大的也是唯一的饮用水源供应地。密云水库有 2 大入库河流，分别是白河和潮河。密云水库也是亚洲最大的人工湖，有"燕山明珠"之称。库区夏季平均气温低于市区 3℃，是一处避暑胜地。

Deemed constructed ones, wetlands around ponds or reservoirs are artificial facilities built for irrigation, hydropower generation, flood control, and other purposes. Examples of such wetlands include Miyun Reservoir and Guanting Reservoir. Located 13 kilometers to the north of the urban area of Miyun County, Beijing, Miyun Reservoir sits amid rolling hills in the Yan Mountains as an artificial lake completed in September 1960. Having a total area of 180 square kilometers and a circumference of 200 kilometers, the reservoir contains about 4 billion cubic meters of water and is 30 meters deep on average. In fact, it is the largest and the sole source of potable water of Beijing, China's capital. Two rivers, the Bai River and the Chao River, supply water to Miyun Reservoir, which is the largest artificial lake in Asia and dubbed the "Pearl of the Yan Mountains." The area around the reservoir is deemed a summer resort thanks to its lower average temperature in summer, which is 3°C lower than the temperature in Beijing's urban area.

6. 湖泊的形成
6. The Formation of Lake

湖泊是湿地的重要类型之一。根据湖泊的成因，可以把湖泊分成牛轭湖、构造湖、堰塞湖、潟湖、冰川湖、水库等，其中：

Lakes are one very important type of wetlands in China and can be divided into cutoff lake, tectonic lake, barrier lake, lagoon, glacial lake, reservoir etc. by the causes of formation.

（1）牛轭湖是一种河成湖。在平原地区流淌的河流，河曲发育，随着流水对河面的冲刷与侵蚀，河流愈来愈曲，最后导致河流自然截弯取直，河水由取直部位径直流去，原来弯曲的河道被废弃，形成湖泊，因这种湖泊的形状恰似牛轭，故称之为牛轭湖。

(1) Cutoff lake is a kind of river-turned-lake. Generally speaking, it is evolved from river winding across plain area. As the river banks are consistently scoured and eroded by the winding river, the river becomes even more winding than ever. At last, normally in flooding period, the river cuts off its most bending section and rushes away straightly with the section deserted to turn into a lake. It is called Yoke Lake in Chinese due to its high resemblance to

yoke in shape.

内蒙古的乌梁素海是典型的河迹牛轭湖，其成因与黄河改道和河套平原发展农业灌溉关系密切相关。

Wuliangsu Lake in the Inner Mongolia Autonomous Region is a typical oxbow lake that formed mainly because of changes in the watercourse of the Yellow River and the development of irrigation works in the Hetao Plain.

（2）堰塞湖是由火山熔岩流，或由地震活动等原因引起山体滑坡等堵截河谷或河床后贮水而形成的湖泊。由火山熔岩流堵截而形成的湖泊又称为熔岩堰塞湖。堰塞湖的堵塞物不是固定永远不变的，它们也会受到冲刷、侵蚀、溶解和崩塌等。一旦堵塞物被破坏，湖水便漫溢而出，倾泻而下，形成洪水。

(2) Barrier lake is the product of geological conformation movement, which forces earth crust rifted, sunk, collapsed to form the lake basin. The tectonic lake comes into being when water is stored within the lake basin. Tectonic lake features striking morphologic characteristics – it takes shape along tectonic line and has steep lakeshore and deep water. It is quite often for us to see a string of tectonic lakes spread along the tectonic line.

四川汶川堰塞湖是由于 2008 年 5 月 12 日四川汶川特大地震，造成北川部分地区被堰塞湖水淹没，形成了大面积堰塞湖泊；唐家山堰塞湖是汶川大地震后形成的最大堰塞湖，地震后山体滑坡，阻塞河道形成的唐家坝堰塞湖位于涧河上游距北川县城约 6 千米处，是北川灾区面积最大、危险最大的一个堰塞湖。

The barrier lakes in Wenchuan County, Sichuan Province, formed due to the 2008 Sichuan Earthquake on May 12, 2008, when some areas in the Beichuan region were inundated to create them. The barrier lake near Mount Tangjia, formally known as the Mount Tangjia Quake Lake, was the largest of its kind to form due to landslides in the wake of the devastating earthquake. Situated in the upper reaches of the Jian River, about 6 kilometers away from Beichuan County proper, Mount Tangjia Quake Lake was the barrier lake to cover the largest area of water and pose the gravest threat to public safety in the Beichuan region.

（3）构造湖是由地壳内力作用，包括地质构造运动所产生的地壳断陷、坳陷和沉陷等产生的构造湖盆，经贮水而形成的湖泊，如青藏高原的纳木错、色林错、加仁错和昂则错等。

(3) The tectonic lake is a product of geological conformation movement, which forces earth crust rifted, sunk, collapsed to form the lake basin. The tectonic lake comes into being when water is stored within the lake basin. Typical examples on the Tibetan Plateau include Namtso, Selincuo, Jiarencuo, and Angzecuo.

（4）潟湖原系海湾，后湾口处由于泥沙沉积而将海湾与海洋分隔开而成为湖泊。如宁波的东钱湖和杭州的西湖。

(4) Lagoon is formed after sediment deposition separates bay from sea at the bay mouth. Dongqian Lake and West Lake are cases in point.

（5）冰川湖是由冰川挖蚀成的洼坑和水碛物堵塞冰川槽谷积水而成的一类湖泊，主要分布在高山冰川作用过的过程，其中的念青唐古拉山和喜马拉雅山区较为普遍。

(5) Glacial lake is formed by water-holding hollow pit dug out by glacier or glacial trough with stagnated moraine during the course of alpine glacier movement. Commonly seen in Nianqing Tanggula mountain area and Himalaya mountain area, glacial lakes sit in places of high elevation and are small in size. They basically have exited as well.

想一想
Give This Some Thought

1. 如果昆明湖没有水，那里会是什么样子？

1. What would Kunming Lake be like if there is no water in it?

2. 试从这一节的湿地类型中选出哪些湿地曾是你亲自走过、见过的？

2. What kinds of wetlands mentioned in this section have you ever seen or heard?

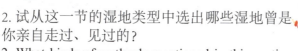

试一试
Give This A Try

看了上文的介绍，你想知道湖泊是怎样形成的吗？根据下面湖泊类型的解释，在后面的图片中填入对应的名称代号吧！

Do you want to know how a lake is formed? Please fill in corresponding lake type codes to pictures shown below after reading the descriptions about lake types.

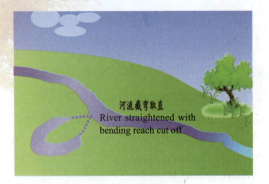

图 1.17

图 1.18

图 1.19

图 1.20

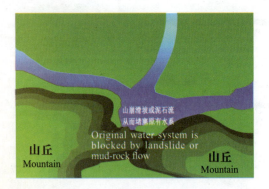

图 1.21

图 1.22

第三节 湿地的生态功能
Section III Ecological Services of Wetlands

　　湿地是孕育人类文明的重要载体。几千年前，我们的祖先"逐水草而居"，在与湿地相互依存的漫长历史过程中，创造了灿烂的人类文明。黄河孕育了华夏文明，西藏的纳木错、玛旁雍错湿地是藏传佛教的朝圣地。中国四大名楼（黄鹤楼、岳阳楼、滕王阁、鹳雀楼）都位于湿地或其周边地区，成就了许多流传千古的诗词歌赋。这些都与湿地的生态特性紧密相连。

Wetlands are the cradle of human civilization. Thousands of years ago, our ancestors started to settle down beside rivers. Over time, the long-standing inter-dependence between human beings and wetlands gave birth to advanced human civilizations. For example, the Yellow River is the cradle of Chinese civilization. Many lakes are revered by different Chinese ethnic groups as "Sacred Lakes" and are often the venue for religious activities. Lake Nam and Lake Manasarovar are pilgrim destinations for believers of Tibetan Buddhism. Besides, the top four famous pagodas in China, namely the Yellow Crane Pagoda, Yueyang Pagoda, Tengwang Pagoda, and Guanque Pagoda, are all located at or around wetlands, and gave inspiration to many famous poets in the nation across the generations. These are closely related to the ecological characteristics of wetlands.

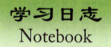
学习日志
Notebook

　　试着说出自己所知道的湿地生态功能，并写在你的学习日志中吧！

Do you know what ecological services wetlands provide to us? Please write down in this notebook.

拓展阅读
Extra Reading Material

　　湿地不仅类型丰富、景色迷人，而且拥有强大的"神奇功效"。湿地的这些"神奇功效"，无时无刻不在发挥作用，为人类的生产和生活提供多样的服务和支持。

In addition to being charming landscape of rich resources, wetlands also have magic power to deliver valuable services and support to better our life.

一、饮水机功能
I. Water Dispenser Function

居民生活用水、工业生产用水和农业灌溉用水大都来源于湿地。溪流、河流、池塘、湖泊中都有可以直接利用的水源，一些泥炭沼泽中的水也可以成为浅水水井的水源。北京的密云水库是亚洲最大的人工湖，是北京市生活和工业用水的主要来源。

The water resources necessary for human living, for industrial manufacture and agricultural irrigation, are frequently sourced from wetlands. Brooks, rivers, ponds, and lakes are endowed with water resources which can be directly used by human beings. Even the water resources found in peat marshes can be used as the water source for shallow wells. The Beijing Miyun Reservoir is the biggest artificial lake in Asia, and is responsible for providing the majority of water resources for Beijing's domestic and industrial activities.

（程兆鹏绘）

图 1.23 湿地饮水机作用
Picture 1.23 Magic power as water dispenser
(Illustration by Cheng Zhaopeng)

（程兆鹏绘）

图 1.24 湿地贮备库作用
Picture 1.24 Magic power as warehouse
(Illustration by Cheng Zhaopeng)

二、贮备库功能
II. Storehouse Function

湿地像一座存贮着大量物资的储备库，给人们提供丰富的生活生产必需品。一方面，它为人类提供肉蛋、鱼虾、蔬菜和水果等食品；另一方面，还供给木材、药材、泥炭、薪柴等多种原材料和能源。例如我国的河流湿地、湖泊湿地和滨海湿地，水温适中，光照条件好，水生生物资源丰富，为鱼类提供了丰富的饵料，所以鱼种类多，经济价值高。

Wetlands are also a huge warehouse with rich life necessities accessible. On one hand, it provides us with nutritious food like meat, egg, fish, shrimp, vegetable and fruit. On the other hand, it also delivers us with countless raw materials and energy like timber, medicinal materials, animal fur, peat, and fuel wood. For example, ample plants of medical value, peat resource, reed resource, salt and alkali resource, fish resource could be found from vast wetlands scattered in mountainous areas to coast areas. Wetlands are especially abundant with various nutritious fish – one of the indispensible food resources in our table. As a result of mild water temperature and sufficient sun ray, rich aquatic biological resources are found across river wetlands, lake wetlands, and coastal wetlands in China. In return, fish gets thrived with such rich aquatic biological resources and turns out to be highly economically valuable.

三、空调器功能
III. Air Conditioner Function

　　湿地有大面积的水域、植被和湿润土壤。湿地具有空调器的功效：水面、土壤的水分蒸发和植物叶面的水分蒸腾，使得湿地与大气之间不断进行广泛的热量交换和水分交换，在增加局部地区的空气湿度、调节气温以及降低大气含尘量等气候调节方面具有明显的作用。例如，北京市密云水库库区夏季平均气温比北京市市区低 3℃，是一处怡人的避暑胜地。

Comprised by large stretch of water surface, rich plants and moistened soil, wetlands can function as a magic air conditioner. Under the joint effect of moisture evaporation taken place in water surface and soil, and moisture transpiration in plant leaf surface, wide range of heat and moisture exchange activities are consistently conducted between wetlands and atmosphere. Thus, regional climate can be adjusted accordingly with enhanced air humidity, regulated temperature, and reduced dust content in air. For instance, Beijing Miyun Reservoir is flocked by holiday-makers in summer as its average temperature in summer days is 3 ℃ lower than in downtown Beijing.

（程兆鹏绘）
图 1.25　湿地空调器作用
Picture 1.25　Magic power as air conditioner
(Illustration by Cheng Zhaopeng)

（程兆鹏绘）
图 1.26　湿地净化器作用
Picture 1.26　Magic power as purifier
(Illustration by Cheng Zhaopeng)

四、净化器功能
IV. Purifier Function

　　湿地拥有强大的水体净化功能，具有滞留沉积物、营养物和降解有毒物质的功能。湿地的水体净化功能依赖于水中生长的各种挺水、浮水、沉水植物，浮游生物以及微生物等各种生物。通过物理过滤、生物吸收、化学合成与分解等过程，将进入湿地的污水和污染物中的有害有毒物质降解或转化为无毒无害的物质，减少经湿地流向下游水体中的有害物种的数量，达到净化水体的作用，湿地也因此被誉为"地球之肾"。人类利用湿地的这种武器，将一些湿地用作小型生活污水处理池，大大提高了水的质量，保障了人们的生活和生产用水安全。

Wetlands are powerful in purifying water by means of retention of sediment and nutrient, and degradation of toxic substance. The water purification services of wetlands are enabled by various wetland-based creatures including emerged plants, floating plants, submerged plants, planktons, and microorganism. After going through processes like physical filtration, biological absorption, chemical synthesis and decomposition, harmful and toxic materials contained in sewage and pollutant which have penetrated into wetlands will be decomposed or converted into non-toxic and non-harmful substances. In such way, detrimental species which might find their way via wetlands to the downstream water body will be reduced, leaving water body purified. So, it is no wonder why wetlands are dubbed as "the Kidney of Earth" as well. To make the best use of the magic power, wetlands have been employed as small-size sewage treatment vehicle in certain areas, with water quality greatly enhanced to ensure water safety in all aspects of our life.

五、缓冲器功能
V. Buffer Function

　　湿地是一个巨大的蓄水库，可以在暴雨和河流涨水期储存过量的雨水，同时均匀地把水流放出。例如中国的淡水湖鄱阳湖，平均可消减长江湖口河段20%左右的洪峰，在枯季每秒可以向长江补充400～500立方米的水量。滨海湿地的植被红树林，可以防止自然力（海啸、风暴潮等）对海岸的侵蚀和破坏。例如，50米宽的白骨壤林带，可使1米高的波浪减至0.3米以下，使林内水流速度仅为潮水流速的1/10。湿地的"缓冲器"功能，有效地保障了人类的生命和财产安全。

Wetlands are also a huge storage reservoir, since they are capable to store excessive rainfall in storm and river flooding seasons, reducing flood threat to downstream areas, discharging such water evenly in days to come, and easing the water insufficiency in dry season. Take Poyang Lake, one freshwater lake in China, for instance, it can bring down about 20% of flood peak of Yangtze River at confluent section on average, and supplement 400—500 cubic meter of water to Yangtze River per second in dry season. Coastal wetlands' plants like mangrove forests are good at preventing coast from the erosion and damage of natural force like tsunami, and storm tide. For example, *avicennia marina* belt measuring 50 meters in width could bring tidewater of 1 meter in height down to less than 0.3 meter, making tidewater velocity reduced by 9/10 when it travels through the belt. The bumper-like power of wetlands effectively safeguards our life and property. So, to protect wetlands is to protect our own security.

(程兆鹏绘)

图 1.27　湿地缓冲器作用
Picture 1.27　Magic power as bumper
(Illustration by Cheng Zhaopeng)

(程兆鹏绘)

图 1.28　湿地能量站作用
Picture 1.28　Magic power as ecological garden
(Illustration by Cheng Zhaopeng)

六、能量站功能
VI. Energy Station Function

湿地不仅是植物生长的理想场所，也是鸟类、鱼类和两栖动物繁殖、栖息、迁徙和越冬的停歇地。存储于湿地中的水，为维持湿地植物的生长和代谢提供了良好的物质条件；湿地植物又为湿地动物提供了丰富的饵料。因此，湿地养育了高度集中的鸟类、哺乳类、爬行类、两栖类、鱼类和无脊椎物种，湿地也是动、植物的家，湿地同时也是遗传物质的重要储存地。

Except of being the Garden of Eden for plants, wetlands are also the paradise for the reproduction, settlement, migration and overwintering of bird, fish, and amphibian. The water stored in wetlands makes the growth and metabolism of wetland plants possible, which in turn provide rich nutrition to wetland animals. Therefore, bird, mammalia, reptile, amphibian, fish, and invertebrate get thrived in wetlands. In addition to being home to both animal and plant, wetlands are also abundant with genetic material.

湿地的"神奇功效"还有很多，它在潜移默化之中影响与改变着人类的生活。而我们也应积极地付出行动来保护它。

In fact, the magic power of wetlands is far beyond what we mentioned above. Wetlands still exert many subtle yet positive influences in the interest of our human society. Thus, timely action is badly needed for wetland protection.

地球之肾
The Kidney of Earth

美丽的地球孕育了无数神奇的生命，无数神奇的生命又组成了无数神奇的景致，这无数神奇的景致错落有致，平衡、美丽、富有生机，组成了我们美丽的大自然！在这颗神奇的蓝色星球上，各种生态系统交相辉映，一起为我们共同的家园添砖加瓦。而湿地生态系统正是无数生态系统中最重要，也是最神秘的一个"家庭成员"。

Our mother earth gives birth to many magic lives, which in return constitute countless magic sceneries as well as beautiful and vibrant nature! In this miraculous blue planet, ecosystems add radiance to each other, and jointly make our homeland more magic. Among these countless ecosystems, wetland ecosystem is doubtlessly the most important and mysterious family member.

人类利用湿地的这种功效，建造了可以由人类控制其运行的人工湿地。人工湿地是一种独特的植物—水—土壤—微生物湿地生态系统，它利用土壤、人工介质、植物、微生物的物理、化学、生物三重协同作用，通过吸附、滞留、过滤、氧化还原、沉淀、微生物分解、转化，对污水进行处理。

Under the control of human, constructed wetlands are built by reference to the magic natural wetlands. As one unique wetland ecosystem with plants, water, soil and microorganism combined together, constructed wetlands will make full use of the triple synergic

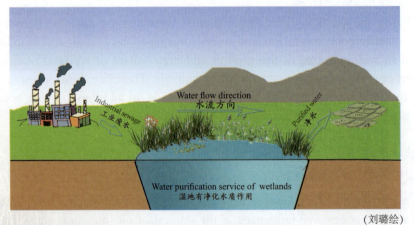

（刘璐绘）

图 1.29 人工湿地净化水质过程
Picture 1.29 Water Purification Process of Constructed Wetlands (Illustration by Liu Lu)

effects (physical, chemical, and biological effects) of soil, artificial medium, plants, and microorganism to treat sewage by means of absorption, retention, filtration, redox, sediment, microorganism decomposition, and conversion.

人工湿地家族
Constructed Wetlands

1903 年，建在英国约克郡的人工湿地被认为是世界上第一个用于处理污水的人工湿地，连续运行到 1992 年。直到 20 世纪 70 年代德国学者 Kichunth 提出根区法理论之后开始，人工湿地才在世界各地逐渐受到重视并被运用。

The wetland built in Yorkshire of UK dated back in 1903 was recognized as the first constructed wetland for sewage treatment purpose in the world. It has served the purpose soundly till 1992 upon retirement. Constructed wetlands has not been duly valued and put into wide use until 1970s when German scholar Kichunth proposed the root-zone-method.

（知识就是力量 ,2014,59(8)）

图 1.30　湿地净化功能
Picture 1.30　Water Purification Service of Wetlands
(Knowledge is Power, 2014, 59 (8))

人工湿地对于污染物的处理效果也较好。对于污水中一些污染元素，如氮、磷等的平均去除率最高可达 70% 以上，在北京市野生动物救护中心的人工湿地对总悬浮物（Total Suspended Solids，TSS）的平均去除率为 75%，对化学需氧量（Chemical Oxygen Demand，COD）的平均去除率为 43%，对总磷的平均去除率为 53%，总氮的平均去除率为 68%。

Constructed wetlands are good at treating contaminant too. They boast an average removal rate over 70% for contaminative elements like nitrogen and phosphor. The constructed wetlands in Beijing Wildlife Rescue & Rehabilitation Center enjoy an average removal rate for Total Suspended Solids (TSS) up to 75%, for Chemical Oxygen Demand (COD) 43%, for total phosphorus 53%, for total nitrogen 68%.

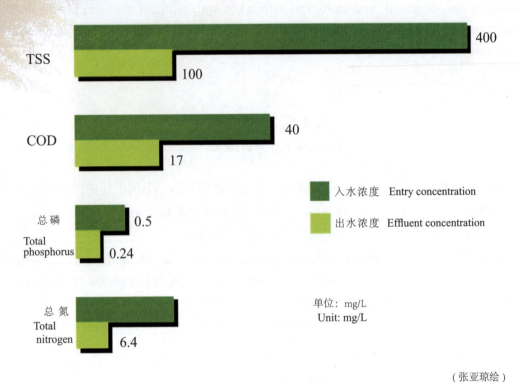

TSS 400
100

COD 40
17

入水浓度 Entry concentration

出水浓度 Effluent concentration

总磷
Total
phosphorus 0.5
0.24

总氮
Total
nitrogen 6.4

单位：mg/L
Unit: mg/L

（张亚琼绘）

图 1.31 人工湿地污染物去除效果
Picture 1.31 Elimination Effect of Pollutants by Constructed Wetlands
(Illustration by Zhang Yaqiong)

湿地的调节作用
Regulating Services of Wetlands

湿地是气候变化的调节器，又是气候变化的指示器。湿地的调节作用表现在很多方面，如大气组分的调节、大气温湿度调节和水分调节等。从某种程度上，我们可以说，湿地影响着气候，是气候的调节器；气候也影响着湿地，湿地是气候变化的指示器。每到盛夏，人们总是喜欢在湖边、河边散步纳凉。这其实与湿地"空调器"的特点密不可分。

Wetlands are both the regulator and the indicator of climate change. The regulating services provided by wetlands can be reflected on many aspects, e.g. regulation to atmosphere component, atmosphere temperature and humidity, humidity control, etc. It can be said, to some degree, wetlands are both the regulator and the indicator of climate as they both influence and are influenced by climate. Lakes and rivers are the places people like to go to enjoy the rare cool in the scorching summer days. This is indeed inseparable from wetlands' magic power as the air conditioner.

（于菁菁绘）

图 1.32 湿地的温度调节作用
Picture 1.32 Wetlands'Temperature Regulation Function
(Illustration by Yu Jingjing)

　　湿地具有明显的降温增湿作用，并且距离湿地越近，其降温增湿的效果也越明显。湿地可以调节局部小气候，对毗邻地区具有增湿、降温的作用，这种现象被称为"冷湿效应"。虽然湿地复杂多变，但是其降温增湿作用的原理却很简单，由于水的热容量小于地面，吸热和放热都比较慢，所以湿地附近气温变化较为缓和，而干燥的地面上气温变化则较为剧烈。而且，大面积湿地水面的蒸发作用以及湿地植物的蒸腾作用要耗去大量的热量，而这部分热量来自周围的空气，因此湿地能够显著降低局部环境的温度。也正是由于湿地的水分蒸发，使得湿地和大气之间不断地进行着能量和物质交换，从而保持和增加湿地及其周边的空气湿度，减少土壤水分丧失，同时有助于促进降水量增加，保持当地的水分平衡，另外湿地植物在蒸腾过程中要耗去大量的热量，在降低温度的同时使大量的水蒸气进入空气，使空气不断地进行着水汽的扩散和交换，增加空气湿度。

Wetlands could do a great job in temperature reduction and humidification. The area is closer to the wetland, and it will be easier for the area to get cooler and more humid. Wetlands are capable to regulate microclimate as they can make the adjacent areas more humid and cooler. This phenomenon is termed Cold-humid Effect. Wetlands might be complicated in forms, but they all comply with one simple principle to make nearby areas cooler and more humid. Since the thermal capacity of water is less than that of ground, the heat absorption and release rate of water are slower than that of ground too. Therefore, temperature change around wetlands is moderate, much less dramatic than that around dry ground. What's more, the evaporation of large stretch of wetland water surface and transpiration of wetland plants will consume a great amount of heat mainly coming from nearby atmosphere. So, the temperature around wetlands is apparently lower than local average temperature. The evaporation of water out from wetlands accelerates the constant exchange of energy and material between wetlands and atmosphere. It helps to maintain and enhance the air humidity of wetlands and its peripheral areas, and reduce the soil moisture loss; meanwhile, it also helps to increase precipitation, and maintain local water balance. What's more, since a good deal of heat will be consumed during the transpiration process of wetland plants, a mass of water vapor will enter into atmosphere when climate becomes lower. The above-mentioned processes make moisture sustainably diffused into and exchange with air, leading to enhanced air humidity.

湿地生态系统作为全球生态系统的重要类型，在减缓全球变化和调节区域气候特征方面发挥着举足轻重的作用。湿地对区域气候的调节影响较大，《湿地公约》和《联合国气候变化框架公约》都特别强调了湿地对调节区域气候的重要作用。此外，湿地晨雾还可以去除大气中的扬尘和颗粒物，净化空气，提高环境空气质量。

As one of the significant ecosystems in the world, wetland ecosystem plays a critical role in mitigating global climate change and regulating regional climate. Both *the Ramsar Convention on Wetlands and United Nations Framework Convention* on Climate Change gave prominence to the ecologic services rendered by wetlands in climate regulation. Besides, the morning fog of wetlands can help wipe off the dust and particulate matters from the air, making air purified with improved quality.

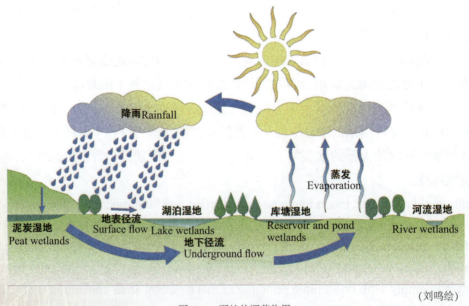

（刘鸣绘）

图 1.33 湿地的调节作用
Picture 1.33 Regulating Services of Wetlands
(Illustration by Liu Ming)

有研究表明，干旱区湿地的气候调节功能尤为明显，其每年调节气候的生态服务价值能够占湿地总生态服务价值的32%，是各项生态价值之首，然而，由于人为干扰和城市快速建设的影响，城市热岛效应逐渐增强，而国内很多城市自然水体面积有限，且水体总面积呈减少的趋势，湿地水体气候调节作用被弱化。

Researches indicate that wetlands can play an even greater role in climate regulation for arid region. Of the total value of ecological services rendered by wetlands, 32% is contributed by wetlands' ecological services in climate regulation – the biggest one in terms of ecological value. However, the ecological service offered by wetlands in climate regulation is weakened under the joint force of man-made interference, facilitated urban construction, and strengthened urban heat island effect, coupled with the continually shrunk natural urban water bodies which were already quite limited even before such shrinkage.

湿地对负氧离子调节功能
Negative Oxygen Ionic Concentration Regulating Services of Wetlands

湿地不仅对温度、空气湿度等有明显的调节作用，还具有调节空气中负氧离子浓度的作用。空气负氧离子水平也是评价空气清洁程度的重要指标。

In addition to temperature and air humidity, Wetlands also can regulate the concentration of negative oxygen ions in air – the significant index to gauge the clean degree of air.

近年来，空气中的负氧离子含量及其保健和净化空气的作用日益受到人们的关注。同样以北京市为例，距湿地越近，负氧离子浓度越高，这些证据都足以证实城市湿地对周围空气中负氧离子含量及空气质量具有明显的调节作用。

In recent years, the role played by negative oxygen ionic concentration in healthcare and air purification has gained increasing attention from the public. Also take Beijing for instance, the closer one place is to the wetland, the higher the negative oxygen ionic concentration it enjoys. All these evidences work to prove urban wetlands can provide powerful regulating services to the negative oxygen ionic concentration of ambient air and air quality alike.

不仅如此，湿地在蓄水、河川径流等过程中也发挥重要的调节作用。湿地是蓄水防洪的天然"海绵"，通过湿地本身的调节作用，达到避免水旱灾害的效果。而湿地中的水分也可以通过蒸发成为水蒸气，并以降水的形式降到周围地区，以保持湿地周边地区的湿度和降水量。

Furthermore, wetlands can accelerate water storage and rive flow. As the natural "sponge" for water storage and flood prevention, wetlands can do a great job to avert flood and drought disasters based on the regulating service it renders. The moisture in wetlands can be transported to neighboring areas in the form of rainfall after being evaporated into water vapor, so as to help maintain the humidity and precipitation of areas around the wetland.

小知识
Tip

带负电荷的氧离子被称为"负氧离子"，它被誉为"空气维生素"，能够通过人的神经系统及血液循环对人的机体生理活动产生影响。"负氧离子"有改善人体心肺功能、促进新陈代谢、增强机体抵抗能力等作用。

Tip oxygen ion with negative charge is called negative oxygen ion – the so-called "air vitamin". It can influence physiological activities of human body via nervous system and blood circulation. Negative oxygen ion is good at improving human's cardio-pulmonary function, facilitating metabolism, and enhancing resistance capacity.

想一想
Give This Some Thought

1. 在日常生活中，你感受到了哪些湿地功能带来的益处？

1. What geologic services of wetlands do you have enjoyed in your life?

2. 湿地还有其他的"神奇功效"吗？你了解的北京的湿地有几种"神奇功效"？

2. Do wetlands have any other magic powers? Do you know how many kinds of magic powers wetlands in Beijing have?

试一试
Give This A Try

1. 根据下列湿地功能与下页所示图片，按表格内容要求填入相应代号。

1. Please fill the corresponding codes of the ecological services provided by wetlands in the following pictures.

2. 下面这些曾在你视线中出现过的湿地，你认为它们为我们提供了怎样的生态功能？

2. In your opinion, what kind of ecological services have these wetlands brought to you?

湿地生态功能
Ecological Services of Wetlands

　　湿地是一个综合的生态系统，具有诸多的生态功能：A. 蓄水、B. 净化、C. 调节小气候、D. 调蓄洪水、E. 补充地下水、F. 维护生物多样性、G. 碳汇、H. 保护海岸、I. 提供水产品等。

Wetlands are the comprehensive ecological system, capable to provide the following ecological services: A.water storage, B.water purification, C.microclimate regulation, D.flood regulation, E.underground water supplement, F.biodiversity assurance, G.carbon sink, H.bank protection, I.aquatic product provision.

图 1.34　　　　　（俞肖剑摄）
Picture1.34 (Photo by Yu Xiaojian)

图 1.35　　　　　（俞肖剑摄）
Picture1.35 (Photo by Yu Xiaojian)

图 1.36　　　　　（俞肖剑摄）
Picture1.36 (Photo by Yu Xiaojian)

图 1.37　　　　　（李伟摄）
Picture1.37　　　（Photo by Li Wei）

图 1.38　　　　　（俞肖剑摄）
Picture1.38 (Photo by Yu Xiaojian)

图 1.39　　　　　（俞肖剑摄）
Picture1.39 (Photo by Yu Xiaojian)

图 1.40　　　　　（刘璐绘）
Picture1.40 (Illustration by Liu Lu)

图 1.41　　　　　（李伟摄）
Picture1.34　　　（Photo by Li Wei）

图 1.42 （俞肖剑摄）
Picture1.42 (Photo by Yu Xiaojian)

图 1.43 （高武摄）
Picture1.43 (Photo by Gao Wu)

图 1.44 （李惠摄）
Picture1.44 (Photo by Li Hui)

图 1.45 （俞肖剑摄）
Picture1.34 (Photo by Yu Xiaojian)

湿地形式 Wetland type	图片代号 Picture code	生态功能 Provided ecological service
滨海 Coast		
沼泽 Marsh		
湖泊 Lake		
天然涌泉 Natural spring		
珊瑚礁 Coral reef		
水库 Reservoir		
池塘 Pond		
稻田 Paddy field		

3. 你认为以上哪种湿地消失后，将对我们带来最大限度的影响？

3. In your opinion, the disappearance of which type of wetlands will exert the most severe impact on our life?

4. 柳宗元《小石潭记》中写道"青树翠蔓，蒙络摇缀，参差披拂……"三言两语间便为我们描绘出一幅潭边碧树轻拂的清秀画面。请试着从其他文言文中摘录几句关于湿地的描述。

4. In the *Little Rock Pond*, Liu Zongyuan described to us, in a very terse yet vivid language, the graceful scenery of a small pond being caressed by gentle tree branches "gently stroked by the swaying branches of green tree, the ripples glister throughout the pond…". Please find similar description about wetlands.

参考文献
References

[1] 崔丽娟,Stephane A.湿地恢复手册:原则·技术与案例分析[M].北京:中国建筑工业出版社,2006.

[1] Cui Lijuan, Stephane A. *The Wetland Restoration Handbook Guiding Principles and Case Studies* [M]. Beijing: China Building Industry Press, 2006.

[2] 崔丽娟,张曼胤,何春光.中国湿地分类编码系统研究[J].北京林业大学学报,2007,29(3):87–92.

[2] Cui Lijuan, Zhang Manyin. He Chunguang, *Wetlands Classification and Its Encoding System in China* [J]., Journal of Beijing Forestry University, 2007, 29 (3): 87-92 .

[3] 崔丽娟,张曼胤,李伟,等.人工湿地处理富营养化水体的效果研究[J].生态环境学报,2010,19(9):2141–2148.

[3] Cui Lijuan, Zhang Manyin, Li Wei, et al. *Research on Effects of Constructed Wetlands Eutrophication Waterbodies* [J]. Ecological Environment Journal, 2010, 19 (9): 2141-2148.

[4] 崔丽娟,李伟,张曼胤,等.北京翠湖人工湿地污水净化的效果分析[J].中国农学通报,2012,28(5):278–282.

[4] Cui Lijuan, Li Wei, Zhang Manyin, et al. *Analysis on sewage Purification Effects of Cuihu constructed wetland,Beijing* [J]. Chinese Agricultural Science Bulletin, 2012, 28 (5): 278-282.

[5] 崔丽娟,张曼胤,王义飞.湿地功能研究进展[J].世界林业研究,2006,19(3):18–21.

[5] Cui Lijuan, Zhang Manyin, Wang Yifei. *The process of Wetland Function Research*[J].world Forestry Study, 2006, 19 (3): 18-21 .

[6] 崔丽娟,张曼胤,张岩,等.湿地恢复研究现状及前瞻[J].世界林业研究,2011,24(2):5–9.

[6] Cui Lijuan, Zhang Manyin, Zhang Yan, et al. *Status and Outlook of Wetland Restoration Research*[J]. World Forestry Study, 2011,24(2):5-9.

[7] 邓侃 . 湿地水文功能及其保护管理 [J]. 林业资源管理 ,2013,3:23-27.

[7] Deng Kan. *Wetland Hydrologic Function and Its Protection and Management* [J]. Forest Resources Management, 2013,3:23-27.

[8] 国家林业局《湿地公约》履约办公室 . 湿地公约履约指南 [M]. 北京 : 中国林业出版社 ,2001.

[8] Implementation Office for *Ramsar Convention on Wetlands of State Forestry Bureau, Guide on Implementing Ramsar Convention in China*[M]. Beijing: Chinese Forestry Press, 2001 .

[9] 陆健健 . 中国湿地 [M]. 上海 : 华东师范大学出版社 ,1990.

[9] Lu Jianjian. *Wetlands in China* [M]. Shanghai: East China Normal University Press, 1990 .

[10] 湿地环境教育工作者手册 [M]. 天下溪乡土环境教育教材系列 , 2006.

[10] *Notebook for Wetland Educators* [M]. Serial Teaching Material for Tianxiaxi Rural Environment Education, 2006.

[11] 王继国 . 艾比湖湿地调节号候生态服务价值评价 [J]. 湿地科学与管理 , 2007, 3(2):38–41.

[11] Wang Jiguo, *Valuation of the Ecological Service of Regulating Climate of Ebinur-Lake Wetland* [J]. Wetland Science and Management, 2007, 3(2):38-41.

[12] 杨一鹏 , 曹广真 , 侯鹏 , 等 . 城市湿地气候调节功能遥感监测评估 [J]. 地理研究 ,2013,32(1):73–80.

[12] Yang Yipeng, Cao Guangzhen, Hou Peng, et al. *Monitoring and evaluation for climate regulation service of urban wetlands with remote sensing*[J].Geographic Study, 2013, 32 (1): 73-80 .

[13]岳泽文 , 徐建华 , 徐丽华 . 基于遥感影像的城市土地利用生态环境效应研究 [J]. 生态学报 ,2006,26(5):1450–1460.

[13] Yue Zewen, Xu Jianhua, Xu Lihua.*An analysis on eco-environmental effect of urban land use based on remote sensing images* [J]. Journal of Ecology, 2006, 26 (5): 1450-1460.

[14] 中华人民共和国国家标准 GB/T24708–2009, 湿地分类 [S].

[14] GB/T24708-2009 National Standard of the People's Republic of China, Wetland Classification [S].

[15] 湿地公约

[15] *The Ramsar Convention on Wetlands*
http://www.ramsar.org/cda/en/ramsar-wetlands-of-world-s/main/ramsar/1%5E16853_4000_0.
http://www.ramsar.org/cda/en/ramsar-documents-guidelines-classification-system/main/ramsar/1-31-105%5E21235_4000_0.

[16] 中国数字科技馆

[16] China Digital Science and Technology Museum.
http://amuseum.cdstm.cn/AMuseum/marsh/page/shouye.html.

第二章　旅行者日志
Chapter Ⅱ Diary of Backpacker

　　假如你是一位背包客、一位旅游爱好者，领略了大自然中的美景，你就会发现中国湿地类型多、面积大、分布广、区域差异显著等特点，一定会情不自禁、由衷地为我国具有如此富饶的湿地资源而感到自豪。

If you are a backpacker and a lover for tourism, after travelling across this nation, you will be deeply impressed by the great diversity, huge size, wide distribution, acute regional disparity of wetlands in China, and feel so proud for the abundant wetland resources owned by our motherland.

第一节　中国湿地概览
Section Ⅰ Overview of Wetlands in China

学习日志
Notebook

　　你了解有关中国湿地的哪些内容？在学习日志中写下以下几个问题的答案，在完成本节的学习之后再来检查这些答案。中国湿地有哪些特点？在我国的分布情况如何？中国湿地若干年来有没有发生变化？发生了哪些变化？

What do you know about wetlands in China? Please write down answers to the following questions and then review your answers after finishing study of this section. Questions: What features do wetlands have in China? What is their geographic distribution? Have such wetlands changed over past years? If any, what changes are they?

学海拾贝
Pearls of Knowledge

一、中国湿地现状
I. The Status Quo of Chinese Wetlands

　　为了了解我国湿地的现状以及满足我国湿地保护管理的需要，更好地履行《湿地公约》，中国政府分别于 1995—2003 年和 2009—2013 年对我国的湿地进行了两次调查。

For the needs of better governance over wetlands in China, sound implementation of the Ramsar Convention on Wetlands, and access to updated knowledge on Chinese wetlands, two comprehensive investigations have been conducted by Chinese government during 1995—2003 and 2009—2013.

根据全国第二次湿地普查结果显示，全国湿地总面积 5360.26 万公顷（另有水稻田面积 3005.70 万公顷未计入），湿地率 5.58%。其中，调查范围内湿地面积 5342.06 万公顷，其中香港、澳门和台湾湿地面积 18.20 万公顷。自然湿地面积 4667.47 万公顷，占 87.37%；人工湿地面积 674.59 万公顷，占 12.63%。自然湿地中，近海与海岸湿地面积 579.59 万公顷，占 12.42%；河流湿地面积 1055.21 万公顷，占 22.61%；湖泊湿地面积 859.38 万公顷，占 18.41%；沼泽湿地面积 2173.29 万公顷，占 46.56%。

According to the statistical data of the second national wetland assessment, China has 53,602,600 hectares of wetlands (excluding an additional 30,057,000 hectares of rice fields), covering 5.58% of the land surface of China. This 53420600-hectare area includes 182,000 hectares of wetlands in Hong Kong, Macau, and Taiwan. A total of 46,674,700 hectares are classified as natural wetlands, accounting for 87.37% of the total area; and 6,745,900 hectares are classified as constructed wetlands, accounting for 12.63% of the total area. Within the natural wetlands, 5,795,900 hectares are offshore and coastal wetlands (12.42% of total area); 10,552,100 hectares are riverine wetlands (22.61% of total area); 8,593,800 hectares are lake wetlands (18.41% of total area); and, 21,732,900 hectares are marsh wetlands (46.56% of total area).

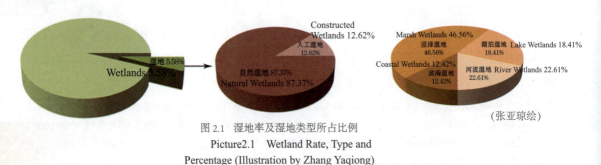

图 2.1　湿地率及湿地类型所占比例
Picture2.1　Wetland Rate, Type and
Percentage (Illustration by Zhang Yaqiong)

二、中国湿地的特点
II. The Features of Wetlands in China

我国湿地具有以下几个方面的特点：

Wetlands in China are characterized by the following features:

1. 类型多。《湿地公约》划分的 42 类湿地在中国均有分布，我国是全球湿地类型最丰富的国家之一。

1. Great diversity: the 42 types of wetlands as defined by *the Ramsar Convention on Wetlands* are all visible in China – one of the countries with the richest wetland diversity in the world.

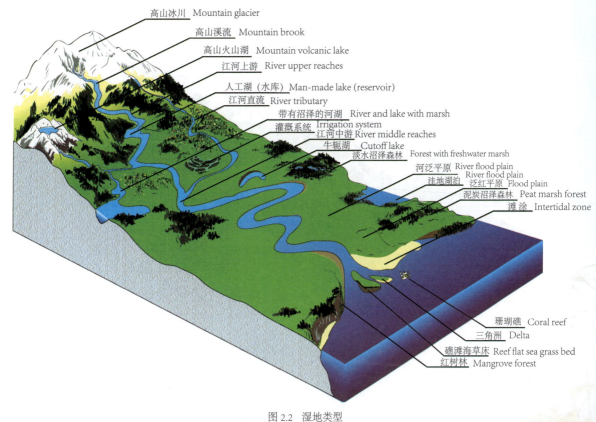

高山冰川 Mountain glacier
高山溪流 Mountain brook
高山火山湖 Mountain volcanic lake
江河上游 River upper reaches
人工湖（水库）Man-made lake (reservoir)
江河直流 River tributary
带有沼泽的河湖 River and lake with marsh
灌溉系统 Irrigation system
江河中游 River middle reaches
牛轭湖 Cutoff lake
淡水沼泽森林 Forest with freshwater marsh
河泛平原 River flood plain
洼地湖泊 River flood plain
泛红平原 Flood plain
泥炭沼泽森林 Peat marsh forest
滩涂 Intertidal zone
珊瑚礁 Coral reef
三角洲 Delta
礁滩海草床 Reef flat sea grass bed
红树林 Mangrove forest

图 2.2　湿地类型
Picture 2.2　Wetland Type

2. 面积大。我国湿地面积大，无论是在亚洲还是世界，总面积都居于前列。

2. Huge size: no matter in Asia or the world, China takes the lead in terms of wetland area.

3. 分布广，从寒温带到热带，从沿海到内陆，从平原到高原都有分布。

3. Wide distribution: wetlands are scattered across China from cold temperate zone to tropic zone, from coastal area to inland area, from plain to highland.

4. 区域差异显著，东部地区河流湿地多，东北部地区沼泽湿地多，长江中下游和青藏高原湖泊湿地多。

4. Acute regional disparity: while East China is dominated by river wetlands, Northeast China by marsh wetlands, the middle and lower reaches of Yangtze River as well as Tibetan

Plateau by lake wetlands.

5. 生物多样性丰富，湿地生境类型众多，不仅物种数量多，且许多为中国所特有。

5. Rich biodiversity: China is endowed with various wetlands of diversified habitats and rich species. And some of these habitats and species are only available in China too.

（刘璐绘）

图 2.3　湿地生物多样性

Picture 2.3　Biodiversity of Wetlands (Illustration by Liu Lu)

拓展阅读
Extra Reading Material

湿地生物之"趣"
Interesting Species among Wetland Creatures

能够捕食的植物——狸藻，属于狸藻科，是具有可活动囊状捕虫结构的小型食虫植物，能将小生物吸入囊中，并消化吸收。

Bladderwort, belongs to the family, and is an unusual carnivorous plant which captures and digests tiny aquatic animals as a source of food by means of a movable baglike structure.

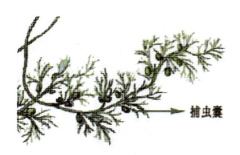

捕虫囊

（改绘自《奥托手绘彩色植物图谱》）
图 2.4 狸藻
Picture 2.4 *Utricularia vulgaris* (Adapted from an illustration shown in the *Color Atlas for Plants Hand Painted by Otto Wilhelm Thomé*)

（梁钊瑞绘）
图 2.5 中华鲟
Picture 2.5 The Chinese Sturgeon (*Acipenser sinensis*)
(Illustration by Liang Zhaorui)

在长江中最大的鱼——中华鲟（*Acipenser sinensis*），被誉为"水中熊猫"。
Acipenser sinensis (Chinese sturgeon) is the biggest fish in the Yangtze River. Due to its'rarity, it has been labelled as the "Panda of the Water".

世界上最小的湿地（种子）植物——"无根萍"（*Wolffia arrhiza*）又称"微萍"，它与浮萍很像，只有它的 1/4 大小，它开的花很小但有一个完整的花序。
Wolffia arrhiza (Micro duckweed) is the smallest wetland (seed) plant in the world. It resembles common duckweed in appearance, but is only 1/4 of duckweed in size. Despite its' tiny size, its' flower is complete in inflorescence.

被誉为"鸟类熊猫"——黑颈鹤（*Grus nigricollis*）。黑颈鹤是我国的三大国宝（大熊猫、金丝猴、黑颈鹤）之一，是人类发现最晚，也是世界上唯一在高原地带生活的珍稀鹤禽。
Grus nigricollis (Black-necked crane) is a rare type of bird, dubbed as the "Panda among birds". Not only is it one of China's three national treasures (together with the panda and the snub-nosed monkey), but it is the rare species to be discovered by man later than any other crane species as well as the only crane in the world to live on plateaus.

"蹄似牛非牛，头似马非马，尾似驴非驴，角似鹿非鹿"——麋鹿（*Elaphurus davidianus*）。
Elaphurus davidianus (Pere David's deer) is a rare deer found in the coastal wetlands of East China. It is unique, as it is said that it is one animal that has the characteristics of many others. Its' hooves resemble the hooves of cattle; its' head resembles a horse; its' tail resembles a donkey's tail; and, its' horns resemble the horns of a deer, which is exactly what it is!

被视为"羽族之宗长，仙人之骐骥"的动物——鹤。

Crane is believed as the chief of feathered birds and the sacred bird for the immortals to ride over amid clouds.

（张曼胤摄）

图 2.6　丹顶鹤
Picture 2.6　The Red-crowned Crane
(Photo by Zhang Manyin)

（梁钊瑞绘）

图 2.7　王莲
Picture 2.7　*Victoria Regia*
(Illustration by Liang Zhaorui)

水上叶子最大的植物——王莲（Victoria regia）。其初生叶呈针状，叶片圆形，像圆盘浮在水面，直径可达 2 米以上，叶面光滑，绿色略带微红。

Victoria regia (Queen Victoria waterlily) has the largest leaf of any aquatic plant. Its acrospire is like a needle in shape and its leaf is circular, like a huge disc, up to over 2 meters across and green in color but with a touch of red, floating on the water.

会仰泳的鱼——倒游鲇（Synodontis nigriventris），鲇鱼的一种，又叫反游猫，上下唇都长有须。除了会仰泳之外，它的全身都是灰黑色，连肚皮也不例外，身上布满黑珍珠似的斑点，人们也叫它"珠点朝天鼠"。

Synodontis nigriventris, one kind of catfish, is nicknamed as backstroke fish or backstroke cat since beards are visible in both of its upper and lower lips. In addition to being good at backstroke, it is gray black all over, including belly. Black pearl like spots are seen over its whole body, so it gains another nickname as belly-up mouse with pearl spots.

被称为清道夫的动物——螃蟹。螃蟹是甲壳纲动物，经常以其他动物尸体为食。繁殖时，一串串卵附在雌蟹的腹部，直到孵出小螃蟹。

Crabs are a type of scavenger. These crustaceans often feed on the bodies of dead animals. During the breeding season, masses of crab spawn (eggs) are attached to the belly of the mother crab until the larval crabs hatch out and float away.

以昆虫、蝌蚪和鱼为食的昆虫——仰泳蝽（*Notonectoidea*）经常在水面躺着，两条腿如船桨一样伸展，捕食时会潜到水下抓住植物或树枝。

Notonectoidea is one kind of insect, which often drifts upon water with face up and two legs extended out like a pair of oars. When preying, it will dive below water to cling to plant or tree branch for body fixation and then capture victims like insects, tadpoles and fishes as food.

（引自香港湿地公园官网）

图 2.8 仰泳蝽

Picture 2.8 Notonectoidea (Quoted from the Official Website of Hong Kong Wetland Park)

（李惠绘）

图 2.9 大鲵

Picture 2.9 The Chinese Giant Salamander (Andrias Davidianus) (Illusttration by Li Hui)

体型最大的两栖动物——大鲵（Andrias davidianus），俗称"娃娃鱼"，栖息在山涧溪流中，肉食性，主要以鱼、虾、蛙等为食，为国家二级保护动物。

Andrias davidianus is the biggest amphibian in the World. It is also known as the giant salamander, and is a carnivorous animal that is considered rare enough to have national second-grade protection in China. It lives in mountain brooks and streams, where it feeds on other steam dwellers such as fish, shrimps, frogs, etc.

丰富多彩的湿地公园
Colorful Wetland Park

1. 西溪国家湿地公园
1. Xixi National Wetland Park

坐落于杭州市区西部的西溪国家湿地公园，横跨西湖与余杭两区，属于罕见的城中次生湿地。该公园是我国第一个也是唯一的集城市湿地、农耕湿地、文化湿地于一体的国家湿地公园，也是我国第一个被列入国际湿地重要名录的国家湿地公园。

Located in west part of Hangzhou City and straddling West Lake and Yuhang districts, Xixi National Wetland Park is a rare urban secondary wetland park. It is also the first and only national wetland park capable to function as urban wetland, agricultural wetland and cultural wetland at the same time. Also, it is the first national wetland park in China being included into the Ramsar List of Wetlands of International Importance.

（俞肖剑摄）

图 2.10　西溪之秋
Picture 2.10　Autumn in Xixi National Wetland Park (Photo by Yu Xiaojian)

　　西溪，古称河渚，"曲水弯环，群山四绕，名园古刹，前后踵接，又多芦汀沙溆"，与西湖、西泠并称杭州"三西"。历史悠久的西溪湿地是古代帝王的青睐之所，雄才大略的秦始皇，躲避东南一隅的南宋高宗赵构，清代盛世的康熙与乾隆都曾经游历西溪并留下墨迹。这里不仅是帝王将相深爱之地，也是文人雅士读书、为文的地方。苏东坡、唐伯虎、冯梦桢、郁达夫、徐志摩等文人墨客都曾寓居于此，久久不愿离去，留下了大批诗词文章。

Xixi, termed as Hezhu in ancient time, is a place "surrounded by winding water and towering mountain, adjacent to famous garden and time-honored temple, and dotted with many waterfront weed shoals." It was jointly acclaimed as "Three Xi" together with Xihu (West Lake) and Xiling. The time-honored Xixi Wetland has long been the favored retreats for ancient emperors. For example, emperors like the aspiring First Emperor of Qin, exiled Emperor Gaozong (Zhao Gou) of Southern Song Dynasty, Emperors Kangxi and Qianlong - the founders of prosperous Qing Dynasty all visited Xixi and left inscriptions to express their appreciation for the beautiful wetland. The place was also deeply beloved by scholars as well who chose to settle there for long with many poems and articles left like Su Dongpo, Tang Bohu, Feng Mengzhen, Yu Dafu, Xu Zhimo, etc.

　　西溪不仅拥有悠久的历史，其景致也毫不逊色。西溪之胜，首在于水。水是西溪的灵魂，正所谓"卢锥几顷界为田，一曲溪流一曲烟"，整个园区六条河流纵横交汇，水道如巷、河汊如网、鱼塘栉比如鳞、诸岛棋布，形成了西溪独特的湿地景致。

In addition to being a place with splendid history, Xixi also boasts breathtaking sceneries. As described by the poem lines that "vast stretch of reeds is bordered by golden field and misty brooks are winding briskly ahead," water is the first eye-striking element widely seen in Xixi. The wetland park demonstrates a unique wetland view thanks to its closely interwoven six rivers, waterways, river branches, fish ponds and islands.

(俞肖剑摄)

图 2.11　西溪之美，首在于水
Picture 2.11　Water: the First Defining Element of Xixi National Wetland Park (Photo by Yu Xiaojian)

西溪湿地保护与利用的平衡点是要做到在保护的前提下进行适度利用，通过适度利用实现更好的保护。坚持国家湿地公园要求的"生态优先、最小干预、修旧如旧、注重文化、可持续发展"六大原则，全面加强湿地及其生物多样性保护，维护湿地生态系统的生态特性和基本功能，保持和最大限度地发挥其各种功能和效益。

To strike a balance between the protection and development of Xixi wetland, efforts should be made to use it rationally under the precondition of sufficient protection. Better protection of Xixi wetland could be realized through proper usage. As guided by the six major principles of "giving priority to ecologic health, ensuring the minimal human intervention, maintaining original look unchanged, valuing cultural service, and achieving sustainable development", overall efforts should be made to enhance wetland and biodiversity protection, safeguard biological features and basic functions of wetland ecological system, so as to have its functions and benefits maintained and employed to the maximum degree.

2. 翠湖国家城市湿地公园
2. Cuihu National Urban Wetland Park

公园位于海淀区上庄镇上庄水库北侧，与稻香湖、上庄水库同属于一个水域系统，其独特的湿地形态宛如嵌在京城中的一块绿色"翡翠"，占地面积约 157 公顷，水域面积 90 公顷，分为封闭保护区、过渡缓冲区、开放体验区。公园内动植物资源丰富，原生、栽植湿地高等植物 371 种，野生鸟类 178 种，鱼类 20 种，两栖动物 7 种，爬行动物 8 种。开放体验区因地制宜地设计了湿地文化长廊、蝴蝶谷、观鸟阁、蛙声伴客、临湖映眺、观鱼区、湿地植物体验区等景点。这里环境优美，湖水清澈，水生植物丰富，成为候鸟在北京过冬或南迁的优选之地。

Located to the north of Shangzhuang water reservoir at Shangzhuang Town of Haidian District of Beijing, Cuihu National Urban Wetland Park falls into the same water system with Daoxiang Lake, and Shangzhuang Water Reservoir. It looks like green emerald embedded in the capital city in virtue of its distinctive wetland morphology. Covering 157 hectare of land area and 90 hectare of water area, the park can be divided into enclosed protection zone, transitional buffer zone, and open experiencing zone. Of the abundant plant and animal resources in the park, 371 species are protogenic and transplanted higher plants, 178 species of wild birds, 20 fish, 7 amphibians, and 8 reptiles. Scenic sights like wetland culture corridor, butterfly valley, bird observatory, flog pond, lakeview zone, fish world, wetland plants observatory are set aside in open experiencing zone. This picturesque park of clean water and rich aquatic plantation is the place favored by migratory birds for wintering or stop in Beijing during their southwards journey.

(李伟摄)

图 2.12　湿地景观
Picture2. 12　Wetland Scenery (Photo by Li Wei)

湿地有溪流、沼泽、天鹅湖、雁鸭湖、鸟岛、芦苇荡、滩涂、荷花池、稻田等景观。公园坚持生态优先、公益为主，以重在保护和最小干预为管理原则，通过多年来的人工修复和封育保护，逐步形成清代著名词人纳兰性德诗中描绘的"野色湖光两不分，碧天万顷变黄云。分明一幅江村画，着个闲庭挂夕曛"的自然湿地景观。

Inviting nature scenes like brook, marsh, swan lake, wild goose lake, bird island, reed marsh, intertidal zone, lotus pond, paddy field are frequently seen in the park. As guided by such key principles as giving priority to ecological health, promoting public interest, valuing proactive protection, and ensuring the minimal human intervention, the park has, after years of recovery and protection efforts, gradually formed a natural wetland scenery as described by Nalan Xingde – a famed poet of Qing Dynasty – the glory scene of golden filed is mirrored upon the limpid lake, suddenly, the transparent sky above is overwhelmed by glowing clouds. Standing in the yard, I was left gasped for the splendid countryside view bathed in the aura of setting sun.

乘船沿着曲折幽静的水道前行，池内大面积各色的荷花（Nelumbo mucifera）和睡莲（Nymphaea tetragona）簇拥，它们有的平卧水面，有的亭亭玉立，高高地凌驾于绿叶之上，纯洁剔透，把水面点缀得绚丽多彩。此时，不由得让人想起宋人杨万里的送行诗《晓出净慈寺送林子方》中的诗句"毕竟西湖六月中，风光不与四时同；接天莲叶无穷碧，映日荷花别样红。"

During your boat tour into the depth of the park along winding and tranquil waterway, you will be greeted by pond of colorful lotuses and water lilies. While some of them lie across water, some stand high above water and green leaves. These pure and elegant flowers make the water surface amazingly colorful. Such a splendid view naturally brings back to us a memory about a poem titled *Farewell to Lin Zifang at Jingci Temple at Dawn* by Poet Yang Wanli of Song Dynasty -"The landscape of West Lake in June is quite different from that in other seasons. While green lotus leaves spread far to the skyline, lotus flowers look even more scarlet under sun."

(李伟摄)

图 2.13　接天莲叶无穷碧，映日荷花别样红
Picture2. 13　Lotus Pond in June (Photo by Li Wei)

3. 香港湿地公园
3. Hong Kong Wetland Park

公园位于天水围北部，建有超过 60 公顷的湿地保护区，以及占地 1 万平方米的室内展览馆"湿地互动世界"，是亚洲首个拥有同类型设施的公园。1998 年，前渔农署（现更名为渔农自然护理署）及前香港旅游协会（现更名为香港旅游发展局）展开了一项有关把该生态缓解区扩展成为一个湿地生态旅游景点的可行性研究，研究的结论是不消弱其生态缓解功能在该生态缓解区建设湿地公园，于是建立了香港湿地公园。

Situated to the north of Tianshuiwei, Hong Kong Wetland Park consists of one wetland nature reserve of more than 60 hectares in area, and Wetland Interactive World – an indoor exhibition hall covering 10,000 square meters of land. As a pioneering park of this kind never seen in other places in Asia, Hong Kong Wetland Park was built followed a study conducted in 1998 and jointly by Fishman Administration Bureau (the predecessor of Agriculture, Fisheries and Conservation Department) and Hong Kong Tourism Association (the predecessor of Hong Kong Tourism Board) on the feasibility to expand a ecological relief area into a wetland ecological tourism attraction. As confirmed by the study, the ecological relief area – turned – wetland ecological tourism attraction will not weaken its original ecological relief function, so, Hong Kong Wetland Park was established with solid ground.

图 2.14 香港湿地公园
Picture 2.14 Hong Kong Wetland Park (Photo by Li Wei)

公园展示了香港湿地生态系统的多样化以及凸显保护它们的重要性。此外，并提供机会建立以湿地功能及价值为主题的教育及休闲场地供人们使用。在 2013 年，香港湿地公园共进行了 117 次生态资源调查。直至 2013 年年底，公园内鸟类物种数目已累积达 246 种，水禽或依赖湿地的鸟类占鸟类物种总数约 47%。除鸟类外，还有多种其他种类的生物，其中与湿地有密切关系的蜻蜓、蝴蝶、两栖类和爬行类动物种类的数目分别为 52 种、161 种、10 种和 29 种。公园经常开展系列湿地保护行动，让公众体验湿地生物的多样性以及生态系统服务的奇趣。在活动中传播湿地知识的同时展示湿地生境孕育着各种人类重要的生活需要，以及种类繁多的湿地野生生物。

Hong Kong Wetland Park will not only demonstrate to visitors the diversity of Hong Kong wetland system and the importance in protecting it, but is an ideal venue to stage mass education about wetland functions and value as well as an ideal venue for leisure seeking. In 2013 alone, Hong Kong Wetland Park conducted 117 ecological resource investigations. As of the end of 2013, there were 246 species of birds available in the park, of which, aquatic birds or birds reliance on wetland for living account for 47% of the total. In addition to birds, the park is also home to many creatures. For example, the park accommodates respectively 52, 161, 10 and 29 species of dragonflies, butterflies, amphibians and reptiles which all bear close relation to wetlands. The park also often hosts series of wetland protection activities, enabling the public to understand the biodiversity of wetlands and their marvelous ecological value and service. In addition to spreading knowledge about wetlands, such activities also help visitors to know the significant role played by wetlands to our life and diversified creatures living in wetlands.

(引自香港湿地公园官方网站)

图 2.15 湿地鸟类保护宣传海报
Picture 2.15 Publicity Poster for Wetland Bird Protection
(Quoted from the Official Website of Hong Kong Wetland Park)

图 2.16 公园全景图（台北市野鸟学会关渡自然公园管理处提供）
Picture 2.16 Panorama of Taiwan Guandu Nature Park
(Photo Provided by Guandu Nature Park of Wild Bird Association of Taipei)

4. 台湾关渡自然公园

4. Taiwan Guandu Nature Park

公园位于台北盆地北端，地处淡水河与基隆河交汇的冲积湿地，面积仅 57 公顷。由于它处于繁华的大都市之中，却有着优越的生态环境，所以被称为台北市都会中心的绿宝石。独特的地理环境赋予了公园丰富的自然资源，河水与潮汐带来的营养物质聚集于此，造就了营养充分的生态环境，为多种生物生存提供了生存条件。自古以来这里就是重要的候鸟栖息地，鸟类记录多达 260 种以上。自 20 世纪 70 年代起，众多 NGO（Non-Government Organization）组织及民众就呼吁希望可以将这个地方予以保护保留。终于在 1996 年，台北市政府拨款规划成立关渡自然公园，并于 2001 年 7 月正式开始营运，由台北市野鸟学会进行经营管理。

Located at the north end of Taipei basin and the alluvial wetland where Danshui River meets with Keelung River, Taiwan Guandu Nature Park is only 57 hectares in area, but acclaimed as the emerald in the heart of bustling Taipei thanks to its superior ecological environment. Abundant with rich natural resources generated by its unique geographic environment, the park enjoys a favorable ecological environment for wetland creatures with sufficient nutrient substances amassed from river and tide. The park has long been an important habitat for migratory birds from ancient time. About 260 species of birds have been recorded to settle here. In response to the consistent call from NGO and local people since 1970s to have the natural habitat well kept and maintained, Taipei City finally allocated fund in 1996 to establish Guandu Nature Park, which was formally put into operation in July 2001 and under the management of Wild Bird Association of Taipei.

图 2.17　湿地亲水（台北市野鸟学会关渡自然公园管理处提供）
Picture 2.17　Taiwan Guandu Nature Park
(Photo Provided by Guandu Nature Park of Wild Bird Association of Taipei)

公园规划有保育核心区、户外观察区、主要设施区及永续经营区 4 个区域。其中的户外观察区、主要设施区和永续经营区都规划设计了如步道、解说系统、赏鸟廊道等可供教学使用的设施，也在主要设施区设置游客中心，为游客学习提供更周到的服务。

The park is comprised by core breeding zone, outdoor observatory zone, major facility zone and sustainable operation zone. Except of core breeding zone, all the three zones are equipped with facilities for mass education purpose like walking path, narrative system, and bird observation corridor, and visitors' center is built in the major facility zone for the convenience of them with more considerate services.

有"赏鸟的天堂，北台湾最后一块净土"美誉的关渡自然公园，其土质松软泥泞且植被丰富，为鸟类提供了良好的栖息环境。每年 10 月至次年 3 月为观鸟旺季，可以在公园中观看到台湾 400 多种鸟类中的 200 种，足见鸟类资源的丰富。公园展示台湾湿地生态系统的多样化以及保护它们的重要性。此外，还提供了建立以湿地功能及价值为主题的教育及休闲场地。

Commended as "the paradise of birds, the last pure land in north of Taiwan", Guandu Nature Park provides excellent settlement environment for birds with its soft and loose sludge grown with dense vegetation. During the best season for bird observation during October to March of next year, visitors can observe about 200 species of birds in the park alone out of 400-strong species of birds available in Taiwan. Also demonstrated in the park are the diversity of wetland ecological system in Hong Kong and the significance to protect the system. Besides, education and recreation venues are set aside in the park to give prominence to the function and value of wetlands.

试一试
Give This A Try

我们知道科学学科的特点就是"用事实说话"，请在本节课的学习内容中找到对我国湿地特点加以描述的数据信息的关键词，完成下面的知识树。
As we all know, science is a discipline stressing on "speaking with facts". Please find out key data describing features of wetlands in this section, and complete the knowledge tree.

图 2.18　中国湿地特点
picture2.18　Features of wetlands in China

想一想
Give This Some Thought

在你周围的湿地有没有随着时间的流逝而发生变化？试举例说明。

Are there any changes happening to wetlands around you over time? Try to find examples, if any.

第二节 绚烂多彩的湿地植物
Section Ⅱ Colorful Wetland Plant

学习日志
Notebook

　　请将你的日志本分成 3 部分，在左侧写出你所知道的湿地植物的名称，在中间一部分写出这些植物的形态结构特征，在最右面写出这些植物的作用是什么？

Please divide the space into three sections, and write down the names of wetland plants you have known on the left side, their morphological features in the middle, and their functions on the right side.

学海拾贝
Pearls of Knowledge

一、湿地植物的概念和分类
I. Concept and Types of Wetland Plants

1. 湿地植物（Wetlands Plant）的概念

1. Concept of Wetland Plants

　　湿地植物资源十分丰富，品种繁多，层次丰富，从陆生植物过渡到沉水植物，包括沼生植物、湿生植物和水生植物。据调查统计，我国湿地高等植物约有 225 科 815 属 2276 种，分别占全国高等植物科、属、种数的 63.7%、25.6% 和 7.7%。

Wetland plants are highly plentiful. They cover wide scope of species ranging from terrestrial plants to submerged plants, and with helophyte, hygrophyte, aquatic plants included. Statistic data show China is home to 2,276 species of wetland higher plants of 815 genuses of 225 families, accounting for 7.7% of total species, 25.6% of total genuses and 63.7% of total families of national high plants.

　　苔藓植物有 64 科 139 属 267 种，其中以凤尾藓科（*Fissidentaceae*）为最多。蕨类植物有 27 科 42 属 70 种，其中金星蕨科（*Thelypteridaceae*）种数最多。被子植物有 130 科、625 属、1919 种，以禾本科（*Poaceae*）种数最多。在中国湿地植物中，有国家一级保护野生植物 6 种：中华水韭（*Isoetes sinensis*）、宽叶水韭（*Isoetes japonica*）、水松（*Glyptostrobus pensilis*）、水杉（*Metasequoia glyptostroboides*）、莼菜（*Brasenia schreberi*）、长喙毛茛泽泻（*Ranalisma rostratum*）；国家二级保护野生植物 11 种。

Bryophyte can be divided into 267 species of 139 genuses of 64 families. Of them, Fissidentaceae is the most widely seen. Pteridophyte can be divided into 70 species of 42 genuses of 27 families. Of them, Thelypteridaceae is the most widely seen. Gymnosperm can be divided into 20 species of 9 genuses of 4 families. Of them, Pinaceae is the most widely seen. Angiosperm can be divided into 1,919 species of 625 genuses of 130 families. Of them, Poaceae is the most widely seen family. Of Chinese wetland plants, 6 wild plants are under first-grade national protection, e.g. *Isoetes sinensis, Isoetes japonica, Glyptostrobus pensilis, Metasequoia glyptostroboides, Brasenia schreberi, and Ranalisma rostratum*; 11 wild plants are under second-grade national protection.

2. 湿地植物的分类

2. Types of Wetland Plants

湿地植物从生长环境看，可以分为水生、沼生、湿生三类；从植物生活类型看，可以分为挺水型、浮水型、沉水型、浮游型；从植物生长类型看，可以分为藻类、苔藓、蕨类、草本类、灌木类、乔木类。

In terms of their ecological niches, wetland plants are classified into aquatic plants, helophytes, and hygrophytes. Wetland plants can also be classified based upon their growing position in the ecosystem, i.e., emergent plants, floating plants, submerged plants, and phytoplankton. In terms of plants genre, wetland plants can also be classified into algae, mosses, ferns, herbs, shrubs, trees, etc.

水生植物（hydrophyte）是指植物体或多或少淹没于水中的植物；沼生植物（helophyte）是指一般生长于沼泽浅水中或地下水位较高的地表植物；湿生植物（hygrophyte）指生长在淹水或过度潮湿环境中的植物。

Wetland plants which grow in are more or less water logged conditions are generally termed as hydrophytes; plants which grow in shallow water marshes or on the surface of a water body with deep underground water are generally termed as helophytes; and, plants which live in water logged areas or excessively humid environments are generally termed as hygrophytes.

下面就植物的生活类型进行分类描述：

Now, let's see how wetland plants are classified by their living status.

（1）挺水植物（Emerged Plant）

(1) Emerged plants

挺水植物就是指根长在底泥中而茎叶伸出水面并在大气中开花的植物，即植物的根、根茎生长在水的底泥之中，茎、叶挺出水面。常分布于 0~1.5 米的浅水处，其中有的种类生长于潮湿的岸边。这类植物在空气中的部分，具有陆生植物的特征；生长在水中的部分（根或地下茎），具有水生植物的特征。常见有：芦苇、水芹、茭白、荷花、香蒲。

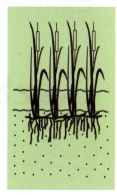

图 2.19 典型挺水植物剖面图（改自 *Treatment Wetlands, Second Edition*）
Picture2.19 Section Drawing of Typical Emerged Plants
(Adapted from *Treatment Wetlands, Second Edition*)

Emerged plants refer to plants whose roots extend into bottom sediments, but whose leaves stretch above the water surface, and whose flowers can be seen above the water surface. Emerged plants are normally distributed across shallow water areas of between 0-1.5 meters in depth. Some species live along the water saturated banks of wetlands, and such species demonstrate features of both terrestrial plants and aquatic plants. Commonly seen emergent plants in China are *reed bulrush, Oenanthe javanica, Zizania latifolia, lotus, and typha.*

挺水植物的适应能力强，根系发达，生长量大，营养生长与生殖生长并存，对氮、磷、钾的吸收能力强。

In short, emerged plants are highly adaptable species with, in general, robust root systems that have a high absorption capacity for nitrogen, phosphorus, and potassium. They often grow in dense stands, and can reproduce both vegetatively and through seed dispersal.

（2）浮水植物（Floating Plant）

(2) Floating plants

一般来说，浮水植物包括浮叶植物和漂浮植物。它们或具有发达的地下根茎或块根，或能产生大量的种子果实，多为季节性休眠植物类型，一般是冬季枯萎春季萌发，生长季节主要集中在 4~9 月。

Generally speaking, floating plants include floating-leaved plants and floating plants. They have either robust underground tuber/root tuber, or can generate a great deal of seeds and fruits. Basically, they are of seasonal dormant plants, withering in the winter and budding in the spring, with growth season concentrated in April to September.

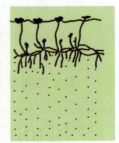

浮叶植物的生长离不开湿地土壤,具有较好的耐淤能力,不易暴发性生长;适宜生长环境的水深一般为40~100厘米。常见的有睡莲、芡实等。

Floating-leaved plants are indispensable from wetland soil for growth and have the ability to rap large quantities of silt and sediments, difficult to grow

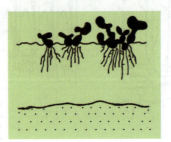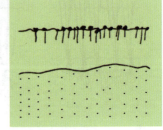

图 2.20 典型浮水植物剖面图
Picture 2.20 Section Drawing of Typical Floating Plants

explosively. They are usually found in water depths of between 40 and 100 cm and include common species such as Nymphaea tetragona, Euryale ferox, etc.

漂浮植物根系发达,生物量大,生长迅速,部分具有季节性休眠现象,如冬季休眠或死亡的水蕹菜,夏季休眠的豆瓣菜等。生长旺盛期主要集中在每年的3~10月或9月~次年5月;漂浮植物的生育周期相对较短,主要以营养生长为主。常见的漂浮植物有藻、李氏禾、浮萍、水蕹菜、豆瓣菜等。

Floating plants have robust root systems, rich biomass, and rapid growth, and as such can survive in most wetland conditions. Some of them normally show seasonal dormancy, for example, *Ipomoea aquatica* is a floating plant which is dormant or dies back in the winter. *Nasturtium officinale* is a floating plant that is dormant in the summer. The main growing season of floating plants falls in March to October or September to May of the following year. Their growth is dominated by vegetative growth as their reproductive growth period is short. Common floating plants include *Pistia stratiotes*, *Leersiahexandra*, *Lemna minor*, *Ipomoea aquatica*, *Nasturtium officinale*, etc.

（3）沉水植物（submerged plant）

(3) Submerged plants

沉水植物是指植物体全部位于水层下面,由根、根须或叶状体固着在水下基质上生活的大型植物。它们的根有的不发达甚至退化,植物体的各部分都可吸收水分和养料,表皮细胞没有角质或蜡质层,能直接吸收水分和溶于水中的氧和其他营养物质,通气组织特别发达,利于在水中缺乏空气的情况下进行气体交换。这类植物

 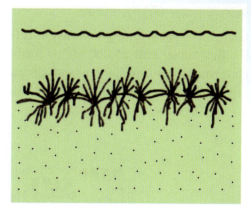

图 2.21 典型沉水植物剖面图（改自 *Treatment Wetlands,Second Edition*）
Picture 2.21　Section Drawing of Typical Submerged Plants
(Adapted from Treatment Wetlands,Second Edition)

的叶子大多为带状或丝状，如苦草（ *Vallisneria spiralis* ）、金鱼藻（ *Ceratophyllum demersum* ）、狐尾藻（ *Myriophyllum verticillatum* ）、黑藻（ *Hydrilla verticillata* ）等。植物体长期沉没在水下，仅在开花时花柄、花朵才露出水面。如狸藻（Utricularia vulgaris ）和眼子菜（ *Potamogeton distinctus* ）等。

Submerged plants refer to plants whose whole body is submerged under water with roots, root hairs, and fronds clinging to the underwater substrates. Their roots are poorly developed or even degenerated. These plants are capable of absorbing water and nutriments directly through their strems, leaves and roots, as their epidermis cells are free from cutinous or waxy coats, and can easily absorb water, soluble oxygen and other nutrients. Their aeration tissues are unusually strong, making gaseous exchange easy when oxygen is depleted in the water column. The leaves of submerged plants (*e.g. Vallisneria spiralis, Ceratophyllum demersum, Myriophyllum verticillatum, and Hydrilla verticillata*) are generally belt- or strap shaped. Submerged plants (*e.g. Utricularia vulgaris and Potamogeton distinctus*) are beneath the water surface most of time, but their anthocaulus and flowers will usually emerge from the water surface when flowering.

很多沉水植物生长有假根，主要是作为固定器官来使用，具有较弱的吸收能力。但也有些沉水植物没有假根，如金鱼藻（ *Ceratophyllum demersum* ）等。

Many submerged plants have a rhizoid that serves to attach the plant to the bottom but displays a weak absorption capability. Some submerged plants, like hornwort *Ceratophyllum demersum,* do not have a rhizoid.

（4）浮游植物（Phytoplankton）

(4) Phytoplankton

浮游植物通常指浮游藻类，全世界约有 40000 种，其中淡水藻类约有 25000 种。这些藻类具有能吸收光能和二氧化碳进行光合作用制造有机物的色素或色素体，是湿地生态系统中的初级生产者。

Generally speaking, phytoplankton refers to floating algae. Of about 40,000 species of floating algae, near 25,000 are of freshwater algae. Such algae have unique pigments or chromatophores capable to absorb optical energy and carbon dioxide for the production of organics. They are primary producers of water area.

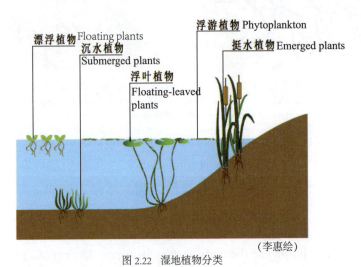

漂浮植物 Floating plants
沉水植物 Submerged plants
浮叶植物 Floating-leaved plants
浮游植物 Phytoplankton
挺水植物 Emerged plants

(李惠绘)

图 2.22 湿地植物分类

Picture 2.22 Types of Wetland Plants (Illustration by Li Hui)

二、湿地植物形态特征
II. Morphological Features of Wetland Plants

为适应湿地环境，湿地植物组织、器官的结构与形态具有以下一些特征：

In order to adapt to wetland environment, wetland plants' tissues and organs feature unique structures and morphology as follows:

发达的通气组织。存在于大多数水生植物及湿生植物中。例如，眼子菜属（Potamogeton）、水鳖（Hydrocharis asiatica）、香蒲属（Typha）、慈姑（Sagiattaria trifolia）、雨久花（Monochoriamorsakowii）等植物。

Advanced aeration tissues: such tissues are widely seen in the majority of aquatic plants and hygrophyte like *Potamogeton, Hydrocharis asiatica, Typha, Sagiattaria trifolia, Monochoriamorsakowii,* etc.

特化或异型的叶片结构。主要存在于水生植物中。为适应水流，沉于水中的叶片多为条形或者线性；为适应漂浮，浮于水面的叶片常变宽，挺水的叶片则因种类而异。一些水生植物的沉水叶、浮水叶或挺水叶常常异型，如浮叶眼子菜（*Potamogeton natans*）有退化为叶柄的沉水叶和宽椭圆形的浮水叶，槐叶萍（*Salvinia natans*）有须状的沉水叶和椭圆形的浮水叶，泽泻（*Alisma plantago-aquatica*）有退化为线性叶柄的沉水叶、具长柄的长圆形浮水叶以及长椭圆形或宽卵形的挺水叶。

Special or meta-typical leaf structure: such structures are widely seen in aquatic plants. The submerged leaves of many aquatic plants are linear in shape, due to their ecological adaption to water flows and currents. Also, leaves that are floating on the water surface are often widened to better facilitate flotation. As the leaves of aquatic plants have evolving to their physical environment, it is common to see submerged, floating or emerged leaves often have a meta-typical appearance. For example, *Potamogeton natans* has stalk-like submerged leaves which and wide elliptic floating leaves, *Salvinia natans* features beard-like submerged leaves and elliptic-shaped floating leaves, *Alisma plantago-aquatica* has linear submerged leaves, long-rounded floating leaves with long stems, and oblong or wide-ovate-shaped emergent leaves.

发达的根茎或不定根。常存在于挺水植物和湿地植物中。由于湿地环境局部的均一性，许多植物常通过发达的根茎或不定根来快速扩充领地，因此许多湿地植物常大片生长，其地下部分就是通过发达的根茎相互连接的。典型的代表植物有芦苇（*Phragmites communis*）、香蒲（*Typha orientalis*）和黑三棱（*Sparganium stoloniferum*）等。

Advanced tubers or adventitous roots: such structures are often seen in emergent plants and hygrophytes. Homogenous wetland environments are conducive for such plants to quickly colonose new areas due to their advanced tubers or adventitous roots. This adaptation is the reason why many wetland plants grow in large patches or beds. Their underground parts are connected by advanced tubers. The most typical wetland plants in this regard are *Phragmites communis, Typha orientalis*, and *Sparganium stoloniferum*, etc.

泌盐结构。植物常吸收过量的盐分，通过叶片或枝条表面的特殊泌盐结构可将多余的盐分排出体外，排出的盐分常在叶片的表面形成粉状结构。如柽柳（*Tamarix chinensis*）、桐花树（*Aegiceras corniculatum*）、盐地碱蓬（*Suaeda salsa*）等。

Salt excretion structures: extra salts absorbed by some wetland plants are often excreted out via their unique salt excretion structures in their leaves and stem surfaces. The excreted salts often remain as salt crusts or powder on the leaf and stem surfaces. For instance, *Tamarix chinensis, Aegiceras corniculatum*, and *Suaeda salsa* are wetland plants with these unique salt excretion structures.

三、湿地植物作用
III. Value of Wetland Plants

很多湿地植物在工农业生产中扮演着重要角色。有些湿地植物具有食用价值。水稻就是典型人工培育的湿地植物，世界上近一半人口，包括几乎整个东亚和东南亚的人口，都以稻米为食。还有很多湿地植物也可以用作食物，例如莲（*Nelumbo nucifera*）、慈 姑（*Sagiattaria trifolia*）、芡 实（*Euryale ferox*）、水 芹（*Oenanthe javanica*）、宽叶香蒲（*Typha latifolia*）等。慈姑的球茎含有大量淀粉，是很好的食材。有些湿地植物是良好的饲料和绿肥，如浮萍（*Lemna minor*）可作为鱼类饵料；满江红（*Azolla imbricata*）等既是草鱼的饵料，又可喂猪、鸭，还可做水稻的肥料。有些湿地植物浑身都是宝，例如芦苇的根部可以入药，有解毒、清凉、镇呕等功能，也是造纸、建材等的良好的工业原料。

Many wetland plants play an important role in industrial and agricultural production. Some wetland plants can be used as food. The rice is a typical wetland plant cultivated by humans. Almost half of the world's population, including almost all of the East Asia and Southeast Asia, rely on rice as a staple. Many wetland plants also can be used as food, like the lotus (*Nelumbo nucifera*), the arrowhead (*Sagiattaria trifolia*), the fox nut (*Euryale ferox*), the water fennel (*Oenanthe javanica*), and the bulrush (*Typha latifolia*). The arrowhead contains a lot of starch in its bulb, making the plant usable as a food material. Some wetland plants are viewed as excellent forage and manure plants, like the duckweed (*Lemna minor*), which can be used as a fish food, and *Azolla imbricata*, which can be used as food by the grass carp and by pigs and ducks and as manure for the rice. Some wetland plants may have each and every one of their parts put to good use. For example, the reed has a root that can be used as an ingredient in medicines to add curative functions like detoxification, refreshing, and vomiting relief; the reed root also can be used as an excellent raw material in industries like papermaking and building materials.

水质指示器。湿地植物的生长、生存和繁殖等情况可以直接或间接地反映出某个水域水体相应的物理化学及其他环境情况，显示水质的变化，如北京水毛茛（*Batrachium pekinense*）、莼菜（*Brasenia schreberi*）等就具有指示水体污染情况的作用。

Working as water quality indicator: the growth, survival and reproduction of wetland plants can, directly or indirectly, reflect the physical, chemical and other environmental circumstances of the concerned water area or water body, thus demonstrating the change of water quality. For example, *Batrachium pekinense* and *Brasenia schreberi* are capable to indicate the pollution degree of concerned water body.

湿地净化功能的核心。湿地植物在污水处理系统方面起着重要的作用，与微生物、基质、水体及动物相互协同，使得整个湿地生态系统平衡运转，发挥良好的净化功能。尤其是植物在人工湿地中作用更加明显：吸收利用和吸附富集污染物质；输送氧气到湿地生态系统，提供根区微生物生长、繁殖和降解所需的氧气；维持和加强人工湿地内的水力传输，维持系统稳定等。

Wetland plants are at the core of wetlands' purification function. Water purifiers: wetland plants in collaboration with micro-organisms, substrates, water chemistry and wetland biology, can play a very significant role in wastewater treatment systems. These processes enable wetland ecosystems to run in a balanced fashion with enhanced water purification effects achieved. The roles played by plants in constructed wetlands are even more diversified. For example, such plants can absorb, utilize, and capture concentrated pollutants; convey oxygen to the wetland ecosystem; provide oxygen needed for the growth, production and degradation of micro-organisms in the root zone; maintain and enhance hydraulic power transportation within constructed wetlands; and, maintain the stability of constructed wetlands.

营造优美的湿地景观。湿地植物的生长环境一般有岸际、岸边、水面、堤、岛等多种形式。湖面上的荷花（*Nelumbo nucifera Gaertn*）、在河岸的芦苇、大片的香蒲（*Typha orientalis*）、慈姑、水葱、浮萍能使水景野趣盎然。湿地中植物的生态习性不同，深水、中水、浅水区，分别生长不同植物。通常深水区在中央，渐至岸边分别是中水、浅水生长有沼生、湿生植物。多种类植物的搭配，在视觉效果上相互衬托，形成丰富而又错落有致的效果。

A beautiful wetland landscape needs to be created. Generally speaking, wetland plants flourish along banks, water surfaces, embankments, islands and various places within the wetland. Wetland plants growing in lakes such as *Nelumbo nucifera* and along river banks, such as common reed, *Typha orientalis, Sagiattaria trifolia, Scirpus tabernaemontan,* duckweed (*Lemna minor*) all contribute to the wetland scenery. Plants with different ecological niches inhabit variable depth water zones. Generally speaking, deeper water zones are located at the center of a water body, with medium depth water zones and shallow water zones located closer to the wetland edges, respectively. The rich tapestry of wetland plants and hygrophytes create beautiful views and water scapes.

拓展阅读
Extra Reading Material

多样的植物形态特征
Diverse Morphological Features of Plants

1. 叶序
1. Phyllotaxis

互生：每节上只着生一片叶子，且各节交互长出
Alternate: only one leaf grows in each section of the stem, and stem sections grow alternatively.

对生：每节上着生 2 叶，相对而生。
Opposite: two opposite leaves grow in each stem section.

轮生：每节上着生3片叶或3叶以上，呈辐射状排列。

Whorled: three or more leaves grow in each stem section in radiation arrangement.

（刘璐改绘自《植物学》）

图 2.23　互生叶、对生叶、轮生叶
Picture 2.23　Alternate Leaf, Opposite Leaf, Whorled Leaf
(Adapted from an illustration shown on *the Botany* by Liu Lu)

2. 叶形
2. Leaf Shape

椭圆形：叶片中部较宽，两端较窄且为等圆，长度约为宽度的2倍或更少。

Elliptic: the leaf has broad middle part, narrow and round sides. Leaf length is about twice or less than twice of leaf width.

卵形：叶片下部圆阔，上部稍狭，长度约为宽度的2倍或更少。

Oval: the leaf has wide and round bottom, shallow upper part. Leaf length is about twice or less than twice of leaf width.

倒卵形：叶片下部稍狭，上部圆阔，长度约为宽度的2倍或更少。

Obovate: the leaf has relatively narrow bottom, round and broad upper part. Leaf length is about twice or less than twice of leaf width.

披针形：叶片较线形宽，由下部至先端渐次狭尖。

Lanceolate: lanceolate leaf is broader than linear leaf and gradually becomes narrow and pointed from bottom to tip.

针形：叶片长似针者。

Aciculiform: the leaf looks like a needle.

（刘璐改绘自《植物学》）

图 2.24 叶形（椭圆形、卵形、倒卵形、披针形、针形）
Picture 2.24   Leaf Shape (Elliptic, Oval, Obovate, Lanceolate, Aciculiform)
(Adapted from an illustration shown on *the Botany* by Liu Lu)

3. 叶缘
3. Leaf Edge

全缘：叶缘平整无齿。
Entire: leaf edge is smooth without prong.

波状：叶缘起伏呈波浪状。
Undulate: left edge fluctuates wavily.

锯齿：叶缘具尖锐的齿，齿尖向前。
Serrate: leaf edge has sharp tooth. Tooth top points forwards.

图 2.25 叶缘类型（全缘、波状、锯齿）
Picture 2.25   Leaf Edge (Entire, Undulate, Serrate)
(Adapted from an illustration shown on *the Botany* by Liu Lu)

（刘璐改绘自《植物学》）
图 2.26 叶裂类型（羽状分裂、掌状分裂）
Picture 2.26   Leaf Lobes
(Pinnation, Palmation)

4. 叶裂
4. Leaf Lobes

羽状分裂：裂片呈羽状排列。

Pinnation: leaf lobes are arranged in pinniform.

掌状分裂：叶片近圆形，裂片呈掌状排列。

Palmation: leaf shape is close to round, with leaf lobes arranged in a palm-like form.

5. 复叶
5. Compound Leaf

奇数羽状复叶：顶端生有一片小叶，小叶的数目为单数。

Odd-pinnately compound leaf: a tiny leaf grows on the top of the leaf. So, the number of tiny leaf is odd number.

偶数羽状复叶：顶端生有两片小叶，小叶的数目为双数。

Even-pinnately compound leaf: two tiny leaves grow on the top of the leaf. So, the number of tiny leaf is even number.

三出复叶：每个叶轴上生 3 个小叶，如果 3 个小叶柄等长，称三出掌状复叶；如果顶端小叶柄较长，两侧较短，称三出羽状复叶。

Ternate compound leaf: three tiny leaves grow on each rachis. The leaf will be called ternate palmately compound leaf if the petioles of the three tiny leaves are same in length. The leaf will be called ternate pinnately compound leaf if the petioles of the middle tiny leaf are longer than that of tiny leaves in both sides.

二回羽状复叶：羽状复叶叶轴分枝一次，各分枝两侧生小叶片。

Bipinnate compound leaf: one branch is sprouted out of each rachis of pinnate compound leaf. Tiny leaves grow at both sides of the tiny branches.

掌状复叶：小叶都生在叶轴的顶端，排列呈掌状。

Palmately compound leaf: tiny leaves grow on the top of rachis in palmate arrangement.

(刘璐改绘自《植物学》)

图 2.27 复叶类型：基数羽状复叶、偶数羽状复叶、三出复叶、二回羽状复叶、掌状复叶
Picture 2.27 Compound Leaf Type: Odd-pinnately Compound Leaf, Even-pinnately Compound Leaf, Ternate
Compound Leaf, Bipinnate Compound Leaf, Palmately Compound Leaf
(Adapted from an illustration shown on the Botany by Liu Lu)

6. 花序类型
6. Inflorescence

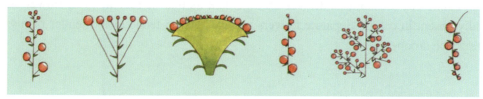

(刘璐改绘自《植物学》)

图 2.28 花序类型：总状花序、伞房花序、头状花序、穗状花序、圆锥花序、荑荑花序
Picture 2.28 Inflorescence: Raceme, Corymb, Capitulum, Spica, Panicle, and Catkin
(Adapted from an illustration shown on the Botany by Liu Lu)

总状花序：花互生排列在不分枝的花轴上，花柄几近等长；

Raceme: flowers are arranged in branchless rachis, with flower stalks basically in same length.

伞房花序：与总状花序相似，但花柄不等长，下部的花柄较长，向上较短，因此，整个花序的花几乎排在同一平面上；

Corymb: flower arrangement is same as that of raceme, but flower stalks are different in length. Flower stalks in lower part are longer than those in upper part. Therefore, flowers of the same flower stalk are arranged in the same plane.

头状花序：花轴呈肥厚膨大的短轴，凹陷、凸出，或呈扁平状；花着于短轴顶端，无柄，花序外层有多数苞片集生呈总苞；

Capitulum: rachis is fleshy, intumescent and short. It can be hollowed or protruded or flattened one. Flowers grow at the top of short rachis without flower stalk. Multiple bracts grow in the outer layer of inflorescence as involucre.

穗状花序：总状花序的一种类型。花序轴较长，排列着许多无柄花。

Spica: as one type of raceme, spica features long rachis with multiple stalkless flowers arranged.

圆锥花序：花轴分枝，每一分枝上形成一总状花序，可成复总状花序；每一分枝若为一穗状花序，则称复穗状花序。两者均属圆锥花序，整个花序开张呈圆锥形状。

Panicle: branches are spouted from rachis, with each branch featuring one raceme. Compound raceme might be formed as well. If flowers in each branch are arranged in the form of spica, it will be called compound spica. Both compound raceme and compound spica are of panicle, with whole inflorescence arranged in the form of circular cone.

葇荑花序：花的排列与总状花序相似，但花无柄或近无柄，单性花排列在细长、柔软的花轴上，花序下垂。

Catkin: catkin features similar flower arrangement as that of raceme. Yet, flower stalk is basically absent in catkin. Separate flowers are arranged in tenuous and tender rachis, with inflorescence drooped.

湿地植物的典型代表
Typical Representatives of Wetland Plants

1. 芦苇
1. Reed

芦苇是湿地的代表植物。芦苇给人的印象是植株是绿色的，芦花是白色的，其实不然。北京湿地的芦苇开花期 8 月下旬至 9 月上旬，秋日下的芦花有着迷人的淡紫色。芦苇多的地方常称为"芦苇荡"或"苇塘"。《诗经》"蒹葭苍苍，白露为霜；所谓伊人，在水一方"中的"蒹葭"指的就是初生的芦苇。现实中，亦有不少作家把情感投射于芦苇中，如法国哲学家帕斯卡尔把人比喻作"会思考的芦苇"。

The reed is a plant commonly seen in wetlands. It gives people the false impression that its body is green and its flowers are white. In Beijing, reeds bloom from late August to early September, and their flowers look charmingly purple under a bright sun in autumn. A place where there are a great many reeds is normally called a reed marsh (pinyin: Lu Wei Dang) or a reed pond (pinyin: Wei Tang). It is the reed in an early stage of development that is referred to in a poem from the Book of Songs that begins by describing a beautiful scene full of beautiful reeds. In reality, many literary figures have put the reed to good use in their works. For example, the French philosopher Pascal liked to compare humans to "reeds that can think".

科：禾本科 Poaceae；属：芦苇属 Phragmites；拉丁学名：*Phragmites australis*
Family: Poaceae; Genus: Phragmites; Latin name: Phragmites australis

(李伟摄)

图 2.29　芦苇
Picture 2.29　Reed (Photo by Li Wei)

图 2.30　芦苇（改绘自《奥托手绘彩色植物图谱》）
Picture 2.30　Reed (Adapted from an illustration shown in the *Color Atlas for Plants Hand Painted by Otto Wilhelm Thomé*)

(李伟摄)

图 2.31　芦苇
Picture 2.31　Reed (Photo by Li Wei)

(李伟摄)

图 2.32　芦苇
Picture 2.32　Reed (Photo by Li Wei)

　　生物学特征：芦苇的植株高大，地下有发达的匍匐根状茎。茎秆直立，秆高 1~3 米，节下常生白粉。叶鞘圆筒形，无毛或有细毛。叶长 15~45 厘米，宽 1~3 厘米。圆锥花序分枝稠密，向斜伸展，花序长 10~40 厘米，小穗有小花 4~7 朵；颖有 3 脉，一颖短小，二颖略长；第一小花多为雄性，余两性；第二外样先端长渐尖，基盘的长丝状柔毛长

6~12毫米；内稃长约4毫米，脊上粗糙。具长、粗壮的匍匐根状茎，以根茎繁殖为主。

Biological characteristics: reed is a tall and huge plant, with well-developed root stock creeping deeply underground. Reed stalk stands upright, measuring 1-3 meters in height. White powder often amasses under knob. Reed has cylindrical sheath, without or only with fine wool. Reed leaves measure 15-45cm in length and 1-3cm in width. Reed panicle has dense branches stretching outwards. The length of reed inflorescence is 10-40cm. 4-7 tiny flowers are arranged in the spikelet. Reed has three glumes, one is short, and one is a little bit longer. The first tiny flower is male, while the left two are bisexual. Reed has long and sharp leaf tip, 6-12mm long of long-thread-shaped pubescence in basal disc. Reed glumelle is 4mm in length with coarse spine. Reed root stock is long and stout, and can creep deeply underground. Reed is basically dependent on root stock reproduction.

分布：较为常见，生于池沼、河旁、湖边等地。

Distribution: common seen in pond, river bank, lake, etc.

用途：芦苇的茎包含大量的纤维，打成浆后可代替木浆造纸。人们利用芦苇编织成苇席、制作芦苇画等手工艺品。苇秆可作造纸和人造丝、人造棉原料，也供编织席、帘等用；嫩时含大量蛋白质和糖分，为优良饲料；花序可作扫帚；花序可填枕头；根状茎叫做芦根，中医学上入药，性寒、味甘，功能清胃火，除肺热；有健胃、镇呕、利尿之功效。

Purpose: the stem of reed contains a large amount of fiber, which can be used to replace wood pulp as raw material for paper-making after being made into thick liquid. Reed is widely used to produce reed mat, and artware like reed painting. Reed stalks are excellent raw material for manufacture of paper, rayon and artificial cotton. It can be waved into mat and curtain as well. The tender and fresh reed contains rich protein and sugar and therefore is ideal to be made into quality feedstuff. Reed inflorescence can be made into broom or made as filler of pillow. Reed root stock is called reed rhizome – a good medicine raw material with cold nature and sweet flavor, capable to reduce lung heat, invigorate the stomach, suppress vomit and accelerate urinate.

2. 莲
2. Lotus

"出淤泥而不染，濯清涟而不妖，中通外直，不蔓不枝，香远益清，亭亭净植，可远观而不可亵玩焉。"宋代周敦颐通过对莲花的爱慕与礼赞，表明自己对美好理想的憧憬，对高尚情操的崇奉，对庸劣世态的憎恶。

In lavishing praise on the lotus in a much-cited poem of his, Zhou Dunyi, a famous scholar from the Song Dynasty, expressed his longing for lofty ideals, his respect for noble moral values, and his hatred for the many ills of society by describing the plant's virtues.

科：莲科　属：莲属　拉丁学名：*Nelumbo nucifera*
Family: Nelumbonaceae　Genus: Nelumbo　Latin name: *Nelumbo nucifera*

别名：荷、芙蕖、鞭蓉、水芙蓉、水芝、水芸、水旦、水华、溪客、玉环

Alias: Water Lily, Fuqu, Bianrong, Fragrant Marshweed Herb, Shuizhi, Shuiyun, Shuidan, Water Bloom, Xike, Yuhuan

（李伟摄）
图 2.33　莲
Picture2. 33　Lotus
(Photo by Li Wei)

（李伟摄）
图 2.34　莲
Picture 2.34　Lotus (Photo by Li Wei)

生物学特征：多年生水生草本，根状茎横生，长而肥厚，有长节。叶圆形，高出水面；叶柄常有刺。花单生在花梗顶端；萼片 4~5，早落；花瓣多数，红色、粉红色或白色；雄蕊多数，药隔先端伸出成一棒状附属物；心皮多数，离生，嵌生于花托穴内；花托于果期膨大，海绵质。

Biological characteristics: As perennial aquatic herbal plant, lotus has horizontally grown root stock, long and fleshy with long sections. Supported by leaf stalk with thorns, the leaves of lotus are round and high above water. Lotus flowers bloom at the top of flower pedicel and are surrounded by 4~5 sepals which will wither far ahead of the bloom of lotus flower.

Normally blooming in red, pink or white, lotus flowers have multiple petals and dominating amount of stamens. A bar-like appendant will be spouted from connective. Multiple carpels will grow separately and are embedded within the cave of receptacle. Of spongeous texture, receptacle will get swollen when lotus flowers get blooming.

分布：较常见，自生或栽培于池塘、湖泊等。
Distribution: commonly growing or cultivated in pond, lake and other places.

用途：根状茎叫藕，可作蔬菜食用或提制淀粉；种子叫莲子，供食用；莲心有清心火、强心降压之效。荷花全株所有部位，都可以食用，亦可入药，简直是宝物。

Function: the root stock of lotus is called lotus root, which is directly edible as vegetable or can be made into starch. The seed of lotus is called lotus seed, edible with special effect to eliminate heart fire, nourish heart and reduce blood pressure.Precious as it is, the whole body of lotus is edible and can be made into medicine.

"莲花" 与 "睡莲" 的区别
Difference between Lotus and Nymphaea Tetragona

莲花又称作荷花，是大家熟悉的水生花卉，原产印度热带地区。而睡莲（Nymphaea tetragona）则原分布在中国、印度、等地区。

Also termed as water lily, lotus is a commonly seen aquatic plant and originates in India, while Nymphaea tetragona is stemming from China, India and other regions.

两者都属睡莲科植物，最容易识别的方法是莲花的叶片表面有绒毛，且成叶会挺出水面，叶片为盾形、没有缺口；睡莲的叶片表面油亮，成叶不会挺出水面，而是漂在水面上，叶片为椭圆形，且有 V 字缺口。花朵的部分，莲花的花朵较大，花瓣基部宽广，颜色有白、红、粉红，集中在清晨开花；睡莲一般的花型比莲花小（大王莲例外），花瓣长狭，颜色有白、黄、紫、粉红、红、紫红、蓝，颜色多，在清晨或夜晚开花。莲花一身都是宝，从花、茎、莲子、莲蓬、莲藕（地下茎）都可拿来食用，不过莲花的花期只限于夏天；睡莲只利用它的花朵来制作睡莲花茶、香水，而且一年四季都开花。

So how can we distinguish these two very similar nympheaceae plants? Remember: lotus is characterized by its finely hairy shield-shaped leaves which emerge from the water surface upon maturity and stand above the water surface. Nymphaea tetragona is characterized by its glossy oval leaves which float on the water surface, and have a V-shaped notch at their base. Supported by a broad petal base, lotus flowers are large and bloom in the morning, either white, red or pink in colour. Nymphaea tetragona flowers are small in size compared with lotus flowers (with the exception of "King" Nymphaea tetragona) and comprise of long and shallow petals. Nymphaea tetragona flowers bloom in the morning and night, and can be a wide variety of colours like white, yellow, purple, pink, red, purplish red, and blue. The entire lotus plant, from flower to stem, seed, seedpod, and root are edible, yet lotus flowers are only seen in summer. Although Nymphaea tetragona blooms all the year around, it is less economically valuable than lotus as only its flowers are of practical value in the production of tea and perfumes.

3. 狸藻
3. Utricularia

湿地中一种"肉食"植物——狸藻，它的生活习性很独特，其捕虫小囊体可以捕捉水中的小虫，并分泌黏液将其消化，是北京唯一的食虫植物。花美丽，可栽培观赏。

There is a carnivorous wetland plant called *Utricularia vulgaris*, which has unique habits. It uses its baglike organ to capture aquatic insects and secrete some mucus to assimilate them, thereby making it the only carnivorous plant in Beijing. The plant has beautiful flowers and can be cultivated as an ornamental plant.

科：狸藻科　属：狸藻属　拉丁学名：*Utricularia vulgaris*
Family: Lentibulariaceae Genus: Utricularia Latin name: *Utricularia vulgaris*

生物学特征：水生草本。匍匐枝圆柱形，多分枝，无毛。叶多数，互生，裂片轮廓呈卵形、椭圆形或长圆状披针形。捕虫囊通常多数，侧生于叶器裂片上，斜卵球状，侧扁，具短柄；花梗丝状，于花期直立，果期明显下弯。

Biological characteristics: *Utricularia* is one kind of aquatic herbal plant, with creeping, cylinder-shaped and hairless branches in great quantity. As an alternate plant, its lobes are mainly in ovoid, oval, long and round lanceolate shapes. Its ampullas for insect-capturing are normally located at the side of lobes, in oblique oosphere shape, with oblate sides and short handle. Its thread-shaped pedicels remain erect before the bloom of flowers and apparently bent during the fruit-bearing season.

分布：狸藻在全世界各温带地区均有分布，生于湖泊、池塘、沼泽及水田中。广布于北半球温带地区。

Distribution: *Utricularia* is widely scattered in temperate regions of the world, especially the temperate regions of the northern hemisphere. Lake, pond, marsh and paddy filed are places it favors very much.

用途：可作观赏植物。
Function: the plant with aesthetical value.

捕虫囊
Ampulla

(李伟摄)

图 2.35 狸藻
Picture2. 35 Utricularia (Photo by Li Wei)

图 2.36 狸藻（改绘自《奥托手绘彩色植物图谱》）
Picture 2.36 Utricularia (Adapted from an illustration shown in the Color Atlas for Plants Hand Painted by Otto Wilhelm Thomé)

4. 水鳖

4. *Hydrocharis Dubia*

《野菜赞》云："油灼灼，苹类，圆大一缺，背点如水泡，一名荇菜，沸汤过，去苦涩，须姜醋，宜作干菜，根甚肥美，即此草也。"

"As quoted in Ode to Edible Wild Herb: glowing with shining brilliance, its leaf is round and big with one notch left and dotted with blister-like spots. The vegetable is also called Fucai and of marsileales family. After boiled, its bitter flavor will be eradicated. It will taste better after mixed with ginger and vinegar. With stout and fleshy root, it is suitable to be made into dried dish."

科：水鳖科　属：水鳖属　拉丁学名：*Hydrocharis dubia*
Family: Hydrocharitaceae　Genus: Hydrocharis　Latin name: *Hydrocharis dubia*

生物学特征：多年生水生植物，有匍匐茎，具须状根。叶圆状心形，全缘，上面深绿色，下面略带红紫色，有长柄。花单性；花丝叉状，花药基部着生。果实肉质，卵圆形，种子多数。

Biological characteristics: *Hydrocharis dubia* is a perennial aquatic plant, with creeping stems and a "beard-like" root. Its round and heart-shaped leaves have an even edge. The upper side of each leaf is dark green, but the underside has a reddish-violet hue. The leaves also have a long leaf stalk. *Hydrocharis dubia* has separate flowers and fork-shaped filaments, and its anthers are hidden in the stem base. It has oval-shaped, fleshy fruits and many seeds.

分布：生静水池沼中，不常见。

Distribution: growing in pond of still water as a rare scene.

用途：植株可作饲料和绿肥，叶柄可食用。

Function: the leaf can be used as fodder and green manure, and the petiole is edible.

图 2.37　水鳖

Picture 2.37　*Hydrocharis Dubia* (Photo by Li Wei)

（李伟摄）

图 2.38　水鳖

Picture 2.38　Hydrocharis Dubia (Photo by Li Wei)

（李伟摄）

5. 槐叶萍

5. Salvinia Natans

槐叶萍，因叶子形似槐树的羽状叶而得名，此外还有蜈蚣萍、山椒藻的别名，是一种常见的浮叶植物。

With a leaf similar in shape to the featherlike leaf of the locust tree, Salvinia natans, also known as the floating fern or the floating moss, is a common floating-leaved plant.

科：水鳖科　属：水鳖属　拉丁学名：*Hydrocharis dubia*
Family: Hydrocharitaceae　Genus: Hydrocharis　Latin name: *Hydrocharis uubia*

生物学特征：茎细长，横走，无根，密被褐色节状短毛。叶 3 片轮生，二片漂浮水面，一片细裂如丝，在水中形成假根，密生有节的粗毛，水面叶在茎两侧紧密排列，形如槐叶。花单性；内轮花被片 3，膜质，白色；花丝叉状，花药基部着生；雌花单生于苞片内；外轮花被片 3，长卵形。果实肉质，卵圆形；种子多数。生静水池沼中。

Biological characteristics: *Salvinia natans* has a thin and long stem, and no obvious roots. As one kind of verticillate plants, it features two leaves floating on water and one leaf as thin as silk in each section. It is covered with brown and nodular fluff. It is characterized by its floating leaves, with leaflets lined along both sides of the stem, It forms rhizoids in water, and is densely covered in nodular fluff. It produces monotropic flowers with three white and membranous sepals in the inner layer of the flower. The filaments are fork-shaped, and the anthers are stored in its roots. Female *Salvinia natans* flowers grow separately within bracts. Three long-oval-shaped sepals are found in the outer layer of the flower. *Salvinia natans* has fleshy fruits, round ovas and many seeds. It grows in ponds of stagnent water.

分布：热带及亚热带，从中国东北到长江以南地区都有分布。

Distribution: *Salvinia natans* floats in water body of tropical and subtropic areas and is widely seen from northeast China regions to areas south of Yangtze River.

(李伟摄)

图 2.39　槐叶萍
Picture 2.39　*Salvinia Natans* (Photo by Li Wei)

图 2.40　槐叶萍（改绘自《奥托手绘彩色植物图谱》）
Picture 2.40　*Salvinia Natans* (Adapted from an illustration shown in the *Color Atlas for Plants Hand Painted by Otto Wilhelm Thomé*)

6. 浮萍

6. *Lemna Minor*

浮萍繁殖迅速，经常大面积覆盖在水面上，明代李时珍曾云："一叶经宿即生数叶。"

Lemna minor multiplies quickly and usually appears in large numbers over vast stretches of water. As Li Shizhen, the great master of traditional Chinese medicine of the Ming Dynasty, put it, "A plant can put out several leaves overnight."

> 科：浮萍科　　属：浮萍属　　拉丁学名：*Lemna minor*
> Family: Lemnaceae　Genus: Lemna　Latin name: *Lemna minor*

生物学特征：浮水小草本。根纤细，根鞘无附属物，根冠钝圆或截切状。叶状体对称，倒卵形、椭圆形或近圆形，两面平滑，绿色，不透明。花单性，雌雄同株，生于叶状体边缘开裂处，佛焰苞囊状；雄花花药 2 室，花丝纤细。果实圆形近陀螺状，无翅或具窄翅。

Biological characteristics: *Lemna minor* is a tiny floating aquatic plant with a slender root, whose root sheath is free from any appendages, and whose root cap is either bluntly rounded or thin in shape. It has symmetrical thalluses which are presented in obovate, oval or basically round shape, with smooth and non-transparent textures on both sides and is green color. Lemna min*or* has monoecism monotropic flowers that emerge from the cracking of the thallus edge and look like spathe capsules. Male *Lemna minor* flower have two anther chambers with slender filaments. Its fruit are round in shape and look like a spinning top, without or with only a narrow wing.

分布：北京各湿地分布普遍，生于池塘、湖边、稻田等。

Distribution: it is widely scattered in various wetlands in Beijing like pond, lake, paddy field, etc.

用途：具药用价值。全草入药，也可作为鱼鸭和猪的饲料。

Function: its whole body can be made into medicine or as fodder for fishes, ducks and pigs.

(李伟摄)
图 2.41 浮萍
Picture 2.41 Lemna Minor (Photo by Li Wei)

图 2.42 浮萍（改绘自《奥托手绘彩色植物图谱》）
Picture 2.42 Lemna Minor (Adapted from an illustration shown in the *Color Atlas for Plants Hand Painted by Otto Wilhelm Thomé*)

7. 香蒲

7. *Typha orientalis*

古人借助香蒲的柔韧性，将其转化为情感的承载物。《诗经·王风·扬之水》："扬之水，不流束蒲。彼其之子，不与我戍许。怀哉怀哉，曷月予还归哉。""蒲"即是香蒲，诗人以"蒲草"为意象，寄托了自己那种对远方人的缠绵思念之情。

In ancient times, typha was often used to imply intimate relations in virtue of its soft texture. The poem of *The Book of Songs • Wang Feng • Rapid River Torrent* is a case in point: "Now matter how rapid it might be, the river torrents still cannot disperse the bundled typha. Now I am stationing in the frontier town lonely. I miss you so much, my darling. When can I return to hometown and you?" In this poem, the author used the image of bundled typha to imply the relations between him and his wife, and expressed his burning lovesickness for his wife far away from him.

科：香蒲科　属：香蒲属　拉丁学名：*Typha orientalis*
Family: Typhaceae　Genus: Typha　Latin name: *Typha orientalis*

别名：狭叶香蒲、蒲草、水烛

Alias: Typha Angustifolia, Scirpoides Holoschoenus, Raupo

生物学特征：多年生沼生草本，直立，高 1~2 米。地下根状茎粗壮，有节。穗状花序圆柱状，雄花序与雌花序彼此连接；雄花序在上，长 3~5cm；雄花有雄蕊 2~4 枚，花粉粒单生；雌花序在下，长 6~15cm；雌花无小苞片，有多数基生的白色长毛，毛与柱头近等长；柱头匙形，不育雌蕊棍棒状。小坚果有一纵沟。

Biological characteristics: *Typha orientalis* is a perennial marsh plant, standing about 1–2 meters tall, and with stout, segmented subterraneous roots. It has cylinder-shaped spica, with staminate inflorescence connected to and above the pistillate inflorescence. Staminate inflorescence measures 3–5 cm in length, and pistillate inflorescence 6–15 cm. Male flowers have 2–4 stamens producing separate pollen grains. Female flowers have no bracteoles, but a great quantity of white hairs which have basically equal length of chapiters. The cochlear chapiter does not give birth to bar-shaped pistil. A longitudinal furrow is visible in the small nutlet produced by the plant.

分布：生于湖泊、池塘、沟渠、沼泽及河流岸带。

Distribution: growing in lake, pond, kennel, marsh and river banks.

用途：香蒲花粉可以入药，名"蒲黄"，用于行瘀利尿；叶片用于编织、造纸等；幼叶基部和根状茎先端可作蔬食；雌花称"蒲绒"，雌花序可作枕芯或坐垫的填充物；叶片挺拔，花序粗壮。香蒲的花晒干后可立即止血，蒲棒晒干燃烧可熏蚊子，香蒲的叶子可以编蒲包、蒲席、扇子等。

Uses: *Typha* pollen is sued as a medicine (called cattail pollen) which is used to dispel stagnation and accelerate diuretic functions. *Typha* leaves can be made into woven goods and used to make paper, etc. The base of tender *Typha* leaves and the tip of the rhizome are also eaten as vegetables. Female *Typha* flowers are called "cattail wool", and are used as stuffing for pillows or cushions. Dried *Typha* flowers are also used to stop bleeding, and dried stems can be burnt to dispel mosquitos. *Typha* leaves can also be woven into bags, mats and fans, etc.

(李伟摄)

图 2.43 香蒲
Picture 2.43 *Typha orientalis* (Photo by Li Wei)

(李伟摄)

图 2.44 香蒲
Picture2.44 *Typha orientalis* (Photo by Li Wei)

8. 慈姑

8. Chinese Arrowhead

慈姑全株柔软，脆弱易折，具有横走根茎，横走根茎的末端为小球茎，在一年中可连生12个子茎，子茎与母根连在一起，有如被慈爱的姑姑呵护着一般，故名"慈姑"。慈姑叶形奇特，似一把剪刀，因此也被称为"三角剪"。

As supple plant, Chinese arrowhead is easy to be broken off. Its horizontally extended root stock has a little corm at the end, and can give birth to 12 branch stems each year. Such branch stems are connected to the mother root stock as being cared by one loving aunt, so its Chinese name has the annotation of loving aunt. Chinese arrowhead's leaf looks oddly like a pair of scissors, so it is called triangle scissor as well.

> 科：泽泻科　　属：慈姑属　　拉丁学名：*Sagittaria trifolia*
> Family: Alismataceae　Genus: Sagittaria　Latin name：*Sagittaria Trifolia*

生物学特征：植株高大，粗壮；叶片宽大，肥厚，顶裂片先端钝圆，卵形至宽卵形；匍匐茎末端膨大呈球茎，球茎卵圆形或球形，可达 5~8×4~6cm；圆锥花序高大，长 20~60cm，有时可达 80cm 以上；果期常斜卧水中；果期花托扁球形，直径 4~5mm，高约 3mm。种子褐色，具小凸起。

Biological characteristics: Chinese arrowhead is a tall, stout and huge plant, with broad, thick and big leaves. The tip of its top lobe features multiple shapes from blunt round, to oval and to broad oval shapes. A corm, either in oval or ball shape and measuring 5–8×4–6 cm, is seen at the end of its swollen stolon. Chinese arrowhead has tall and huge panicle which usually measures 20–60 cm in length and in some case even measures over 80 cm. During fruit-bearing duration, Chinese arrowhead is often seen obliquely lying in water, with spheroidicity-shaped receptacle measuring 4-5mm in diameter and 3mm in height. Chinese arrowhead has brown, tiny and bulged seeds.

分布：慈姑在北京湿地不难找到，正如它的英文名"Chinese Arrow-head"所提示。叶的形状如"矛头"一般，生长在三角形的茎上，叶面略带光泽。

Distribution: Chinese arrowhead is not rare in Beijing's wetlands. Just as its name suggests, it has arrowhead-shaped and slightly glossy leaves growing out of triangular stem.

用途：慈姑的块茎可食用，含丰富淀粉质，它在农历新年期间尤其受欢迎。慈姑通常伴以冬菇、黄芽白、芹菜及胡萝卜，成为一道可口的传统开年菜。另一方面，慈姑亦为不少人带来美好的回忆，就是与家人共度佳节的温馨片段。

Uses: The tubers of Chinese arrowhead are edible and rich in starch. It is mixed with snake butter, Chinese cabbage, celery, and carrot to produce a popular dish during the Spring Festival. Chinese arrowhead brings us many sweet memories related to family reunion during the Spring Festival.

(李伟摄)

图 2.45　慈姑

Picture 2.45　Chinese Arrowhead (Photo by Li Wei)

图 2.46　慈姑（改绘自《奥托手绘彩色植物图谱》）

Picture 2.46　Chinese Arrowhead (Adapted from an illustration shown in the *Color Atlas for Plants Hand Painted by Otto Wilhelm Thomé*)

9. 千屈菜
9. Willow Herb

在爱尔兰千屈菜被称为湖畔迷路的孩子，因为千屈菜常多生长在沼泽地、沟渠边或滩涂上等近水地带，它不是群生植物，而是掺杂在其他植物丛中，单株单株地生长。花色淡雅，其花语是孤独。

In Ireland, willow herb is called Lost Kid in Lake Bank. As not social plant, willow herb often grows individually amid other plants at belt close to water like marsh, trench, intertidal zone, so such elegantly-colored plant is usually deemed as the token of loneness.

> 科：千屈菜科　　属：千屈菜属　　拉丁学名：*Lythrum salicaria*
> Family: Lythraceae　Genus: Lythrum　Latin name: *Lythrum salicaria*

别名：水枝柳、水柳、对叶莲
Alias: Shuizhi Willow, Water Willow, Lythrum

生物学特征：多年生草本，高达1米左右。茎直立，多分枝，四棱形或六棱形，被白色柔毛或变无毛。叶对生或3枚轮生，狭披针形，长3.5~6.5cm，宽1~1.5cm，无柄，有时基部略抱茎。总状花序顶生；花两性，数朵簇生于叶状苞片腋内，具短梗；花萼筒状，长4~6mm，萼筒外具12条细棱，被毛，顶端具6齿，萼齿之间有长约1.5~2mm的尾状附属体；花瓣6，紫色，生于萼筒上部，长6~8mm；雄蕊12，6长6短，排成2轮，在不同植株中有长、中、短三种类型，与雄蕊三种类型相应，花柱也有短、中、长三种类型；子房上位，2室。蒴果包截于萼内，2裂，裂片再二裂。

Biological characteristics: willow herb is perennial herb, standing about 1 meter in height. It features straight stem and multiple branches, in either four or six prism form, and is covered with white pubescence or no hair at all. It has opposite or verticillate leaves of shallow lanceolate shape, measuring 3.5–6.5cm in length and 1–1.5cm in width. Sometimes, willow herb leaves which are lack of handles will embrace stem at base. With raceme spouted from top, willow herb has both female and male flowers, which will grow in clusters with short peduncles inside leaf-shaped bract axil. Willow herb has 4–6mm long of canister-shaped calyx. 12 tiny ridges are seen outside calyx tube, which is covered with hair and has 6 calyxes at top. Tail-shaped appendant of 1.5–2mm long is seen growing among calyxes. Willow herb's six-pedal and purple flowers bloom at the top of calyx tube, measuring 6–8 mm. It has 12 stamens arranged in two layers, of which, six are short and six are long. Long, middle and short stamens are seen in different willow herbs. Accordingly, willow herbs also feature long, middle and short styles. With two chambers, the ovary of willow herb grows above calyxes and petals. Capsule is wrapped inside calyx, with two lobes, each of which will be split into two lobes as well.

用途：全草入药，有收敛止泻之效。
Function: the whole body of willow herb can be made into medicine, good at arresting diarrhea.

(李惠摄)
图 2.47 千屈菜
Picture 2. 47 Willow Herb
(Photo by Li Hui)

图 2.48 千屈菜（改绘自《奥托手绘彩色植物图谱》）
Picture 2.48 Willow Herb (Adapted from an illustration shown in the *Color Atlas for Plants Hand Painted by Otto Wilhelm Thomé*)

看不见的"小山头"——不沾水、不惹尘
Invisible Mountains Secret behind Unsullied and Water-proof Lotus Leaves

"出淤泥而不染,濯清涟而不妖"形容的是莲花洁身自好的品质,然而可曾有人想到,那一顶顶如华盖般擎着的莲叶也是一样的洁净无瑕。而且不管莲叶上洒下多少水,也只会在它们表面形成如落玉盘似的大珠小珠,不会留下一点水渍,还是那么光洁干爽。

As noted by the poem "Lotus is born of sludge yet unsullied by its humble origin. It is washed by water without any bewitching trace left in its lofty beauty", lotus is the epitome of purity and morality. Do you know, the towering lotus leaf is as pure and immaculate as lotus? The lotus leaf has always remained permanently clean and dry no matter how much dew might drop to its surface.

（李伟摄）

图 2.49　莲叶的自清洁效应

Picture 2.49　Self-cleaning Effect of Lotus Leaf (Photo by Li Wei)

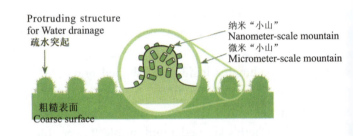

图 2.50　莲叶表面局部放大图（引自《知识就是力量》）

Picture 2.50　Partial Enlarged Details of Lotus Leaf Surface (Quoted from *Knowledge is Power*)

莲叶为什么会有这种功能呢?最开始人们认为是莲叶上那层白色蜡质决定的。但是很多植物的叶子都有蜡质,水滴上去,很快就铺平、蔓延开了,更达不到水珠在莲叶上四处滚动的效果。所以除了蜡质之外,莲叶不沾水一定还另有原因。直到 20 世纪 90 年代,德国的科学家首先用扫描电子显微镜观察了莲叶表面的微观结构,才解开了莲叶的不沾水之谜。放大 1000 倍,会发现莲叶的表面竟然是由一些突起构成的,这一个个的突起平均大小约为 10 微米,只有一根头发直径的 1/10。再继续放大 1000 倍,这一个个的小突起上面竟然还有一排排更微小的突起,它们小得要用纳米去衡量,只有一根头发直径的 1/250。莲叶表面就是这么精细的微米加纳米双重结构。在看似光滑的莲叶表面上,其实是一个个我们肉眼看不到的微米"小山"再叠加上纳米"小山"组成的,"山"与"山"之间的空隙非常窄,那些尺寸远远超过"小山"的水滴,只能在"山头"上跑来跑去。

What does it make lotus leaf so magic? At the beginning, it is attributed to the white wax layer on lotus leaf. But such wax layer is found in many plant leaves as well, on which, water drops will immediately spread all over. No leaf, except of lotus leaf, could have water drop rolled all around. So, it must be something else rather than wax layer making lotus leaf water-proof. The riddle has not been deciphered until 1990s when Germany scientists glimpsed into the microstructure of lotus leaf with scanning electron microscope. Via the microscope, which could magnify the observed object 1,000 diameters, scientists found that lotus surface was comprised by protuberant components, whose average diameter is around 10 micrometer, only about 1/10 wide of the diameter of one hair. To continue magnify 1,000 times, scientists found, with astonishment, that rows of even tinier protuberant components were lined above such tiny protuberant components. They were so tiny that they fall into the measurement scale of nanometer as their diameter is only 1/250 of that of hair. The surface of lotus leaf is comprised by such refined double structure of micrometer and nanometer scale. Above the seemingly smooth surface of lotus leaf is an invisible world to our eyes which is superposed by micrometer-scale mountains and nanometer-scale mountains. The gaps between such mountains are so narrow – far less than water drops. Therefore, such water drops have to run hither and thither above such mountains.

水滴之所以能在"山头"上跑来跑去，还不单是因为"山"之间的缝隙太小，更为关键的是"山"和"山"之间都被空气填充的严严实实，形成了一个类似气垫的东西。因为隔着一层气垫，当水落在莲叶的表面，在自身张力的作用下，形成的水滴就在这层气垫上自由滚动，在滚动的过程中带走了莲叶表面的尘土。莲叶的这种不依靠外力就可以让自己变得很清洁的现象，科学家称之为"莲叶效应"。

In addition to such extreme narrow gaps, the air tightly filling up such mountain gaps also forces water drops to roll about on such mountains as the thing like an air cushion is thus formed on lotus leaf. When water drops onto the surface of lotus leaf, due to the existence of the air cushion, the formed water drop will roll freely onto the air cushion under the effect of its own tense. The dust left on lotus leaf will be taken away by the rolling water drops. The phenomenon for lotus leaf to clean up itself without the introduction of external force is called Lotus Leaf Effect by scientists.

小实验
Experiment

我们做一个实验，在南瓜叶和莲叶上都洒满灰尘，再用水冲叶片，结果会发现在水和尘土的作用下，南瓜叶子变得很脏，而莲叶却不受任何影响。莲的生长离不开淤泥，可是破水而出的莲叶上，不但淤泥、灰尘不粘，就连水滴也很难在上面安安稳稳地待上一会儿，仿佛自己就能把自己打扫干净。这种现象叫莲叶的自清洁效应。

Now, let's do an experiment – to spray dust onto pumpkin leaf and lotus leaf, and then wash them with water. From the experiment we will find that under the joint effect of water and dust, pumpkin leaf will be very dirty, while the lotus leaf will still remain impeccable. The growth of lotus is indispensible from sludge. Yet, the lofty lotus leaf is unsullied by either sludge or even dust. Even water drops will find it is hard for them to linger on lotus leaf for long enough. It seems that lotus has a magic power to clean itself up automatically. Such phenomenon is called the self-cleaning effect of lotus leaf in scientific community.

会吐泡的"鼻子"—— 呼吸
Bubble-spitting Nose Magic Respiration Organ

所有的植物都要进行光合作用和呼吸作用，需要吸收并释放大量气体，莲也不例外，但是它的呼吸作用要直观得多。

Without exception, all plants are indispensible from photosynthesis and respiration, during which, a great amount of gas will be absorbed and released. This is true for lotus as well. But its respiration is much more perceptible.

在与叶秆相连的莲叶中心有一个泛黄的部位，长得有些像鼻子，而且是呼吸最强的部位，被形象地称为莲鼻。在上面扎几个小孔，不一会就会出现一个白色小泡，如果倒些水，马上就会发现水底咕嘟嘟地冒出气泡来了。

The most powerful respiration organ, the yellow intersection region between lotus leaf and lotus stalk somewhat resembles a nose. Thus it gains a highly vivid nickname as lotus nose. By leaving several tiny holes in the region, you will find soon enough a white tiny bubble will appear. By pouring some water into the holes, you will find immediately the appearance of bubbles from water below.

将莲叶的秆剖开，可以看到里面是几条粗细不一的管道，就像藕里面的孔洞一样，气泡就是顺着这些管道冒出来的。莲为什么要采用如此神奇的呼吸方式呢？植物的生长需要阳光、水和空气，而莲的地下茎——藕，尤其需要进行高强度的呼吸才能贮藏足够的养分，但是它生长在池塘底的淤泥中，几乎接触不到空气，莲叶和莲花的秆都是空心的，这一个个通道通过，进到藕里，藕也有着一个个气孔，空气在藕的这些气孔中自由流动，传给藕节上的根，从而保证了莲藕生长所需的空气。对于一株完整的莲，它的呼吸结构是一个连通的整体，因为藕节里也有同样的孔洞将两段相邻的藕连接起来，从而保证呼吸系统的整体效率。在长期的进化中，莲形成了这种独特而神奇的呼吸结构，也保证了它能够代代繁衍，生生不息。

Several pipes of different widths will be revealed after the stalk of lotus leaf is split off. Bubbles come out of such pipes which have same function as air holes inside lotus root. Why does lotus adopt such a magic way for breath? We all know that the growth of plant is indispensible from sun, water and air. Lotus root – the underground stem of lotus – is especially in bad need of strong respiration for storage of sufficient nutrients. However, it is buried deeply in the bottom of pond by sludge, an environment basically deprived of the circulation of atmosphere. It is the special inner structure of lotus that helps overcome the problem: air will travel freely along such pipes through the hollow stalks of lotus leaf and flower into the air holes inside lotus root, therefore it guarantee the necessary air provision for the growth of lotus. For a complete lotus, its respiration structure is a connected entirety - air holes embedded in lotus subterraneous node will have adjacent lotus roots connected, guaranteeing the overall efficiency of lotus respiratory system. Such unique and magic respiratory structure of lotus has formed after long-term evolvement and also ensures its proliferation over generation.

（李伟摄）

图 2.51 鼻泡泡
Picture 2.51   Cross Section of Lotus Stem
(Photo by Li Wei)

（李伟摄）

图 2.52 藕断丝连
Picture 2.52   Connected Fibres of Broken Lotus
(Photo by LiWei)

图 2.53 荷叶（引自《知识就是力量》）
Picture2. 53   Lotus Leaf (Quoted from *Knowledge is Power*)

（李伟摄）

图 2.54 荷叶参差错落
Picture 2.54   Graceful Deployment of Lotus Leaves
(Photo by Li Wei)

　　莲的地下茎（藕）横生在泥中，节上生根和芽，节间肥大（即我们吃到的食用部分），里面有多条气腔（也就是藕里面的气生通道），与叶秆、花秆气腔相连通，通过叶秆顶端的莲鼻与外界进行气体交换，完成呼吸过程。
Growing horizontally in sludge, the subterraneous stem consists of large sections (namely the edible part to us), on which adventitious roots and lateral buds are visible. For respiration, air cavities (namely the inner atmogenic passages of lotus) embedded in lotus root are connected with those embedded in louts leaf and stalk, and conduct gas exchange with the external environment via the lotus noses located at the top of lotus leaf stalk.

　　莲叶高矮交错，有的紧紧漂浮在水面，有的亭亭玉立在水面之上。莲是由一粒种子在淤泥中长出来的，从淤泥到水面，莲叶经过了怎样的历程，才形成这样高高低低、错落有致的景观呢？
As we see, lotus leaves are well-deployed across space magnificently - while some lotus leaves keep floating on water leisurely, some dash out of water toweringly. What kind of

process has lotus ever experienced before lotus leaves pop out from water to form such a splendid view from a tiny seed deeply buried under sludge?

在淤泥中，莲子开始萌芽，由于不能进行光合作用，所以钻出水面之前的大部分养分要依赖种子本身。从莲子发芽到莲叶长出水面，必须在3天之内完成。小小的莲子养分有限，必须与时间赛跑才能完成这段生死攸关的旅程。

Lotus has to rely on the nutrients contained in its seeds when it buds in the depth of sludge where it can't conduct photosynthesis. Due to its highly limited nutrients contained within seeds, lotus has to complete the life journey - budding from a seed and growing into the leaf and dashing out of water - within three days. It is a life-and-death race against time.

第一片莲叶要第一时间破水而出，所以它在水下像锥子一样卷起，这是阻力最小的状态，因此才有"小荷才露尖尖角，早有蜻蜓立上头"的景致。等它刚刚露出水面，卷着的叶子就迅速展开。这主要是因为莲子的养分不足以支撑莲叶继续向上生长，所以莲叶必须快速打开并进行光合作用，以制造养分来维持生命。这片叶子在水面上漂浮，被形象地称为浮叶。

In order to lift its head out of the water at the earliest possible moment, the lotus plant has its first leaf curled up under water like an awl, so that it only needs to overcome the smallest possible resistance against water to push itself upwards. The poem that "no sooner than the curled lotus leaf emerges out of water, a dragonfly rests upon it impatiently" describes the scene of fledging lotus leaves. After it emerges out of the water, the curled leaf will quickly unfold and conduct photosynthesis to produce more nutrients for the growth of the rest of the plant, as the seed nutrients become more and more depleted. This first lotus leaf lays on the water surface and has no need to push itself high above the water, its sole function is to photosynthesis and give life to the rest of the plant. The leaf is thus vividly called floating leaf since its flotation over water.

(李娜摄)
图 2.55　莲
Picture 2.55　Lotus (Photo by Li Na)

(李惠摄)
图 2.56　莲
Picture 2.56　Lotus (Photo by Li Hui)

这是一片重要的叶子，它提供的养分开始让种子生根并长出一条地下茎，形成日后的藕。藕与藕之间的藕节上同样可以长出莲叶，它们按照同样的方式破水而出。因为已经有了光合作用的养分，藕节上长出的叶子露出水面后并不急于展开，它们要继续向上生长。充足的养分和粗壮的茎秆孕育出肥大的藕叶，足以支撑淤泥里藕的生长。

The first lotus leaf is very significant, since the nutrients generated by it will enable lotus seed to take root and grow out the first subterraneous stem before lotus finally comes into being. More curled lotus leaves will grow on the lotus subterraneous nodes and dash out of water following the same manner of the first lotus leaf. As beneficiaries of sufficient nutrients generated by photosynthesis, these lotus leaves are not anxious anymore to unfold themselves after breaking the water surface. Instead, they keep grow upwards till they grow into corpulent lotus leaves high above. Such towering leaves, which are supported by sufficient nutrients and stout lotus stalk, in turn give nutrients to accelerate the maturity of lotus root amid sludge below.

如果从一片莲塘中取出一株完整的藕，就会发现莲叶的生长都遵循着一个不变的规律。莲子长出的第一片叶子浮在水面上，叶片最小，而随后长出来的叶柄越来越高，叶片越来越大，第五片叶子是叶柄最高、叶片最大的叶子。从这时起，以后生长出的叶柄会越来越矮，叶片也会越来越小，最后一片叶子像第一片叶子一样大小，而且也浮在水面上，形成了神奇的对称。

A close observation of lotuses completely took out of pond will reveal to us one invariable rule followed by all lotus leaves: the first lotus leaf, also the smallest one, will float on the water surface and is followed by four lotus leaves which keep grow higher and bigger one by one. After the fifth lotus leaf, which is the highest and biggest leaf among all of its counterparts, the lotus leaves born afterwards will become shorter and smaller one by one. Magic enough, the last lotus leaf will grow into the same size as that of the first lotus leaf and float on water as well, forming a stunning symmetrical scene.

莲有雅致的花朵和沁人的清香，更有亭亭的莲叶。从"小荷才露尖尖角"到"留得残荷听雨声"，莲叶见证了莲的整个生命周期，滋养着莲花，孕育出莲藕和莲子，为它们提供空气和养料，自己却如此谦逊而低调。虽然甘做配角，却练就了许多不平凡的神奇之处，莲叶蕴含的奥秘更值得我们在人生中细细品味。

Lotus is a magic plant with rich combination of gracious flowers, smoothing fragrance, and towering leaves. Lotus leaves ranging from the curled first one which takes lead to emerge out of water to the last one which still refuses to wither after all lotus components have gone, are all witnesses to the life circle of lotus. In spite of their great significance in seeing to the growth of lotus flowers, roots and seeds by provision of air and nutrients, they remain modestly low-profile only as a supporting role. However, their extraordinary characters are what we should learn from and ponder over in our life journey.

想一想
Give This Some Thought

回顾一下你以前学过的古诗，看看里面哪些植物是湿地植物？
Take a look back on the poems you learned before to see if there are any wetland plants in them.

试一试
Give This A Try

你会制作芦苇画或植物叶片画吗？让我们动手试一试！
Do you know how to make painings with reeds or
other plant leaves? Let's give it a try!

你需要准备：芦苇（Phragmites communis）（或其他植物叶片）、剪刀、小刀、清水、报纸、电熨斗、粘胶等。
Materials to be prepared: reed (Phragmites communis) or other plant leaves, scissors, knife, water, newspaper, iron, viscid gum, etc.

制作步骤：
Steps:

1. 根据自己要制作的内容选择芦苇（或其他湿地植物）。
1. Choose the ideal parts of reed or other wetland plant leaves in light of your requirements.

图 2.57　制作植物叶片贴画
Picture 2.57　DIY for plant leaf pinup picture

2. 用剪刀或小刀取材（注意保护植物，只选取需要的部分，不要破坏其他部位）。
2. Cut such parts with scissors or knife carefully (please do not damage other unnecessary parts of such plants in the interest of plant protection).

3. 剪成需要的形状，用水将芦苇（其他植物叶）完全浸没，约10分钟后取出用电熨斗烫平整（或者将材料叶放在一叠报纸中间，再用一本书压住它们，记住隔一天要把报纸换一换，尽快吸收叶中的水分，一周左右就可以了）。
3. Cut the needed parts into ideal shapes. Soak the cut reed or other plant leaves into water for ten minutes and then take them out to have them ironed (or insert each of the soaked leaves between newspapers and put them under a book. Do remember to renew newspaper every other day, so as to hasten the dried-up process quickly. About one week is needed for the water drying-up process).

4. 继续修剪芦苇叶（或其他植物叶）原料，刻成丝或剪成毛，或与纸拼对黏合。
4. Trim reed or other plant leaves into threads or feathers, or paste such leaves to paper to cater to your requirements

5. 根据已设计好的画稿，再进行造型，组合叠压，完成芦苇画（或叶画）。
5. Make final modeling and combination in light of designed drawing to finish the reed painting or leaf painting.

第三节 种类繁多的湿地动物
Section III Diversified Wetland Animals

学习日志
Notebook

试着在你的学习日志本中写出你所知道的湿地动物吧。如果你是一位动物的兴趣爱好者，还可以介绍一下这些动物有哪些生理特点和生活习性是和它所生活的湿地环境相适应的。

Please write down the names of wetland animals you have known on the notebook. Also, you are welcome to introduce their physiological characteristics, life habits and how they adapt to wetland environments they live in, if you are an interested animal lover.

学海拾贝
Pearls of Knowledge

一、我国湿地动物资源概况
I. Overview of Wetland Animal Resources in China

我国拥有丰富多样的湿地野生动物。现有湿地兽类共 7 目 12 科 31 种，湿地鸟类 12 目 32 科 271 种，全世界共有鹤类 15 种，我国有 9 种，占 2/3；爬行类 3 目 13 科 122 种，我国两栖类共有 3 目 11 科 300 种。此外，鱼类、甲壳类、虾类、贝类等脊椎和无脊椎动物种类繁多，资源丰富，我国湿地有鱼类 1000 多种，鱼类总数占全国总数的 37.1%，世界淡水鱼总数的 8% 以上。

Many wetland wild animals inhabit China. In total, China has 31 species of wild animal of 12 families and 7 orders. China is home to 271 species of wetland birds of 32 families of 12 orders. Of 15 species of cranes found in the world, 9 (or 2/3) are found in China. In addition, China is home to 122 species of reptiles of 13 families and 3 orders. At present, China has 300 species of amphibians of 11 families of 3 orders. What's more, China has abundant vertebrate and invertebrate animals like fish, shellfish, shrimps, and has more than 1,000 species of freshwater fish, accounting for 37.1% of total fish species in the nation, over 8% of total freshwater fishes in the world.

二、湿地动物的常见类型
II. Common Categories of Wetland Animals in China

1. 湿地鸟类

1. Wetland birds

湿地鸟类是湿地野生动物中最具代表性的类群，是湿地生态系统的重要组成部分，灵敏和深刻地反映着湿地环境的变迁。

Wetland birds are the most representative category of wetland animals in China and the most significant component of China's wetland ecological system. They profoundly and sensitively reflect the vicissitude of China's wetland environment over history.

湿地水鸟是指在生态上依赖于湿地，即某一生活史阶段依赖于湿地，且在形态和行为上对湿地形成适应特征的鸟类。它们以湿地为栖息空间，依水而居，或在水中游泳和潜水，或在浅水、滩地与岸边涉行，或在其上空飞行，以各种特化的喙和独特的方式在湿地觅食。无论它们在湿地停留的时间是长还是短，是日栖还是夜宿，是嬉戏还是觅食与筑巢，湿地水鸟在喙、腿、脚、羽毛、体形和行为方式等方面均会显示出其相应的长期适应湿地环境的特征。

Wetland aquatic birds refer to birds which are ecologically dependent on wetlands, namely birds which rely on wetlands for living over certain stage of life circle and whose morphologies and actions are adaptive to wetlands. Such birds take wetlands as their settlements and live by water. They are seen swimming or diving in water, wading across or flying over shallow water, beach, and bank. They forage about with special beaks or in special manners. No matter how long, what time span (day or night), for what purpose (playing, foraging or nesting) they linger in wetlands, they all share features for long adaptivity to wetland environments in terms of beak, feet, leg, feather, figure, action, etc.

湿地水鸟包括了潜鸟目（Gaviiformes）、鸊鷉目（Podicipediformes）、鹳形目（Ciconiiformes）、红鹳目（Phoenicopteriformes）、雁形目（Anseriformes）和鸻形目（Charadriiformes）（海雀除外）的所有种类，以及鹈形目（Pelecaniformes）、鹤形目（Gruiformes）和佛法僧目（Coraciiformes）的部分种类。此外，与湿地关系密切、经常栖息于湿地的鸟类还有隼形目（Falconiformes）、鹃形目（Cuculiformes）、鸮形目（Strigiformes）、䴕形目（Piciformes）和雀形目（Passeriformes）的许多种类。因此，将依赖于湿地和经常栖息于湿地的鸟类一并统称为湿地鸟类。

Wetland birds include all species of birds from Gaviiformes, Podicipediformes, Ciconiiformes, Phoenicopteriformes, Anseriformes, to Charadriiformes (with puffin excluded), as well as partial species of Pelecaniformes, Gruiformes and Coraciiformes. Besides, birds which bear close relations with and often settle on wetlands include many species of falconiformes, cuculiformes, strigiformes, piciformes and passeriformes. In short, birds which depend on and frequently use wetlands are collectively termed as "wetland birds".

（俞肖剑摄）
图 2.58 灰雁
Picture 2.58 Greylag Goose (*Anser Anser*)(Photo by Yu Xiaojian)

（俞肖剑摄）
图 2.59 赤麻鸭
Picture2.59 Ruddy Shelduck (*Tadorna Ferruginea*) (Photo by Yu Xiaojian)

（俞肖剑摄）
图 2.60 黑尾塍鹬
Picture 2.60 Black-tailed Godwit (*Limosa Limosa*) (Photo by Yu Xiaojian)

（张词组摄）
图 2.61 白鹈鹕
Picture 2.61 White Pelican (*Pelecanus Onocrotalus*) (Photo by Zhang Cizu)

（范忠勇摄）
图 2.62 白胸苦恶鸟
Picture 2.62 White-breasted Waterhen (*Amaurornis Phoenicurus*) (Photo by Fan Zhongyong)

（王树青摄）
图 2.63 白枕鹤
Picture 2.63 White-naped Crane (Photo by Wang Shuqing)

（郑永富摄）
图 2.64 青脚鹬
Picture2.64 Greenshank (*Tringa Nebularia*) (Photo by Zheng Yongfu)

（陈建中摄）
图 2.65 白额燕鸥
Picture 2.65 Little Tern (*Sterna Albifrons*) (Photo by Chen Jianzhong)

（范忠勇摄）
图 2.66 黄嘴白鹭
Picture 2.66 Swinhoe's Egret (*Egretta Eulophotes*) (Photo by Fan Zhongyong)

(张词组摄)

图 2.67　彩鹳
Picture 2.67　Painted Stork (*Mycteria Leucocephalus*)
(Photo by Zhang Cizu)

(陈水华摄)

图 2.68　黑尾鸥在孵蛋
Picture 2.68　A Black-Tailed Gull Sitting on Eggs
(Photo by Chen Shuihua)

(陈水华摄)

图 2.69　黑水鸡幼鸟
Picture 2.69　A Moorhen (*Gallinula Chloropus*)
Chick (Photo by Chen Shuihua)

(朱英摄)

图 2.70　黄苇鳽
Picture 2.70　Yellow Bittern (*Ixobrychus Sinensis*)
(Photo by Zhu Ying)

(陈建中摄)

图 2.71　凤头潜鸭
Picture 2.71　Tufted Duck (*Aythya Fuligula*)
(Photo by Chen Jianzhong)

(王树青摄)

图 2.72　凤头麦鸡
Picture 2.72　Northern Lapwing (*Vanellus Vanellus*)
(Photo by Wang Shuqing)

（王树青摄）
图 2.73 大天鹅
Picture 2.73 Whooper Swan (*Cygnus Cygnus*) (Photo by Wang Shuqing)

（郑永富摄）
图 2.74 翻石鹬
Picture 2.74 Ruddy Turnstone (*Arenaria Interpres*) (Photo by Zheng Yongfu)

（陈建中摄）
图 2.75 大杓鹬
Picture 2.75 Far Eastern Curlew (*Numenius Madagascariensis*) (Photo by Chen Jianzhong)

鹤属 *Grus*　　鹈鹕属 *Pelecanus*　　天鹅属 *Cygnus*　　鹭属 *Ardea*　白鹭属 *Egretta* 雁属 *Anser*
图 2.76 湿地鸟类尺度对比图
Picture 2.76 Comparison Chart on Wetland Birds of Grus, Pelecanus, Cygnus, Ardea, Egretta, and Anser

2. 鱼类

2. Fishes

（1）内陆湿地中的鱼类种类多，有 13 目 38 科约 770 种（包括亚种，下同）。其中北方区以鲑科（Salmonidae）、茴鱼科（Thymallida）、狗鱼科（Esocidae）、江鳕科（Gadidae）等耐寒性较强的鱼类为主，此外还有一些鲤科（Cyprinidae）、鳅科（Cobitidae）和刺鱼科（Gasterosteidae）的种类；西北高原区，生活着适应高原急流、耐旱耐盐的鳅科（Cobitidae）；江汉平原区的鲤鱼类特别丰富，是我国淡水渔业中心；华南区和西南区均以鲤科（Cyprinidae）、鳅科（Cobitidae）和鲇科（Siluridae）种类为主。沼泽湿地是多种鱼类产卵和繁殖场所，如三江平原沼泽湿地是冷水性鱼，如鳇鱼（*Acipenser sinensis*）、大马哈鱼（*Oncorhynchus keta*）、鲟鱼（*Sturgeon*）的繁殖地。

(1) Wetland fishes in China are dominated by inland wetland fishes. Of 770 species (including subspecies, the same below) of inland wetland fishes of 38 families of 13 orders, North China is dominated by such cold endurance fish species like Salmonidae, Thymallida, Esocidae, Gadidae, and other fish species like Cyprinidae, Cobitidae and Gasterosteida. Plateau areas in Northwest China are dominated by cobitidae which can adapt to rapid torrent, drought and salty soil here. As the center of China's freshwater fishing industry, Jianghan Plain area is dominated by carp. South China and Southwest China are dominated by Cyprinidae, Cobitidae, and Siluridae. Marsh wetland is the egg-laying and breeding places

for multiple fish species. For example, marsh wetlands in Sanjiang Plain are the breeding places for cold water fishes like *Acipenser sinensis, Oncorhynchus keta*, and Sturgeon.

（2）河口半咸水鱼类共有 60 种，过河口洄游性鱼类 20~30 种。

(2) China is also home to 60 species of estuary brackish water fishes, 20—30 migratory fishes across estuary.

图 2.77：鲫鱼   鲢鱼   鳙鱼   青鱼   中华鲟
Carassius auratus   *Hypophthalmichthysmolitrix*   *Hypophthalmichthys nobilis*   *piceus*   *Acipenser sinensis Gray*
Picture 2.77 Crucian Carp (*Carassius Auratus*), Silver Carp (*Hypophthalmichthys Molitrix*), Bighead Carp (*Hypophthalmichthys Nobilis*), Black Carp (*Mylopharyngodon Piceus*), Chinese Sturgeon (*Acipenser Sinensis*)

3. 两栖类

3. Amphibians

两栖动物是脊椎动物中从水到陆的过渡类型，它们除成体结构尚不完全适应陆地生活，需要经常返回水中保持体表湿润外，繁殖时期必须将卵产在水中，孵出的幼仔还必须在水内生活；有的种类甚至终生在水内生活，所以两栖动物全部归入湿地动物。据统计，我国两栖动物共有 3 目 11 科 45 属 300 种。

从动物区划来看，东洋界成分占优势，古北界成分次之，广布种较少。国家重点保护种类有 2 目 3 科 7 种。主要分布于秦岭、淮河以南，其中西南地区种类最多。两栖类中无足目（Apoda）仅有版纳鱼螈（*Ichthyophis bannanicus*）1 种，生活于云南西双版纳地区湿地；有尾目大多是水栖湿地种，如大鲵（*Andrias davidianus*）、贵州疣螈（*Tylototriton kweichowensis*）等；无尾目（Anura）数量较多、分布甚广。

More than most species, amphibians rely on the wetland environment, due to their life histories of movement between terrestrial and aquatic systems. They have to lay their eggs in water during the breeding season, and newly hatched amphibians also need to live in water during their early life stages or even throughout their whole life stage. Therefore, amphibians are classified as wetland animals. According to statistic data, China has 300 species of amphibians of 45 genuses of 11 families of 3 orders. Judged from zoning distribution, amphibians are dominated by these originating from oriental realm, and then from palearctic realm. Amphibians of cosmopolitan species are rarely seen in China. 7 species of amphibians of 3 families and 2 orders are under key national protection and mainly distributed to the south of Qinling Mountains and Huaihe River, and especially in southwest region. *Ichthyophis bannanicus*, the sole species under Apoda recorded in the nation, is seen in wetlands in Xishuangbanna of Yunnan Province. Caudata like *Andrias davidianus* and *Tylototriton kweichowensis* are mainly aquatic marsh wetland amphibians. Anura are widely seen across the nation in great quantity.

（高武摄）

图 2.78 濒临灭绝的北京一级保护动物——金
线蛙

Picture 2.78 Eastern Golden Frog (*Pelophylax Plancyi*), an Endangered First-Grade Protected Species in Beijing (Photo by Gao Wu)

（刘鸣绘）

图 2.79 扬子鳄

Picture 2.79 Chinese Alligator (*Alligator Sinesis*) (Illustration by Liu Ming)

4. 爬行类

4. Reptiles

我国湿地爬行野生动物有122种，龟鳖目（Chelonia）［除陆龟科（Testudinidae）外］、蛇亚目（Serpentes）、游蛇科（Colubridae）的部分种类都分布于我国南部，广布种不多，常见的有乌龟（*Chinemys reevesii*）、鳖（*Trionyx sinensis*）等。

China has 122 species of wetland reptiles. South China is home to all species (except of Testudinidae species) of Chelonia reptiles, all species of Serpentes reptiles, and some species of Colubridae reptiles. Reptiles of cosmopolitan species are rarely seen in China. The mostly common seen reptiles in China are *Chinemys reevesii* and *Trionyx sinensis*.

5. 湿地兽类

5. Wetland animals

我国湿地兽类有31种，隶属于7目12科，约占我国兽类总种数的6.2%。国家重点保护种类有5目9科23种。与湿地中的两栖类和爬行类不同，湿地兽类的广布种成分较多。生活在水中或经常活动在河湖湿地岸边；如白鳍豚（*Lipotes vexillifer*）、江豚（Neophocaena）、水獭（*Lutra lutra*）、水貂（*Mustla vison/lutreola*）等；适合潮湿多水生活条件，如麋鹿（*Elaphurus davidianus*）等。

China is home to 31 species of wetland animals of 12 families of 7 orders, accounting for 6.2% of total animal species in the nation. 23 wetland animals of 9 families of 5 orders are under key protection of the nation. Different from wetland amphibians and reptiles, wetland animals in China have many cosmopolitan species. While *Lipotes vexillifer*, Neophocaena, *Lutra lutra, Mustla vison/lutreola* are wetland animals living or basically living in the bank of river or lake wetlands, wetland animals like *Elaphurus davidianus* prefer to live in humid land with ample water resources.

(张曼胤摄)

图 2.80 江豚（http://opinion.hexun.com/
2012- 04 -19/140580137.html）

图 2.81 麋鹿
Picture 2.81 Mi-lu (Photo by Zhang Manyin)

Picture 2.80 Cowfish（http://opinion.hexun.com/
2012- 04 -19/140580137.html）

6. 无脊椎动物甲壳类

6. Invertebrate crustaceans

无脊椎动物甲壳类属于节肢动物门（Arthropoda）、甲壳纲（Crustacea），全世界共有 7500 多种，是一个比较庞大的动物类群，大部分种类为海产，淡水种类不多。甲壳类不仅种类繁多，而且生态类型多样。按生态习性大体可分为浮游甲壳类和底栖甲壳类两大类，前者一般个体小，营浮游生活，后者常营底栖生活。

Under Crustacea of Arthropoda, invertebrate crustacean is a quite huge animal group in the world. Of its over 7,500 species in the world, the majority is marine species and a few are freshwater species. Invertebrate crustaceans are not only rich in species, but highly diversified in ecological forms. They can be further divided into planktonic crustacean and demersal crustacean by ecological habits. While the former group is normally small in size and lives a planktonic life, the latter group mainly lives a demersal life.

拓展阅读
Extra Reading Material

中国湿地水鸟的迁徙路线
Migratory Routes of Wetland Aquatic Birds in China

鸟类迁徙是自然界中最引人注意的生物学现象之一，鸟类离开繁殖地，迁往对它们来说更为适宜的栖息地。在这整个飞行过程中，除了伤病困扰和人类的残害，候鸟们都会坚持完整的迁徙。它们一起掠过宁静的湖面，驰过金黄的麦田，飞过巍峨的高山，穿过无尽的丛林……

Bird migration – birds leave their breeding places and migrate to places more suitable for settlement — is one of the most prominent biological phenomena in the natural world. Except of being troubled by disease or injured by human beings, migratory birds will endure the whole migratory journey no matter how distant it might be. Together, they will skim over serene lakes, sweep across golden cornfields, fly over towering mountains, and pass through vast jungles…

(张曼胤摄)　　　　　　　　　　　　　　　　(张曼胤摄)

图 2.82　湿地鸟类迁徙　　　　　　　　　图 2.83　湿地鸟类迁徙
Picture 2.82 Migration of Wetland Birds　　Picture 2.83 Migration of Wetland Birds
(Photo by Zhang Manyin)　　　　　　　　(Photo by Zhang Manyin)

鸟儿们选择的旅程长短不一，从几百公里到上万公里不等。除了翅膀和脂肪，它们没有任何行李。大多数鸟类迁徙的飞行高度不会超过 1000 米，小型鸣禽的迁徙高度则低于 300 米。

The distances of migratory journeys vary with different migratory bird group and range from several hundreds of miles to tens of thousands of miles. Except of their own wings and body weights, they have no other luggage. For the majority of migratory birds, their flight altitude will not be higher than 1,000 meters. For small-size songbirds, their flight altitude is normally within 300 meters.

候鸟在中国的迁徙路线主要分为东部、中部和西部 3 条，其中东部迁徙路线是东亚—澳大利西亚迁徙路线的重要组成部分，西部迁徙路线为中亚—印度迁徙路线的重要组成部分。

As for migratory routes, wetland aquatic birds in China normally follow three routes, namely eastern migratory route, central migratory route and western migratory route. While the eastern migratory route and the central migratory route are significant components of East Asian- Australasian Flyway route, the western migratory route is the significant component of Central Asia- India Flyway.

东部迁徙路线是水鸟最重要的迁徙路线。在俄罗斯、日本、朝鲜半岛和我国东北与华北东部繁殖的水鸟，春、秋季节主要通过我国东部沿海地区进行南北方向的迁徙。春季，来自南洋群岛和大洋洲的北迁鸟类到达中国台湾后，分为两支，一支沿中国大陆扩散或继续沿东部海岸北上，另一支经琉球群岛到日本或继续北迁。沿中国大陆东部沿海北迁的鸻鹬类等水鸟在到达长江口以后，又分两条北上迁徙路线。一条经江苏、山东到东北、俄罗斯，另一条则越海向朝鲜半岛或日本迁飞。秋季，水鸟沿中国东部沿海向南迁飞至华东和华南，远至东南亚各国，或由俄罗斯东部途经中国向东南亚至澳大利亚迁徙，其南下迁徙路线大致与春季北上路线相似。

The eastern migratory route is the most significant migratory route for wetland aquatic birds in China. Wetland aquatic birds whose breeding places are in Russia, Japan, Mongloia, Korean Peninsula, Northeast China and eastern regions of North China, will migrate in the spring and the autumn along south-north routes via the eastern coastal areas of China. In spring, after arrival at Taiwan, the northwards migratory birds which started their journey from the South Sea Islands and Oceania will be divided into two branches. While one branch will diffuse along the mainland of China or continually fly northwards along eastern coastal line, the other branch will head for Japan via Ryukyu Islands or continually fly northwards. After arrival at Changjiang Estuary, the wetland aquatic birds like shorebirds which have traveled northwards along the eastern region of mainland China will be further divided into two groups. While one group heads for Northeast China and Russia from Jiangsu and Shandong, another heads for Korean Peninsula or Japan. In autumn, wetland aquatic birds will fly southwards along the eastern coastline of China to East China and South China, or even farther to Southeast Asian countries; or fly from the east part of Russia via China to Southeast Asia and Australia. The places they will travel along their southwards migratory route in autumn are basically the same as those of northwards migratory route they have travelled in spring.

西部迁徙路线。内蒙古西部、甘肃、青海和宁夏的湖泊、草甸等湿地繁殖的候鸟，在秋季可沿阿尼玛卿山、巴颜喀拉山和邛崃山脉向南迁飞，然后沿横断山脉南下至四川盆地西部和云贵高原越冬，有些候鸟可飞至中南半岛越冬。新疆地区的湿地水鸟可向东南汇入该西部迁徙路线，或向西南出境，或向南进入西藏。西藏地区的湿地水鸟主要沿唐古拉山和喜马拉雅山向东南方向迁徙，亦可以飞越喜马拉雅山脉，至印度、尼泊尔等地越冬。

Westwards migratory route. Wetland migratory birds, whose breeding places are lakes and meadows in west regions of Inner Mongolia, Gansu, Qinghai and Ningxia, will fly southwards in autumn along Amyes rma- chen, Bayan Har Mountains, and Qionglai Mountain Range before they continually fly southwards along Hengduan mountains to spend a warm winter in west regions of Sichuan Basin and Yunnan-Guizhou Plateau. Some of them will fly farther to Indo-China Peninsula for wintering. Wetland birds whose breeding places are in Xinjiang regions will either fly southeastwards to join the westwards route; or fly southwest to leave China behind; or enter into Tibet southwards. Wetland birds whose breeding places are Tibet regions will travel southeastwards along Tanggula Mountains and Himalaya Mountains; or fly over Himalaya Mountains to reach India and Nepal for wintering.

中部迁徙路线是候鸟在我国境内的另外一条迁徙路线。在内蒙古东部、中部草原、华北西部和陕西地区繁殖的候鸟，秋季沿黄河流域、吕梁山和太行山南下，越过秦岭和大巴山区进入四川盆地越冬；或继续沿大巴山东部向华中或更南的地区越冬。

The central migratory route is another major migratory route for wetland birds in China. Wetland birds, whose breeding places are eastern regions of Inner Mongolia, Central region grassland, western regions of North China and Shannxi regions, will fly southwards in autumn along Yellow River basin, Luliang Mountain and Taihang Mountains via Qinling Mountains and Daba Mountain area into Sichuan Basin for wintering; or fly along eastern regions of Daba Mountain towards Central China or more southwards places for wintering.

你知道吗?
What You May Not Know

白鹤

Siberian Crane (Grus leucogeranus)

白鹤在中国主要分布在从东北到长江中下游，迁徙时见于河北、内蒙古、辽宁、吉林、黑龙江、安徽等地，鄱阳湖是白鹤的重要越冬栖息地，越冬种群数量 2500 余只，占世界总数的 95% 以上，夏天它们则会回到东北、俄罗斯的西伯利亚。在世界范围内，白鹤有 3 个分离的种群，即东部种群、中部种群和西部种群；东部种群在西伯利亚东北部繁殖，在长江中下游越冬；中部种群在西伯利亚的库诺瓦特河下游繁殖，在印度拉贾斯坦邦的克拉迪奥国家公园越冬；西部种群在俄罗斯西北部繁殖，在里海南岸越冬。

In China, the siberian crane is mainly distributed in Northeast China and the middle and lower reaches of the Yangtze River. It can be seen, however, in other provinces during its

(郭玉民摄)

图 2.84 白鹤
Picture 2.84 Siberian Crane (*Grus Leucogeranus*) (Photo by Guo Yumin)

migratory season, including Hebei, Inner Mongolia, Liaoning, Jilin, Heilongjiang, and Anhui. Poyang Lake is the most important winter habitat of the species, whose population there may be as high as over 2,500 in winter, a figure that accounts for more than 95% of the entire population around the world. When summer comes, the birds there fly back to Northeast China and Russian Siberia. In the world there are three separate populations, namely the eastern, the middle, and the western populations. The eastern population multiplies in northeastern Siberia but winters in the middle and lower reaches of the Yangtze River; the middle population multiplies in the lower reaches of the Kunovat River in Siberia but winters in the Keoladeo National Park in Rajasthan, India; the western population multiplies in northwestern Russia but winters on the south bank of the Caspian Sea.

黑嘴鸥

Saunders's Gull

黑嘴鸥仅分布于东北亚地区，其越冬地分布于中国南部沿海地区，其繁殖地除在韩国有少数种群数量外，主要分布在中国江苏盐城自然保护区、辽宁双台河口国家级自然保护区、辽宁丹东鸭绿江口国家级自然保护区等。其中，位于盘锦境内的辽宁双台河口国家级自然保护区内栖息的种群数量最多，有 6000 余只，占全球种群分布数量 8000 余只的 70% 以上。

The bird is only distributed in North Asia and East Asia, and its winter habitats are mainly distributed in southern Chinese coastal regions. Aside from a small number of breeding grounds in South Korea, most of the breeding grounds of the bird are protected as nature reserves in China, including Yancheng Nature Reserve in Yancheng City, Jiangsu Province, Shuangtai Estuary National Nature Reserve in Panjin City, Liaoning Province, and Yalu River Estuary National Nature Reserve in Dandong City, Liaoning Province. Of all these nature reserves, Shuangtai Estuary National Nature Reserve is home to the largest population of the bird, which stands at over 6,000 birds, a figure that accounts for more than 70% of the global population of over 8,000.

（丁洪安摄）

图 2.85　丹顶鹤
Picture 2.85　Red-crowned Crane (Grus Japonensis)
(Photo by Ding Hongan)

丹顶鹤
Red-crowned Crane (*Grus japonensis*)

丹顶鹤在中国繁殖于东北的黑龙江、吉林、辽宁和内蒙古达里诺尔湖等地。越冬于江苏、上海、山东等地的沿海滩涂，以及长江中、下游地区，偶尔也见于江西鄱阳湖和台湾。扎龙自然保护区是我国最大的以鹤类等大型水禽为主体的珍稀鸟类和湿地生态类型的国家级自然保护区，尤以丹顶鹤居多，故有"仙鹤之乡"美称。

The red-crowned crane multiplies in Heilongjiang, Jilin, Liaoning, Dalinuoer Lake in Inner Mongolia, and other places, but winters mostly in coastal shoals in Jiangsu, Shanghai, Shandong, and other provinces and in the middle and lower reaches of the Yangtze River. The bird is also occasionally seen wintering on Poyang Lake in Jiangxi Province and Taiwan. Zhalong National Nature Reserve is China's largest wetland ecological nature reserve designed to protect rare bird species, mostly large aquatic birds like cranes. It is acclaimed as the "Hometown of the Red-crowned Crane" because the population of the bird is larger than that of any other protected bird at the nature reserve.

遗鸥

Relict Gull (*Ichthyaetus relictus*)

遗鸥分布于欧亚大陆及非洲北部，包括整个欧洲、北回归线以北的非洲地区、阿拉伯半岛以及喜马拉雅山—横断山脉—岷山—秦岭—淮河以北的亚洲地区。内蒙古鄂尔多斯遗鸥国家级自然保护区属于高原内陆湿地生态类型自然保护区，主要保护对象是以国家一级保护野生动物遗鸥为主的 83 种鸟类。

The relict gull is distributed in northern Africa and in Eurasia, including Europe in its entirety, the African land north of the Tropic of Cancer, the Arabian Peninsula, and the Asian land north of the line formed by linking the Himalaya Mountains, the Hengduan Mountains, the Min Mountains, the Qinling Mountains, and the Huai River together. The Relict Gull National Nature Reserve in Ordos City, Inner Mongolia, is an inland plateau wetland reserve dedicated to the protection of 83 birds including the relict gull, which is a First-Grade Wild Animal protected at national level.

常见的水生昆虫——蜻蜓和蚊子
Commonly Seen Aquatic Insects – Dragonfly and Mosquito

健康的湿地，孕育了不少生物，有的昆虫整个或部分生命周期以水维生，我们称之为水生昆虫。常见的水生昆虫有蜻蜓稚虫和孑孓等，它们是食物链中重要的一环。通过调控水质和水位，可以使更多不同的水生昆虫生活在湿地中，也会使湿地更健康。

Healthy wetlands have given birth to many creatures. Among them, some are aquatic insects dependent on water for living during whole or partial life circle. The commonly seen aquatic insects include, among others, dragonfly naiads and wigglers. They form a very significant link in food chain. By means of water quality and water level regulation, more aquatic insects could be attracted to wetlands and make wetland healthier as well.

蜻蜓的一生

Life of Dragonfly

蜻蜓将卵产于植物内、枯木内甚至干土中，或随意产于水面上；蜻蜓稚虫从卵孵化，需要经过多次的脱壳才变成成虫；蜻蜓羽化成虫后，根据品种不同，可有几星期至几个月的寿命；交尾时，雄虫会用肛附器抓着雌虫头部后侧或前胸的背板。

Dragonfly prefers to lay eggs amid plants, dead woods, dry soil, or water surface. Only having its shell dropped for many times after egg incubation, could the dragonfly grow into an adult insect. Afterwards, it will live for weeks or months with species as deciding factor. When mating, male dragonfly will seize female dragonfly's head rear side or precordial tergum with its caudal appendages.

蚊子的一生

Life of Mosquito

蚊子爱在静止的水中产卵，雌蚊每次在水中产下 30~300 粒卵不等；蚊子的幼虫成为孑孓，以水中微生物为生；幼虫变成蛹，在水中停止进食；雄性蚊子约有 1 星期寿命，以植物汁液为生；雌性则有 2~3 星期寿命，以吸血为生。

Mosquito prefers to lay eggs, which vary from 30-300 each time, to still water. The larva of mosquito is called wiggler, dependent on microorganisms in water as food. It will stop food consumption from water upon its growing into pupa. While male mosquito will live for one week by juice from plants, female mosquito will live for two and three weeks by blood.

图 2.86 蜻蜓的一生
Picture 2.86 Life of Dragonfly

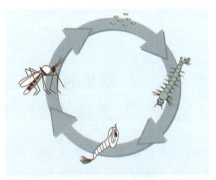

图 2.87 蚊子的一生
Picture 2.87 Life of Mosquito

蜻蜓和豆娘的区别
Difference between Dragonfly and Damselfly

特征 Feature	蜻蜓 Dragonfly	豆娘 Damselfly
体型 Body shape	较粗大 Bulked	较细小纤幼 Slender
眼睛 Eye distance	双眼相连 Connected eyes	双眼明显分开 Apparently separated eyes
翅膀 Wing	后翅基部较前翅宽阔 Underwing base is broader than forewing	前翅跟后翅的大小及形状都非常接近 The underwing and forewing are highly similar in size and shape
休息的姿态 Rest posture	翅膀张开 Opened wings	大部分豆娘会把翅膀合起来 Closed wings in most cases

图 2.88 蜻蜓和豆娘的体型对比图
Picture 2.88 Comparison on Body Shape of Dragonfly and Damselfly

图 2.89 蜻蜓和豆娘眼睛距离对比图
Picture 2.89 Comparison on Eye Distance of Dragonfly and Damselfly

图 2.90 蜻蜓和豆娘的翅膀对比图
Picture 2.90   Comparison on Wings of Dragonfly and Damselfly

图 2.91 蜻蜓和豆娘休息姿态对比图
Picture 2.91   Comparison on Rest Posture of Dragonfly and Damselfly

想一想
Give This Some Thought

针对某一特定湿地鸟类建设的湿地保护区有哪些，想一想告诉大家！
Could you tell us some wetland protected areas which are especially built for protection of wetland birds?

试一试
Give This A Try

1. 试着在纸上将湿地动物按鱼类、鸟类、兽类、两栖类等分类，然后写出你所知道的种类，越多越好。

1. Please try you best to list as more as possible creature names of wetland animals in different classifications like fishes, birds, animals, amphibians, etc.

2. 为你喜欢的湿地动植物画幅画吧！
2. Please draw a picture for your favorite wetland animal.

参考文献
References

[1] 高广元. 莲叶配角也神奇 [J]. 知识就是力量，2014，499(6)：68-71.

[1] Gao Guangyuan. *The Magic Supporting Role of Lotus Leaf* [J]. Knowledge is Power, 2014, 499(6):68-71.

[2] 徐景先，赵良成，林秦文. 北京湿地植物 [M]. 北京科学技术出版社，2009.

[2] Xu Jingxian, Zhao Liangcheng, Lin Qinwen. *Wetland plants in Beijing*[M]. Beijing Science and Technology Publishing Co., Ltd., 2009.

[3] 严承高. 中国湿地资源特点与保护对策 [J]. 林业资源管理，1995，24(6)：2.

[3] Yan Chenggao. *Features of Wetlands in China and Protection Measures* [J]. Forest resources protection, 1995, 24(6):2.

[4] 赵学敏. 湿地：人与自然和谐共存的家园 [M]. 中国林业出版社，2005.

[4] Zhao Xuemin. *Wetland: the Shared Hometown of people and the Nature* [M]. China Forestry Publishing House, 2005.

[5] 方炎明. 植物学 [M]. 中国林业出版社，2006.

[5] Fang Yanming. *Botany* [M]. China Forestry Publishing House, 2006 .

[6] 中国网：http://www.china.com.cn/zhibo/zhuanti/ch-xinwen/2014-01/13/content_31170323.htm

[7] 湿地中国网：http://www.shidi.org/lib/lore/animal.htm

[8] 环境生态网：http://www.eedu.org.cn/Article/eehotspot/everglade/200404/14.html

[9] 湿地中国：http://www.shidi.org/lib/lore/animal-beasts.htm

[10] 湿地之友：http://www.wowcn.org.cn/common.asp?id=185

[11] 新华网：http://news.xinhuanet.com/2012-12/03/c_113877992.htm

[12] 湿地中国网：http://www.shidi.org/sf_b2e06ef52e484b8b9a648d05e6cac7a5_151_animal.html.

[13] 湿地中国网：http://www.shidi.org/lib/http://wx.pkone.cn/item_view_photo.aspx?photoid=257769. http://www.wowcn.org.cn/common.asp?id=185

第三章　湿地的倾诉
Chapter Ⅲ　Wetlands' Sadness

　　湿地宛若一位淡泊温婉的少女，在人们或关注或漠然的目光中静静地承受着人类给予她的一切。湿地是一块大自然赐予人类的瑰宝，然而现在，这块瑰宝在为人类提供着各种保障的同时，却面临着来自人类与日俱增的威胁与挑战。

Whether people are interested in them or not, wetlands silently accept whatever is given to them as a gentle young lady would. Wetlands are ubiquitous, serving mankind at all times, being one of the many treasures that nature makes available to him, but at the same time facing ever-increasing threats and challenges as they provide man with their various services.

第一节　数据告诉我们中国湿地的现状
Section I Data Tell Us the Status Quo of China's Wetlands

学习日志
Notebook

　　观察一下你身边的湿地，并在你的学习日志中简要分析一下这些湿地的现状，例如她的水体是否清澈、她的动植物种类是否丰富等？

Take a close look at the wetlands around you, and make a brief analysis of the status of those wetlands in your notebook, for example by recording whether the bodies of water they are associated with are clear and whether there are a lot of animal and plant species in the wetlands.

学海拾贝
Pearls of Knowledge

　　由于人类对湿地盲目开垦，对水资源过度利用，甚至在湿地中大量排放污染物等，再加上自然环境的不断变化，中国的湿地面积正日趋减少，湿地资源遭到了一定程度的破坏，水体水质也呈现出恶化趋势。

The total area of wetlands in China is decreasing every day. The decrease is mostly due to human factors such as land reclamation; the overuse of water resources; and, the discharge of various pollutants into the ecosystem. Wetlands are also decreasing due to factors such as global climate change. In fact, China's wetland resources have not only suffered direct damage and loss of area, but the water quality of the sources of water supporting them, have also deteriorated significantly.

一、湿地数量变化
I. Changes in the number of wetlands over time

中国湿地丧失和退化的现象主要发生在 20 世纪 50 年代中期到 80 年代初，在这段时间内，中国的淡水湖泊面积减少了约 11%，围垦湖泊的面积达到 1.30×10^6hm² 以上，仅因围垦而消亡的天然湖泊就将近 1000 个。除此之外，在 20 世纪 40 年代末至 70 年代初，每年因围垦而减少的湖泊面积超过了 4000 hm²，其中长江中下游流域因围垦而丧失湖泊面积达 1.2×10^5km²，鄱阳湖因围垦损失的库容达 4.522×10^9m³，而曾作为中国最大的淡水湖的洞庭湖天然湖面则从 1852 年的近 6.27×10^3km² 缩减到 2006 年的 2.625×10^3km²，退化成了中国的第二大淡水湖泊。同样被厄运波及的还有中国的第七大湖泊——洪湖，因受到气候变化以及人类的围湖造田和过度捕捞等活动的影响，洪湖的水面面积由历史最大时的 1.88×10^3km² 锐减到了 2006 年的 309.95km²。

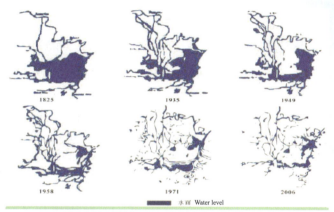

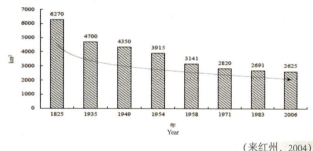

（来红州，2004）

图 3.1 洞庭湖水面变化
Picture 3.1　Changes in Water Level at Dongting Lake over the Years
(Lai Hongzhou, 2004)

Historical records show that the number and area of China's wetlands have significantly deteriorated and decreased between the mid-1950s and the early 1980s. During this period an 11% decline in the total area of freshwater lakes in China was recorded, statistics show that over 1.30×10^6 hectares of wetlands was reclaimed for land; and, a total of nearly 1,000 natural freshwater lakes disappeared because of land reclamation. Beyond that, from the late 1940s to the 1970s, the annual decrease in the total area of freshwater lakes due to land reclamation stood at 4,000 hectares a year, with a total area of 1.2×10^5 km² of lakes lost in the middle and lower reaches of the Yangtze River alone. Poyang Lake lost 4.522×10^9 m^3 of storage capacity due to land reclamation, while the original area of Dongting Lake shrank from 6.27×10^3 km^2 in 1852 to 2.625×10^3 km^2 in 2006. Thus by 2006, China's largest freshwater lake (Dongting Lake) was significantly reduced in size, and could no longer hold the title as the largest lake in China. Correspondingly, the area of Hong Lake, China's seventh largest lake, decreased from 1.88×10^3 km^2 at its maximum recorded level, to 309.95 km^2 by 2006 due to a combination of global climate change, land reclamation, implementation of intensive fisheries, and other factors.

诗仙李白在其《游洞庭湖》一诗中曾写道："洞庭西望楚江分，水尽南天不见云"，描绘中尽现洞庭湖湖面的辽阔、气势的雄浑。但是，在近100多年来，这曾被视为"衔远山，吞长江，浩浩汤汤，横无际涯"，于朝晖夕阴间，变幻着万千气象的"八百里洞庭"，由于被过度的围湖垦殖，湖域面积也在急剧缩小。除此以外，长江中大量的泥沙经由松滋、太平、藕池、调弦"四口"进入到洞庭湖，并沉积湖盆中，致使洲滩发育和扩展，湖泊日益萎缩。

"While I stand on Dongting Lake looking towards the Yangtze River in the distance, an endless stretch of water extends as far as my eyes can see under a cloudless sky," wrote Li Bai, the famous Chinese poet who lived during the Tang Dynasty, in a poem titled Tour Dongting Lake to depict the vastness and majestic grandeur of Dongting Lake. Over the recent 100 years, however, the magnificent Dongting Lake once Water level lavishly praised in lots of literature has witnessed a sharp drop in the area of water due to excessive land reclamation and cultivation for agricultural purposes. At the same time, huge amounts of silt from the Yangtze River enter the lake by way of four entrances, at Songzi, Taiping, Ouchi, and Tiaoxian, respectively, settling on the bottom of the lake and resulting in the development and expansion of its surrounding sands and the shrinkage of the lake over time.

洞庭湖的演变主要受构造沉降、泥沙淤积和人类活动影响三大因素的制约。目前，湖区围湖垦殖活动已经得到严格控制，泥沙淤积则成为洞庭湖萎缩的主要因素。

In summary, the evolution of Dongting Lake is mainly affected by three major factors, namely structural subsidence, silt sedimentation, and human activity. At present, land reclamation and cultivation activity around the lake has been placed under strict control, and silt

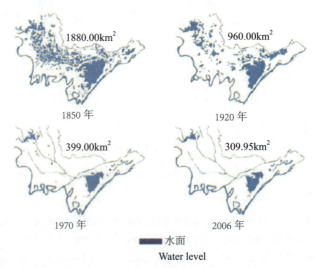

图 3.2　1850—2006 年洪湖水面变化（俞立中等，1993；赵淑清等，2001；尹发能，2008）

Picture 3.2　Changes in Water Level at Hong Lake from 1850 to 2006 (Yu Lizhong, 1993; Zhao Shuqing, 2001; Yin Faneng, 2008)

sedimentation has become the main reason for the shrinkage of its area.

　　洪湖形成于 2500 年之前的春秋战国时期，之后的沉淀过程和面积都发生过较大的变化，早期的洪湖主要是以静水湖泊为主。直至 1850 年，尚为一个通江的敞水湖，湖泊面积达到 $1.88 \times 10^3 km^2$，而在接下来的 70 年里，洪湖就缩小了近一半的面积。Formed about 2,500 years ago, during the Spring, Autumn and Warring State periods, Hong Lake has experienced relatively large changes in its sedimentation process and the area of surface water ever since. Originally Hong Lake was a static-water lake, and as recently as 1850, it was still an open water lake connected to a river, measuring about 1.88×10^3 km² in area. However, over the next 70 years (up to 1920) its area had shrunk by nearly 50 percent.

　　新中国成立后，人们在洪湖湖区先后进行过 3 次大规模的围湖造田活动，并且兴修了大量的水利设施，建成了洪湖隔堤、螺山电排河、新滩节制闸等，水利设施的兴建在为人们带来便利的同时，也严重地改变了洪湖湖区的土地利用及土地覆盖类型，导致洪湖湖泊面积锐减。如今，这块曾经拥有着"瑕苇弥望"景观的湖泊却早已不足 1850 年时洪湖面积的 1/5 了。

After the founding of the People's Republic of China, three large-scale reclamation campaigns were launched on the lake, and irrigational works were built on a large scale, including embankments, Luoshan Pump Station, and Xintan Regulator. These works and campaigns seriously altered the land use situation around Hong Lake as well as the soil covering there, resulting in a sharp drop in the wetland area of the lake. Hong Lake, once widely acclaimed as a spectacular sight full of plants and waters, is now less than one-fifth its size in 1850.

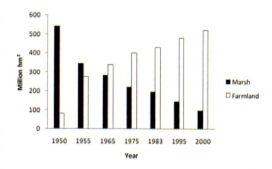

图 3.3　近 50 年三江平原沼泽湿地和农田变化比较柱状图 (2004)
Picture 3.3　Changes in the Area of Marshy Wetland and That of Farmland in the Sanjiang River over 50 Years Illustrated by Histogram (Liu, H.Y.,)

　　除了湖泊湿地退化的问题较为突出外，其他类型的湿地同样面临严重威胁。在过去 40 年间，中国的红树林湿地面积减少了约 75%。青藏高原拥有着典型的高寒湿地，在 1969~2004 年，这一特殊的湿地类型萎缩了 10% 以上，其中，以长江源区的沼泽湿地退化最为严重，退缩的幅度达到了 29%。吉林向海湿地位于科尔沁草原中部，它的"向海鹤舞"被誉为"吉林八景"之一，但在近 15 年间，由于降水量的减少和蒸发量的增加等，使其面积大幅减缩了 735.61km²。此外，大规模湿地围垦或牧场开发，也同样使三江平原、松嫩平原及若尔盖草原等沼泽湿地在近 50 年里出现了大面积的萎缩现象，仅三江平原沼泽湿地在 1950~2000 年间就因农业开垦而丧失近 73.6% 的面积；长江河口湿地也在由 20 世纪 50 年代起的 40 年间，因围垦而丧失滩涂面积达 $7.85 \times 10^4 hm^2$。

The rather grim situation in which China's lakes and their associated wetlands find themselves, is mirrored by several other types of wetlands within the country. Over the past 40 years, China's mangrove wetlands have shrunk in area by about 75%. On the Tibetan Plateau, the total area of original high altitude wetlands shrank by more than 10% in the period 1969 to 2004, with the highest levels of deterioration, as high as 29%, taking place in the wetlands around the source of the Yangtze River. Located in the center of the Horqin Grassland, Jilin Xianghai Nature Reserve boasts Xianghai Crane Dance, one of Jilin's "Eight Spectacles". Wetlands Xianghai Nature Reserve have shrunk by 735.61 km^2 over the recent 15 years due to a drop in levels of rainfall; an increase in rates of evaporation; and' other reasons. A major factor in wetland loss has been the large-scale reclamation of wetlands for agricultural purposes. Wetland reclamation for use as pastureland has caused the great marsh wetland ecosystems once found in the Sanjiang Plain, the Songnen Plain, and the Ruoergai Grasslands to shrink greatly in the past 50 years. The Sanjiang Plain wetlands have perhaps experienced the largest losses of any Chinese wetlands, with a decrease of 73.6% in the original area (in 1950) by the year 2000. A corresponding decline in the wetlands around the estuary of the Yangtze River has been observed from the 1950s to the 1990s, with 7.85×10^4 hm^2 of wetlands lost to reclamation of the inter-tidal wetlands along the coastal zone.

经过第一、第二次全国湿地资源调查，并对相同类型、相同范围和相同起点的调查面积的湿地进行对比得出：近 10 年来，我国湿地面积已减少了 339.63hm^2，其中自然湿地面积减少了 3.3762hm^2，减少率达到 9.33%。

The results of the 1st and 2nd national wetland resources censuses provide an excellent barometer of wetland loss in China during the last decade. Through comparison of data on different wetland types throughout the country, it clearly shows that China's wetland area has shrunk by 3,396,300 hectares, and that significantly total includes 3,376,200 hectares of natural wetlands, amounting to a 9.33% loss over nearly 10 years.

二、湿地质量现状
II.Status quo of the wetland quality

1. 湿地水质污染严重
1.Water pollution is serious in the wetlands

湿地水质恶化是湿地退化的重要标志，也是中国湿地所面临的最严重威胁之一。2013 年的中国环境状况公报显示，所调查的十大流域国控断面中，Ⅰ～Ⅲ类、Ⅳ～Ⅴ类和劣Ⅴ类水质断面比例分别为 71.7%、19.3% 和 9.0%，其中长江水质总体良好，黄河、松花江、淮河与辽河流域为轻度污染，海河流域为中度污染，主要污染指标为化学需氧量、高锰酸盐指数和 5 日生化需氧量。而 122 个国控的重点湖泊（水库）水质调查中，优良、轻度污染、中度污染和重度污染的比例分别为 60.7%、26.2%、1.6% 和 11.5%，且富营养、中营养和贫营养的湖泊（水库）比例分别为 27.8%、57.4% 和 14.8%，主要污染指标为总磷、化学需氧量和高锰酸盐指数。国家水利部发布的 2013

年中国水资源公报则表明，全国 67.6% 的河流湖泊已遭受了污染。

Changes in water quality in wetlands provide a good measure of overall wetland health. Water quality deterioration appears to be one of the most serious threats to China's wetlands. According to the 2013 Bulletin of China's Environmental Situation, which reported the results of monitoring for different sections within 10 major drainage basins, the water quality classes corresponding to Grades I~III, Grades IV~V, and Grades V and below, account for 71.7%, 19.3%, and 9.0% of the sections in general. Water quality is considered to be generally "good" in the Yangtze River basin; "lightly polluted" in the Yellow River, Songhua River, Huai River, and Liao River basins; and, the Hai River was "moderately polluted", with the chemical oxygen demand (COD), the permanganate index, and the biochemical oxygen demand after 5 days (BOD_5) as the major pollution indexes. In a survey involving 122 major lakes (and reservoirs) under national control, 60.7% of lakes were considered to have "excellent" water quality; 26.2% were "lightly polluted"; 1.6% were "moderately polluted"; and, 11.5% were "heavily polluted". In addition, 27.8% were deemed "highly eutrophic"; 57.4% as "moderately eutrophic"; and, 14.8% as "slightly eutrophic", using the total phosphorus levels, the chemical oxygen demand, and the permanganate levels as the major pollution indexes. According to a bulletin released by the Ministry of Water Resources of the People's Republic of China on China's water resources in 2013, 67.6% of the country's rivers and lakes have suffered pollution to varying degrees.

2013 年重点湖泊（水库）水质状况
Water Quality Situation of Major Lakes (Reservoirs) in 2013

湖库类型 Type of lake or reservoir	优（个） Excellent	良好（个） Good	轻度污染(个) Lightly polluted	中度污染(个) Moderately polluted	重度污染（个） Heavily polluted
三湖（太湖、滇池、巢湖） Three lakes (Tai Lake, Dianchi Lake, Chao Lake)	0	0	2	0	1
重要湖泊 Important lakes	5	9	10	1	6
重要水库 Important reservoirs	12	11	4	0	0
总计 Total	17	20	16	1	7

2013 年，中国海洋环境质量公报监测结果表明，我国近海海域水质一般，鱼、虾和贝类的产卵场、索饵场、洄游通道及自然保护区主要污染指标为无机氮和活性磷酸盐。而长江口无机氮和活性磷酸盐超标较重，珠江口则无机氮超标较重，杭州湾活性磷酸盐超标较重。部分养殖水域无机氮和活性磷酸盐超标较重，其结果不仅破坏了滨海湿地景观，也直接造成了生物多样性丧失。

China's offshore waters are considered "moderately good" in water quality, according to the Bulletin of Marine Environmental Quality of China, 2013; and, inorganic nitrogen and active phosphates constitute the major pollutants in important fisheries and shell fisheries areas, and in the country's coastal nature reserves. Levels of inorganic nitrogen and active phosphates are both much higher than the permissible levels in the estuary of the Yangtze River. In the Pearl River estuary, levels of inorganic nitrogen far exceed the legal limits; whilst in Hangzhou Bay high levels of active phosphates is a major environmental issue. In areas where there are high levels of agricultural activity and run-off, levels of both inorganic nitrogen and active phosphates tend to exceed permissible levels by a wide margin, resulting in a generally polluted coastal wetland landscape, and subsequent loss of biodiversity in these zones.

2. 湿地生物多样性减少

2. Biodiversity is decreasing in the wetlands

中国湿地类型的多样性造就了中国湿地丰富的生物多样性，而被列入了世界受威胁鸟类名录的中国湿地鸟类就有 23 种。湿地不合理的开发利用、全球变化和污染物的滥排等破坏了湿地生态系统的生态平衡，导致生物多样性严重下降，甚至有的物种已濒临灭绝。

High diversity of wetland habitating in China ensures that the country supports high levels of biodiversity at these wetlands. China's wetlands are known to support 23 endangered bird species. However, unsustainable practices such as over-exploitation of natural resources, global climate change, and the discharge of pollutants into wetlands, have all contributed to a decline in wetland ecosystem health in China, and a corresponding drop in biodiversity levels at wetlands. In fact, some wetland species are now on the verge of extinction.

中国内陆湿地生态系统中白鳍豚（*Lipotes vexillifer*）、中华鲟（*Acipenser sinensis*）、达氏鲟（*Acipenser dabryanus*）、白鲟（*Psephuyrus gladius*）和江豚（*Neophocaena*）等已成为濒危物种，长江鲟鱼（*Acipenser dabryanus*）、鲥鱼（*Tenualosa reevesii*）和银鱼（*Hemisalanx prognathus*）等经济鱼种种群也已接近灭绝；长江中下游湿地区域内的洞庭湖湿地因围垦和过度捕捞，其天然鱼产量在持续下降；洪湖湿地的鱼类则从 20 世纪 50 年代的 100 余种已降为 90 年代的 50 余种，其湿地植物和植被类型也都明显降低；青海湖截止 1999 年已有 34 种野生动物消失。除以上案例外，在我国重要的滨海湿地，也因着酷渔滥捕的现象频发，使湿地鱼类资源受到很大的破坏，同时严重影响到了这些滨海湿地的生态平衡，并威胁着其他水生物种的安全。

Already listed as endangered species in China's inland wetland ecosystems are the white-flag dolphin (*Lipotes vexillifer*), the Chinese sturgeon (*Acipenser sinensis*), Dabry's sturgeon (*Acipenser dabryanus*), the Chinese paddlefish (*Psephuyrus gladius*), and the finless porpoise (*Neophocaena phocaenoides*); moreover, some economic fish species, including Dabry's sturgeon (*Acipenser dabryanus*), the reeves shad (*Tenualosa reevesii*), and the whitebait (*Hemisalanx prognathus*), are close to extinction as they are experiencing sharp drops in numbers; the wetlands of Dongting Lake, located in the middle and lower reaches of the

Yangtze River, are seeing constant drops in the production of natural fishes because of reclamation and overfishing; at Hong Lake, the number of wetland fish species decreased significantly, from over 100 in the 1950s to a mere over 50 in the 1990s, and so did the number of wetland plant species and that of available types of vegetation there; by 1999, a total of 34 wild animals had become extinct at Qinghai Lake. In addition, excessive fishing and hunting prevails in China's important coastal wetlands, resulting not only in serious damage to their fish resources but also in the ecological balance in these wetlands and the safety of the other aquatic species.

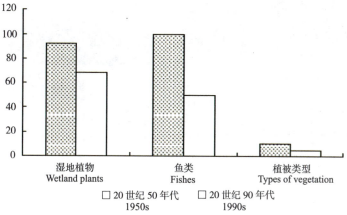

图 3.4　20 世纪 50 年代和 90 年代洪湖湿地植物，
鱼类和植被类型比较（An et al, 2006；2007；
安娜，2008；尹发能，2008）

Picture 3.4　A Comparison of the Number of Wetland Plants, the Number of Fish Species, and the Number of Types of Vegetation in the 1950s and in the 1990s (An et al, 2006; 2007; An Na, 2008; Yin Faneng, 2008)

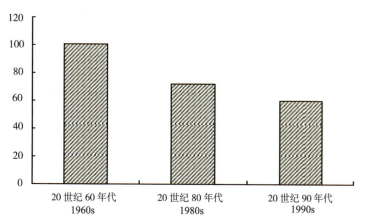

图 3.5　20 世纪 60 年代、80 年代和 90 年代太湖鱼类种类变化
（An et al, 2006；2007；安娜，2008；尹发能，2008）

Picture 3.5　A Comparison of the Number of Fish Species at Tai Lake in the 1960s, 1980s, and 1990s (An et al, 2006; 2007; An Na, 2008; Yin Faneng, 2008)

三、其他湿地功能退化
III. Other Wetland Functions Are Deteriorating

中国的湿地功能退化除上述两个主要内容外，也表现在生物生产力下降，湿地蓄水拦洪能力降低等方面。

Apart from the two aforementioned issues, the deterioration of wetland functioning in China is also reflected in aspects such as a decrease in biological productivity and a decrease in the water storage and flood mitigation capacities of wetlands.

图 3.6　左图：大量泥沙在汉江水源区南沙河河床上堆积成 1~2 米高的沙山；右图：南沙河流域局部
地区泥沙堆积严重，占据河床的 80%（来源：长江水利网 摄影：杨林）

Picture 3.6　(Left) Huge amounts of silt have created on the bank of the Nansha River within the Han River water source zone sand piles that are 1 to 2 meters high; (Right) Silt sedimentation is severe in some sections of the watercourse of the Nansha River, with the area affected by the process sometimes accounting for 80% of the riverbed. (Source: http://www.cjw.com.cn/ Photo by Yang Lin)

"断流导致湖泊水位下降，加速湿地萎缩"，这一直是中国湿地面临的突出问题。近 20 年来，因降水减少、气温升高和蒸发量增加等原因，青海湖泊水位逐年降低，致使湖泊出露面积已多达 100km²，在调节区域气候等方面的生态功能面临严重威胁；中国的呼伦湖由于入湖河流水量明显减少或断流，湖水水位下降近 2m，已经危及呼伦贝尔草原和大兴安岭林区的生态安全。

"Interruptions to the supply of water lead to reduced levels of water at lakes, thereby speeding up the shrinkage of wetlands," the report says, referring to the most prominent problem to dog China's wetlands for long. In the past 20 years, the water level at Qinghai Lake has been dropping every year due to factors like reduced rainfall and increased temperature and evaporation, and over 100 km² of water has become exposed land, meaning the lake's ecological function of regulating regional climate and others are under serious threat; due to greatly reduced or interrupted inflows from the rivers feeding it, Hulun Lake has seen its water level drop by nearly 2 meters, which has in turn posed a threat to the ecological safety of Hulunbuir Prairie and the Greater Khingan Mountains region.

"泥沙淤积填平湖底，导致湖泊湿地丧失蓄水拦洪能力"，也是中国湿地面临的重要问题之一。如三门峡库塘湿地和洞庭湖湖泊湿地因多年泥沙淤积逐渐填平了库（湖）底，使蓄水拦洪能力严重丧失；向海自然保护区由于湿地水源的不足导致湿地蓄水和调节径流能力退化，湿地调蓄功能大幅度下降，引起该地区旱灾、水灾经常交替发生，生物生产力和湿地自净能力明显降低。

The same report as quoted above, states that "deposition of silt and sediments cause significant changes of the bottom topography of lake basins, leading to significant reductions in the water storage capacity of many lake wetlands, and in turn their ability to mitigate downstream flooding". Examples of these phenomena include Sanmenxia Reservoir, and Dongting Lake, which have both suffered a catastrophic decline in water storage capacity due to high levels of sedimentation of their basins. Another example of a similar problem can be seen at the wetlands of the Xianghai Nature Reserve, where an insufficient water supply has led to significant decreases in the area of water in the basin, and a loss of lake wetland functions, and periods of longer drought in the area. There has also been a corresponding loss of biological productivity within the nature reserve and loss of function of natural water treatment by its wetlands.

(李伟摄)

图 3.7 水体富营养化
Picture 3.7 Bodies of Water Undergoing Eutrophication (Photo by Li Wei)

　　除此之外，人类肆意的围垦滥伐和环境污染，也不同程度地降低了湿地的功能，如对红树林的围垦和砍伐，使红树林大面积消失而丧失了其防护海岸的生态功能；多年来因无度和无序地对滨海湿地开发，已使部分滨海湿地的珊瑚礁受到严重破坏，致使其丧失了护岸功能和旅游价值；再如，近 20 年来，太湖流域因工业污染，生活污水及池塘养殖等所带来的各类污染，使其洪水调蓄、旅游等生态功能受到严重威胁。

Human activities such as land reclamation, forestry in river catchments and environmental pollution have all contributed to a loss of wetland functions to varying degrees. For instance, coastal land reclamation, forestry and other forms of overuse, have contributed to significant loss of mangrove forests, and corresponding loss of coastal ecological functions. In the last 20 years, unsustainable exploitation has caused severe damage to coastal wetlands and coral reefs in China, resulting in significant losses of wetland functioning such as coastal protection, fisheries and tourism. In addition, various sources of pollution (e.g., industrial pollutants, domestic sewage, agricultural runoff, etc.), as well as aquicultural land conversion have overwhelmed the Tai Lake drainage basin, severely affecting the aquatic environment of the lake wetlands, and posing a grave threat to their functions as a source of potable water, as natural storage basins and flood mitigation areas, and as a tourist destinations.

想一想
Give This Some Thought

想一想在维护滨海湿地健康的大任中，除了红树林，还有哪些湿地植物参与到了其中？

Think which wetland plants in addition to mangroves play a part in the important task of maintaining the health of coastal wetlands?

试一试
Give This A Try

跟朋友一起调查一下身边的湿地较之其最初的面积、外貌，都发生了哪些变化吧!

Investigate with your friends what changes have happened to the wetlands around you in terms of area and appearance.

第二节 现状背后的原因
Section II Potential Damage-causing Factors

学习日志
Notebook

中国的湿地正面临着不同程度的威胁与损害，北京的湿地也不例外。在你闲暇的时间里，走到室外、走进湿地，尝试实地探访调查，去发现你身边的湿地都承受着哪些伤害吧！

Nowadays, China's wetlands, including those in Beijing, are confronted with threats and suffering damage to varying degrees. Go out in your spare time, to spend time in the outdoors by setting foot on wetlands to make an on-the-spot investigation, to find out for yourself what sorts of harm man is doing to the wetlands around you!

所谓"工欲善其事，必先利其器"，这句话提醒我们，在进行每一项调查研究之前都需要事先做好完善的知识储备，目前搜集资料的方式是多种多样的，诸如上网、查询书籍及文献等。那么，请你利用最适合你的方式针对上面提到的问题搜集相关的资料，并整理记录到你的学习日志中。

Just as "To do a good job, one must first sharpen their tools," the Chinese saying goes, so we need to accumulate a sufficient amount of knowledge before launching any investigation. There are many ways to collect data, like Web surfing and looking them up in books and other types of literature. So, please use the most appropriate way of yours to collect data on the topics discussed above, and sort them out and put them down in your notebook.

学海拾贝
Pearls of Knowledge

一个健康的湿地生态系统具有自我的调节能力，即保持系统平衡的能力。但这个调节能力也是有限度的。当外力的影响超出了这个限度，生态平衡就会遭到破坏，湿地生态系统就会在短时间内发生湿地的环境、生物，以及湿地内部信息上的一系列变化，比如一些物种种群的规模会发生剧烈的变化，而另一些物种则可能会消失等，并且这一系列的变化总的结果也往往是不利的。像这一类超越限度的影响对湿地生态系统造成的破坏将是长远的，而要重新回到和原来相当的状态则往往需要相当长的时间，甚至湿地生态系统的一些变化所造成的转变还将是不可逆转的，这便是湿地生态平衡的破坏。

A healthy wetland ecosystem has the capability of making adjustments (or maintaining its balance) on its own, but there are limits to that capability. When external forces exceed those limits, the ecological balance will be damaged to a certain degree, leading to significant changes in the wetland environment, the makeup of the ecosystem with respect to species, and the internal information system of the ecosystem over a short period of time, like drastic changes in the size of the population of a particular species and the disappearance of certain species. Such changes usually represent a turn for the worse. Damage caused by influences that exceed the limits of the ecosystem lasts long, making it impossible to complete any process of restoring the system to its original state within a short period of time. And processes caused by some changes are sometimes irreversible, which is what we usually refer to as permanent damage to the wetland ecological balance.

破坏湿地生态平衡的因素可以分为自然因素和人为因素两大类：自然因素主要包括洪水的侵蚀、旱灾、地震，以及台风、海啸等；人为因素则包括废水排放、污染、乱捕滥猎，以及排水填埋等。目前，在这两者之中的人为因素已成为湿地生态平衡失调的主要原因。下面，就让我们一起来看看这自然和人为因素中的几个重要方面的概要分析吧。

Contributing factors to wetland ecological damage may be divided into two major categories, namely natural factors and artificial factors. Natural factors may include floods, droughts, earthquakes, typhoons, and tsunamis, while the artificial ones include wastewater discharges, pollution, excessive hunting and fishing, and reclamation or land conversion. At present, the artificial category plays a more critical role than the natural one in disturbing the ecological balance of wetlands in China. Now, let's make a brief analysis of the several major threats to the ecological balance from both categories.

一、自然威胁
I. Natural Threats

21 世纪以来，大气平均温度比 20 世纪升高了 0.4℃ ~0.8℃，促使极地和高寒地带冰川融化力度加大而导致海平面已上升 15~50cm。而当海平面升高到一定程度时则会导致沿海湿地的分布状况发生较大的变化，例如滩地、红树林和其他沼泽会在因海平面上升而带来的水淹和冲蚀中消失掉，其他湿地则将发生向内陆移动的趋势。其次，随着海水温度的升高和 CO_2 浓度的增加，也将对珊瑚礁产生严重的威胁，这主要是因为珊瑚礁对温度的变化非常敏感，如果在短时间内海水温度升高了 3℃ ~4℃ 的话，就将会造成珊瑚的大面积死亡。此外，近海与海岸湿地作为野生动物栖息地的价值也将随着湿地的变化而被削弱，湿地的生物多样性则亦将随之减少。

Since the beginning of the 21st century, average atmospheric temperatures have climbed by 0.4℃ ~0.8°C from where they stood in the 20th century. This has resulted in rapid melting of the polar ice caps, glaciers, and in other cold regions, which has led to an increase of between 15 −50 cm in sea levels. When sea levels rise to a certain level, rather big changes will occur in the distribution of wetlands along our coasts. For instance, the seaward edge of current seashores will be permanently submerged by seawater, or will result in increased erosion of this zone, resulting in wetland habitats found in this zone retreating further inland. This will impact inter-tidal mangrove forests and salt marshs in particular. As sea water temperatures and concentrations of carbon dioxide in seawater rise, coral reefs will also be seriously threatened, because they are very sensitive to temperature changes. If sea water temperatures rise by about 3℃－4℃ over a short period of time, large areas of coral reef are likely to die. Moreover, the significance of coastal waters and the wetlands and wildlife they support will likely decrease as a result of global climate change.

　　全球变化会导致一些地区的降水量减少，部分区域的气候趋于干旱，这将使当地的湿地面临着退化或消失的命运。例如，中国新疆境内的冰川在过去40年里，因为全球变化而带来的面积消融量达到了20%，而冰川逐渐消失的直接后果就是以冰川为补给水源的河流的来水量将直接减少，导致河流断流现象的发生。由于源头青藏高原冰川消融的影响，黄河流域从20世纪90年代以来就经常性地发生断流，直接造成黄河中下游的湿地因缺水而大范围萎缩和退化。被誉为"华北之肾"的白洋淀湿地作为我国华北地区典型的内陆湖泊湿地，历史上水量是十分充沛的，但在近几十年，由于上游流域频发干旱并且修建了较多的水利工程，进一步加剧了整个湖区的缺水现象，全球自然环境的变化和人为的影响共同造成了白洋淀"干淀"的威胁。

Global climate change is also predicted to cause rainfall in some areas to decrease. This will lead to drier weather conditions, thereby aggravating the deterioration or disappearance of wetlands. For example, the total area of glaciers in Xinjiang AR, China, has dropped by 20% in the past 40 years (as is believed to be limked to global climate change). The direct result of this decrease in glacier formation and growth has been seen in the water supply to rivers basins and more severe interruptions in seasonal flows associated with snow and glacial melt waters. Interruptions to flows in the Yellow River drainage basin have frequently occurred since the 1990s due, in part, to the melting and disappearance of glaciers at the source of the river on the Tibetan Plateau. This has resulted in the middle and lower reaches of the river suffering from shrinkage and deterioration due to a shortage of water. Baiyangdian Lake and its surrounding wetlands, widely acclaimed as the "Kidney of North China," are typical inland lake wetlands in North China, and historically, have always had an abundant supply of water. However, in the past decade or more, the lake has suffered from a chronic shortage of water due to prolonged drought, and also due to increased use of lake basin water for irrigation throughout the ctachment. Indeed, global climate change combined with human impacts, continue to threaten Baiyangdian Lake and its wetlands, and there is a danger that the wetlands will eventually become a dry lake bed.

二、泥沙淤积
II. Silt Sedimentation

　　长期以来，一些大江、大河上游水源涵养区的水土流失正不断加剧，严重影响了江河流域的生态平衡。河流中的泥沙含量逐渐增大，造成河床、湖底不断淤积，湿地面积不断缩小，湿地功能逐渐衰退。近年来，长江中下游及东北地区的洪涝灾害频繁发生，这与这些地区湿地水文的变化、湖泊拦蓄洪水功能的下降是有着直接关系的。

For decades, soil erosion in the major river catchments of China has been worsening and has seriously effected the ecological balance within the river drainage basins. Deposition of silt and sediments poses a serious problem for riverbeds because the continuous but gradual increase in deposition slowly reduced the river's functional capacity to hold water and mitigate flooding along the river course. In recent years, floods have been frequent in the middle and lower reaches of the Yangtze River and throughout Northeast China as well, due in large measure, to changes in the hydrological conditions of these rivers, and decreases in the functional capacity of the river channels to store water and mitigate flooding.

　　根据水利部门全国实测河流泥沙资料及历年《中国河流泥沙公报》数据显示，每年平均约有 12 亿吨泥沙淤积在外流区下游平原的河道、湖泊和水库中，或被引入灌溉区以及分洪区内。古书曾有"黄河斗水，泥居其七"的记述，黄河每年携带的泥沙量就多达 16 亿吨之巨，位居世界河流输沙量之冠，而这其中，绝大多数泥沙来自于中游的黄土高原。在这众多的泥沙中，有 4 亿吨沉积在下游河道，4 亿吨进入了海洋，8 亿吨沉积在河口三角洲和近海水下三角洲，其结果便是三角洲地区经常改道，平均每年可以向外伸展约 50 米。

According to data collected on silt sedimentation status in rivers across the country by national water resources authorities and the *Bulletin on Silt Sedimentation Status in Rivers across China, a report released annually that is based on those data*, about 1.2 billion tons of silt is either deposited in watercourses, lakes, and reservoirs in the plains which function as the lower reaches of rivers or diverted to irrigation and flood-diversion areas each year. In ancient literature the Yellow River is sometimes described as "containing in its river water more silt than water." In fact, the river carries off an alarming over 1.6 billion tons of silt each year, which makes it the river in the world to carry off the largest amount of silt. Of the 1.6 billion tons of silt, nearly all comes from the Loess Plateau. Roughly speaking, 0.4 billion tons of silt is deposited in the watercourse in the final section of the river, another 0.4 billion discharged into the sea, and 0.8 billion deposited on the delta around the estuary and on the one beneath the coastal waters. The result of all this silt sedimentation is that the delta frequently changes its position, extending outward by about 50 meters each year on average.

三、外来物种入侵

III. Invasion of External Species

外来物种入侵，已是一种全球现象，是 21 世纪三个最棘手的环境问题之一。这些异域杀手，一旦在湿地安家落户，便凭着其较强的繁殖能力，在新的几无天敌的环境中，爆发性的生长，迅速蔓延，占领地盘，将湿地原有的动植物赶尽杀绝。

The invasion of alien species is a global phenomenon, which has been highlighted as one of the three most serious environmental problems of the 21st century. Many alien species are considered "invasive" as they may have no natural predators in their new environment, they are usually highly adaptable to a wide range or environmental contitions, and can produce large numbers of seeds or have high levels of repoductive potential. Thus, such species can often spread quickly throughout their new environment and greatly impact native species, often threatening the survival of native animals and plants which have evolved over millions of years without competition from the alien species, and in extreme cases leading to local extinction.

(a)

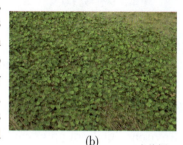
(b)　　　　　　（李伟摄）

图 3.8 (a) 互花米草侵占原有红树林；
(b) 幼苗滋生
Picture 3.8 (Above) Mangrove Woods Being Invaded by Spartina Alterniflora;
(Below) Seedlings Running Wild (Photo by Li Wei)

这些入侵杀手中鼎鼎大名的互花米草（*Spartina alterniflora*）沿中国大陆海岸线分布面积已达 35995.2 公顷，它原产于美国大西洋沿岸与墨西哥湾，主要生长在潮间带，根茎发达，能够促进泥沙快速沉降和淤积，原本是为了保滩护堤而引进的，却因为生长迅速已被重点防控。同样臭名昭著的还包括凤眼莲（*Eichhornia crassipes*，水葫芦）、空心莲子草（*Alternanthera philoxeroides*）等，它们在我国南方省份分布较广，危害极大。

One of the most notorious alien invasive species is the smooth cordgrass (*Spartina alterniflora*), a species that has severly impacted inter-tidal wetland ecosystems along the east coast of China. Native to the Atlantic coast of the United States and the Gulf of Mexico, the smooth cordgrass mainly grows in marshlands and its advanced roots and stem help to trap silt and promote coastal deposition and accretion of the inter-tidal zone. The species was originally introduced into China as a method to protect the seashore and its coastal protection embankments, but has quickly spread and is now threatened native ecosystems in several East coast provinces. There are many similarly notorious species that have established themselves throughout the wetlands of China, these include the water hyacinth (*Eichhornia crassipes*), and the alligator weed (*Alternanthera philoxeroides*), which are both widely distributed in the southern Chinese provinces, and have caused great damage to wetland ecosystems.

2013 年《中国环境状况公报》就有这样一组数据：目前中国有约 500 种外来入侵

物种，常年大面积发生危害的物种有 100 多种。对待外来入侵物种，我们应根据其特点区别对待，在充分评估引进其所带来风险的前提下，再对其进行合理的利用。

According to the 2013 *Bulletin on China's Environmental Situation*, there are in China about 500 external species that are believed to have originated from sources outside China, of which over 100 are deemed to cause damage over large areas each year. When it comes to external species, we should treat them differently by taking their respective features into account, in order that proper use can be made of them after assessing the risks they could introduce.

四、环境污染
IV. Environmental Pollution

环境污染（Environmental pollution）易导致环境质量恶化，扰乱和破坏生态系统的稳定性及人类的正常生活条件，影响和改变环境原有的性质或状态。例如水环境污染、空气污染、垃圾污染等都属于环境污染。

Environmental pollution causes environmental quality to deteriorate, disrupts or damages the stability of ecosystems and man's normal living conditions, and affects and changes the environment's original nature or condition. For instance, environmental pollution exists in a number of different forms, including water pollution, air pollution, and waste pollution.

污染是中国湿地面临的最严重威胁之一，不仅使湿地的水质恶化，也对湿地生物造成严重危害，而且这些危害正随着经济的迅速发展而不断加剧。中国部分天然湿地因受周边地区的农业污染、工业污染与生活污染的影响，已逐渐沦为工农业废水、生活污水的承泄区，这种状况在经济发达地区尤为明显，其结果便是导致了湖泊的富营养化（由于氮、磷等营养物质过量所引起的水质污染现象），藻类"水华"（由于水体富营养化而引起的浮游生物大量繁殖使水面呈现不同颜色的自然现象）等现象的频发。

Environmental pollution is one of the most serious threats to China's wetlands. In fact, not only has it led to serious deterioration of water quality, but it has caused significant damage to wetland biodiversity. These impacts have become increasingly more severe as the country's economic development continues its high speed growth. China's wetlands are the "sinks" for much of China's agricultural, industrial, and domestic pollution, and as a result many of our natural wetlands have degenerated into *de-facto* dump sites. This phenomenon tends to be more prominent in the economically developed regions of China, and inevitably leads to the occurrence of other phenomena associated with pollution. Most prevalent amongst these is "eutrophication", a type of water pollution caused by excessive levels of nitrogen, phosphorus, and other nutrients in the water; coupled with sunlight; and, the rapid growth of green algal blooms in response to the nutrients and sunlight.

(a)   (李惠摄)   (b)   （新京报记者 郭铁流摄）
图 3.9 (a) 北京某湿地中遭污染水体；(b) 某湿地水岸垃圾污染
Picture 3.9 (Left) A Polluted Body of Water in a Wetland in Beijing (Photo by Li Hui); (Right) Pollution Caused by
Wastes Dumped into a Body of Water in a Wetland (Photo by Guo Tieliu of The Beijing News)

五、不合理利用
V. Improper Use

目前，湿地开垦、湿地资源滥用、改变自然湿地用途和城市开发占用自然湿地已成为中国自然湿地面积削减、功能下降的主要原因。

At present, land reclamation on wetlands, the misuse of wetland resources, and the use of natural wetlands for industrial purposes or for development projects are the main reasons China's natural wetlands dropping in size and in function.

1. 对湿地的盲目开垦和改造
1. Unsustainable wetland reclamation and conversion to other land uses

长期以来，由于人们对湿地生态价值和社会效益认识不足，加上保护管理力度薄弱，一些地方仍在开垦、围垦和随意侵占湿地。中国历史上曾一度将沼泽湿地作为荒地或未利用地来看待，并将它纳入了农业生产的后备资源而进行过大规模的开发和利用，这一不合理的利用模式不仅破坏了大量的湿地资源，也导致部分沼泽湿地的功能逐渐下降，甚至消失。

People are still reclaiming or encroaching on the wetlands in their parts of the country due to an insufficient knowledge of the importance of the ecological and social value of wetlands coupled with weak control over their protection. Marshlands and wetlands were once viewed as wastelands or uncultivated land in Chinese history and, treated as some sort of reserve resources for agricultural production, were exploited on a large scale. Not only did such improper use of wetland resources cause damage to huge amounts of wetland resources, but it leads to decreases in function in some marshlands and wetlands or even the disappearance of such lands.

(a)　　　　　　　　　　　　　　　　　　　(b)　　　　　　(李伟摄)

图 3.10　(a) 红树林湿地周边的城建占地；(b) 湿地挖沙

Picture 3.10　(Left) Land on the Edge of a Mangrove Wetland Allocated for Development Work; (Right) Sand Excavation in Wetlands (Photo by Li Wei)

2. 水资源不合理利用

2. Unsustainable use of water resources

湿地水资源不合理利用现象多发生在湖泊和沼泽，主要表现为：过度的从湿地取水或开采地下水；注重工农业生产和生活用水，而不关注生态环境用水（Ecological environment water use）；在湿地内挖沟排水，导致湿地水文发生变化，湿地不断萎缩甚至消失等。

Improper use of wetland water resources normally occurs at lakes and marshlands, mainly taking one of a number of forms, including extracting surface or underground water from the wetland excessively; paying more attention to water allocated for agricultural, industrial, and domestic purposes than to water required for the proper functioning of the ecological environment; and draining the wetland by digging up ditches, which may lead to changes in its hydrological conditions or even its shrinkage or disappearance.

(a)

(b)　　　　　　(李伟摄)

图 3.11　(a) 过度抽取湿地水体；
　　　　　(b) 湿地干涸

Picture 3.11　(Above) Excessive Extraction of Water from a Wetland Body of Water (Below) A Dried-up Wetland (Photo by Li Wei)

湿地是工农业和居民生活等的主要水源地，过度的和不合理的用水已使中国湿地供水能力受到重大影响。例如，中国西部地区的湖泊也因上游地区超负荷的截水灌溉，而导致湖泊加剧萎缩，水质不断咸化，像新疆准噶尔盆地西部的玛纳斯湖，到 20 世纪 50 年代湖体面积尚为 550 平方千米；60 年代，注入该湖的河道已断流；而到了现在，该湖区早已变成了干涸的盐碱地和荒漠。除此之外，因过度从湿地取水、开采地下水及水资源的不合理利用，也已使西北地区塔里木河、黑河等重要的内陆河的下游出现严重的缺水现象。

Wetlands serve as one of the major sources of water used for agricultural, industrial, and domestic purposes. Excessive and improper use of water has greatly affected the water supply capability of China's wetlands. In fact, many lakes in Western China have been shrinking at increasing rates, and becoming increasingly salty, due to the excessive diversion of water for irrigation and other purposes. For example, Manas Lake, which lies to the east of the Zhunge'er Basin, had a water surface area of 550 square kilometers in the 1950s, but by the 1960s, the main catchment river supplying water to the lake basin was dry. Much of the original lake bed has now become saline or desert land. In other parts of China, excessive extraction of surface and ground water from wetlands, along with other forms of unsustainable water resource use , have caused severe water shortages in some major inland river basins, including the Tarim River in Northwest China and the Hei River.

3. 生物资源无序和过度利用

3. Unsustainable use of biological resources

　　水中无鱼何以为水？但你是否曾经见到过这样的景象：一片清清的湖水，却是水中无鱼、水上无鸟。此时这片湿地的鱼类很有可能已经被捕捞殆尽，鸟儿也不愿再来觅食，也许你会感到痛心失望，但是一定不要忘记，我们的任务正是让这些曾经的飞鸟与鱼儿回归到这片土地。

Can any body of water be viewed as a pleasant sight if there are no fishes in it? Have you ever seen a sight like this: there is a large area of clear water in a lake but no fish or bird swimming in or flying above it? If you did, it was very likely that the fishes once growing

（李伟摄）

图 3.12 围垦红树林湿地
Picture 3.12 Land Reclamation on Mangrove Wetlands (Photo by Li Wei)

in abundance there had all been captured, thereby making it meaningless for the birds to come for food. Such a grim sight might sadden you beyond expression, but it is far more important for you to bear in mind that our task is to bring those fishes and birds back to where they once swam or flew.

　　湿地以"生物宝库"而著称，而过度的捕捞采集让湿地丰富的物产被肆意掠夺，最终不但影响了湿地的生物多样性，更破坏湿地健康的生态平衡。根据国家林业局的调查，我国 323 处受到监测的重要湿地中 40.7% 的湖泊、26.4% 的近海岸湿地和 19.8% 的沼泽湿地均受到了过度捕捞的威胁。一些被承包的内陆湖泊型湿地中，大鱼小鱼都被捕捞殆尽，大量的小鱼被用来作为动物的饲料；现如今，渔民的渔网网眼越来越密，滩涂相连的很多近海鱼虾都已被打捞得干干净净；还有一些地区则采用抽水捕鱼、电鱼、虾笼等残忍的捕捞方式，给湿地的鱼虾带来了灭顶之灾，导致湿地鱼类的种类日趋单一，种群结构出现了低龄化和小型化。所谓"涸泽而渔"，最终却可能是水未竭而鱼已尽。

Wetlands have been widely acclaimed as "biological treasure houses," but unfortunately, their resources are often plundered at will to suit the greed of man. Such activities not only effect the levels of biodiversity supported at the wetland, but ultimately, also damages the healthy wetland ecological balance. According to a survey by the State Forestry Administration of the People's Republic of China, of 323 major wetland ecosystems monitored, 40.7% of the lakes, 26.4% of the coastal wetlands, and 19.8% of marshes are suffering from over-fishing to varying degrees. Some freshwater lakes are managed and leased for fisheries producion, resulting in the complete loss of natural fish populations and their replacement with industrial fisheries systems. At other wetlands, more and more fishermen are using smaller mesh fishing nets, enabling the capture of all sized fish, and preventing small fish from becoming adults that will breed and continue the production cycle. Other unsustainable fisheries practices include the drainage of ponds and lakes to remove all fish; electrofishing to stun and kill fish with electricity; and extensive cage (trap) fishing. These techniques cause devastation to natural fish and shellfish populations in wetlands, which results in a less diverse fish community in these wetlands and trends showing that individual fish are getting smaller and smaller with each new generation. The grim conclusion of adopting these unsustainable practices is that no fish will remain in the wetland even before the water is completely drained.

图 3.13　某湿地不同年份的对比状况
Pictures3.13　The Status of the Same Wetland over the Years
(a) 2007 年 9 月摄，原有湿地状况
Picture (a)　Taken in September 2007, to record the original status of the wetland
(b) 2009 年 4 月摄，原有湿地上方铺设一条土路
Picture (b)　Taken in April 2009, to record what the wetland looked like after a dirt road was built on it
(c) 2012 年 3 月摄，土路改建为 8m×550m 的水泥路
Picture (c)　Taken in March 2012, to record what the wetland looked like after the dirt road was converted into an 8m×550m concrete road

4. 基建侵占

4. Encroachment by construction projects

现阶段，基建占用是导致湿地面积大幅度减少的关键因素之一，而且我国受此影响的湿地范围占有较大比例。基建占用主要发生在沿海地区，据不完全统计，我国沿海地区因围垦和基建占地的原因，累计丧失和被严重破坏的滨海湿地近 220 万公顷，约占滨海总湿地面积的 50%。根据第一、第二次全国湿地资源调查显示，近 10 年间，我国受基建占用威胁的湿地面积已增长了近 10 倍。

In today's world, allocation of wetlands for development projects is one of the major reasons for a sharp decline in China's wetlands. Conversion of wetlands to development areas is perhaps the largest cause of wetland loss in modern China. Much of this land conversion has taken place in the coastal regions. According to incomplete statistics, nearly 2.2 million hectares of coastal wetlands have been lost or severely damaged due to land reclamation for construction projects, accounting for about 50% of the total area. According to the first and second national surveys of China's wetland resources, the total area lost due to reclamation projects has increased 10 fold in the last decade.

新中国成立后开展过全国范围内的大规模水利工程建设，仅长江流域就修建了近 4.6 万座水坝、7000 多座涵闸，但由于缺乏规划和措施，这些水利工程设施也对湖泊和河流湿地生态系统带来了不利的影响。例如，20 世纪 50 年代，在与长江连通的湖口地区所修建的闸坝，切断了洄游鱼类的通道，造成了洄游鱼类资源的衰竭，妨碍了湖水与江水发生直接交换，使湖水植物群落发生变化，导致沼泽化进程加剧；巢湖原来属通江湖泊，湖泊内洄游和半洄游性鱼类的产量占总产量的 40%，自 20 世纪 60 年代兴建巢湖、裕溪口两闸后，致使洄游鱼类几乎绝迹，而定居性鱼类却占据绝对优势；我国西部内陆干燥地区的湖泊，与入湖河流的水量补给关系密切，特别是上游拦河筑坝、发展灌溉农业后，致使位于河流下游的一些湖泊、泡沼因上游拦水得不到足够的水量补充而逐渐萎缩、水质咸化，甚至消亡。此外，在一些郊野湿地上，因为原有湿地得不到有效的重视与保护，大量的道路建设直穿湿地而过，破坏了当地湿地。

Shortly after its founding China carried out large numbers of irrigation and water conservancy works across its territory. A total of nearly 46,000 dams and over 7,000 culverts and sluices were built in the Yangtze River drainage basin, one of its many regions; due to a lack of proper planning and preventive measures, those irrigation and water conservancy facilities have caused damage to the wetland ecosystems of the lakes and rivers affected. For example, a gate dam was built in the Hukou Region, where a lake joins the Yangtze River, in the 1950s, cutting off the migration path for some fish species and due to permanent disruption to the direct exchange between the lake water and the river water, resulting in the serious depletion of the resources of these species and marked changes in the plant species makeup of the lake, which in turn aggravated its transformation into a large area of swampland. Chao Lake, which had originally been linked to the Yangtze River and where migratory and semi-migratory fishes had accounted for 40% of its fish output, saw most if not all of its migratory species wiped out after two dams, called Chaohu Dam and Yuxikou Dam, respectively, were built in the 1960s, resulting in the absolute dominance of its non-migratory fish species. As for the lakes in the typically arid regions in West China, all of them depend heavily on rivers supplying water to them, and if dams and other irrigation works are carried out on such rivers for agricultural and other purposes, they gradually shrink, become saltier, and even die out due to a lack of water. Moreover, due to insufficient attention and protection paid or given to wetlands, a large number of roads pass through some suburban wetlands, causing serious damage.

想一想
Give This Some Thought

你是否还听到过其他的生物入侵案例，跟朋友讨论一下吧！

Tell us if you have heard of cases of invasion by other organisms. If so, share them with your friends!

试一试
Give This A Try

对你周边被污染的湿地，试着进行局部的改造，并在纸上画出你想象中的蓝图。

Try to restore a small part of a polluted wetland near you, and put down on paper the blueprint you have developed for your endeavor.

第三节 病症的表象
Section III Symptoms

学习日志
Notebook

　　当我们在湿地中陶醉于她碧波荡漾的美景、清新的空气时，也许不会意识到，在中国还有很多如她般美丽的湿地正遭受着各种各样的煎熬，面临着重重的危机，让她娴静美好的外表出现了不同形式的疾患征兆，请试着在学习日志中写下你认为的湿地病征吧！

If you are lucky enough to be strolling around a pristine or natural wetland in one of China's national nature reserves, you may not realize that many wetlands in other parts of China are being degraded by development, pollution and other factors. What are the symptoms of such degradation? Try to jot down in your notebook all the problems Chinese wetlands are facing.

学海拾贝
Pearls of Knowledge

　　湿地也有她脆弱的一面，湿地的"敌人"无时无刻不在威胁着她的"生命"和"健康"。如果不好好爱护和保护湿地，她也会像人类一样"生病"，而湿地一旦"生病"，其功能就会衰退，如果不能对湿地实施有效的"救治"，湿地也终将会"死亡"。那么，湿地"病症"到底都存在着哪些"病因"呢？首先，让我们看看湿地都患上了哪些"病症"吧。毕竟只有对症下药，才是治"病"良策。

Wetlands, just like anything else in our environment, have inherant weaknesses. The "enemies" of wetlands pose a grave threat to its "life" and "health", and if left unprotected and uncared for, wetlands may become "sick", just as we do. If a wetland becomes sick, its functions will deteriorate, and if no effective "treatment" is provided, it may eventually die. So, what "causes" are there to the "diseases" of wetlands? Let's find out what diseases wetlands are suffering from. Only by finding out the causes can any "disease" be cured.

一、"贫血"——过度利用
I. "Anemia"— Overuse

水是湿地的"血液"。缺少了水的湿地，就像缺少了血液的人体一样。如果人类从湿地中抽取大量的"血液"，将导致湿地"血液"供给不足，湿地就会产生严重的"贫血"。

Water is the "blood" of the wetland. Just as a human body afflicted with a blood shortage cannot function normally, so a wetland afflicted with a water shortage cannot function. If man extracts a large amount of "blood" from it to such a degree that it suffers from an insufficient supply of "blood," the wetland may contract serious "anemia."

（程兆鹏绘）
图 3.14　湿地"贫血"
Picture 3.14　A Wetland Afflicted by "Anemia" (Illustration by Cheng Zhaopeng)

水是湿地存在的基础，没有了水的"湿地"如何再称为湿地？此外，湿地缺水还会导致湿地生态系统的退化，最终造成湿地生命的消亡。

Water is one of the prerequisites for the existence of the wetland. There will be no wetland if there is no water. If there is a lack of water, the wetland ecosystem of the wetland will deteriorate, thereby resulting eventually the loss of all the life in it.

二、"高血脂"——过度积累
II. Excessive Accumulation — "Hyperlipidemia"

如果接收过多的营养物质，湿地会患上"高血脂"，影响湿地的"代谢"，而湿地的"代谢"功能一旦受阻，就会产生一系列的"健康"问题，甚至可能失去她的"生命"。湿地营养物质的过多积累，在专业上称之为"富营养化"（Eutrophication）：即氮、磷等营养物质大量进入湖泊、河口和海湾等湿地水体，引起藻类及其他浮游生物迅速繁殖，水体溶解氧量下降、水质恶化，进而导致水中鱼类及其他生物大量死亡。

（程兆鹏绘）
图 3.15　"高血脂"
Picture 3.15　"Hyperlipidemia" (Illustration by Cheng Zhaopeng)

If it has received too many nutrients, the wetland may contract "hyperlipidemia," which in turn may cause disruption to its "metabolism." A series of "health" problems, including "death," may occur if the metabolic function of the wetland is suppressed in any way. The excessive accumulation of nutrients in the wetland is known as "eutrophication" in science, referring in the context of the wetland to the entry of nutrients like nitrogen and phosphorus compounds into any body of water that forms part of the wetland ecosystem, like lakes, estuaries, and bays. Eutrophication causes algae and plankton to multiply quickly, resulting in sharp decreases in the level of dissolved oxygen in the water and in the level of water quality, which in turn leads to the death of fishes and other organisms in the wate.

引起湿地富营养化的营养物质主要是氮和磷，它们的产生与我们的生产生活密切相关。氮、磷等营养盐主要来源于工业废水、生活污水、有机垃圾、家畜家禽粪便以及化肥等。因此，日常生活的吃穿住行都可能直接或间接产生营养物质，而其中，农田里施用的大量化肥则是湿地营养物质的重要来源。保护和爱护湿地，需要我们从身边做起，从控制生活污水、垃圾的排放做起。

The main substances involved in this process are nitrogen and phosphorus compounds, whose generation is closely related to human activities. Because nitrogen and phosphorus compounds come mainly from industrial wastewater, domestic wastewater, organic wastes, the dung of cattle and fowl, and chemical fertilizers, it is fair to say that any human activity may directly or indirectly generate some nutrients, with chemical fertilizers spread on farmland constituting the largest source of nutrients to the wetland. To protect and care for the wetland, we need to pay attention to everything we do, starting with placing the discharge of domestic wastewater and wastes under control.

(李伟摄)

图 3.16 湿地 "高血脂"
Picture 3.16   A Wetland Afflicted by "Hyperlipidemia" (Photo by Li Wei)

三、"感染" ——受毒害
III. Poisoning —"Infection"

一些城市中的湿地，满眼绿色的芦苇丛下也许是泛着泡沫的城市污水，水边偶尔会出现漂浮的死鱼，这所有一切无不在讲述着那掩盖在绿色之下的湿地被污染的现状。

Urban wetlands in some cities can present a grim sight. Beneath a sea of green reeds there may be a sea of bubbling domestic wastewater, with dead fish bobbing up and down from time to time on the surface. A scene like

(程兆鹏绘)

图 3.17 湿地水体 "感染"
Picture 3.17   A Body of Water Becoming Infected in a Wetland
(Illustration by Cheng Zhaopeng)

this shows how gloomy the situation for many wetlands has become as they are continuously under assault from in-flowing pollutants.

湿地本身是拥有着强大的净化功能的，但超负荷的废水、垃圾等也会让它自身受到污染。随着城市建设的扩张，大量工业废水、废渣、生活污水等有害物质被排入湿地，甚至降水也会把城市中的垃圾和污染物及农业活动产生的化肥、农药和动物垃圾等带入河流，带进湿地。这些有毒物质会危害到水生生物的存活，而过量的营养物质又会导致水体的富营养化，令藻类灾害爆发，导致鱼类、水草等因缺氧而死。

In natural situations, wetlands possess powerful self-cleaning mechanisms, however most wetlands cannot withstand too high concentrations of pollutants before these mechanisms start to break down. In today's world, with such huge amounts of industrial and domestic wastewater, and solid wastes, being dumped into wetlands the situation is even more serious. Urban development further aggravates the situation with flushing of pollutants into urban drains and channels a common sight. Domestic waste and pollutants and agricultural wastes such as chemical fertilizers, agricultural chemicals, and animal wastes are all dumped into our wetlands. These substances harm aquatic organisms, and excessive concentrations of nutrients may lead to eutrophication and algal blooms, which can cause mass fish kills, death of aquatic plants, and other organisms to die from a sudden lack of oxygen in the water.

另外，养殖污染的威力也不容小觑。以海参的人工养殖为例，人们在滩涂养殖海参的过程中，从幼苗到出产一直都需要用药，这些药物会杀死大量贝类及其他生物，影响水中鱼类的生存、繁殖，加速部分细菌的繁殖，致使水草丛生，产生厌气发酵，形成恶臭，严重破坏滨海湿地的生态平衡。

（程兆鹏绘）
图 3.18　湿地植物渐少
Picture 3.18　Plants on the Decline in a Wetland (Illustration by Cheng Zhaopeng)

Pollution due to activities such as fish cultivation and animal husbandry is another source of pollution to be reckoned with. The cultivation of sea cucumber in large-scale, coastal aquaculture farms is an example of how polluting chemicals are used throughout the process of artificial cultivation. Chemicals are used to supress predatory shellfish and other aquatic organisms, and these chemicals directly effect the growth and breeding of local fish populations, as well as increase bacteria populations. These factors eventually lead to the rapid growth of seaweeds, and promote anaerobic conditions, which both cause serious damage to the ecological balance of the coastal zone.

不论是湿地水体，还是湿地动植物，都是整个湿地有机体的重要组成部分，它们相互关联，维持着一种牵一发则动全身的关系。如果一味地不加限制地对湿地进行过度"感染"，再加上其他"疾患"的影响，湿地的各部分共同维持的这一独特的生态系统就会受到严重破坏，会导致鸟类失去栖息的环境，鱼儿失去嬉戏的乐园，湿地的美观和健康也都会受到严重影响。继续任其发展，那么我们身边这些绮丽的湿地风景就将逐渐消失。

Every part of a wetland, including its water and the fauna and flora that live in it, are integral to the functioning of the system in an organic way. In fact, they are so closely interrelated that any change in any part will affect all the other parts of the wetland. If wetlands becomes seriously "infected" due to unsustainable human activities, and at the same time are assaulted by other "ailments," the ecological balance will be seriously damaged, and both the beauty and health of the wetland will be seriously affected. If such deterioration is left unchecked, the beautiful wetland scenery we enjoy today will gradually disappear for future generations.

四、"萎缩"——受挤压
IV. Being Squeezed — "Shrinkage"

当我们陶醉在湿地的秀丽景色中时，当你因眼前湿地的广阔无垠而发出慨叹时，你可能想不到，在其他的地域，有多少曾比她壮丽得多的湿地现在却只能瑟缩在人类为她余留的狭小空间内。

When enjoying a beautiful wetland scenery or landscape in one of China's many wetland nature reserves, it may not occur to you that in many other areas, spectacular wetlands have disappeared and shrunk due to human activity.

都怪你们不爱惜我，我现在都变小了。呜呜呜……
I am becoming smaller and smaller because you treat me roughly. Boo-hoo...

（程兆鹏绘）

图 3.19　湿地"缩水"
Picture 3.19　A Shrinking Wetland
(Illustration by Cheng Zhaopeng)

由于人口和经济的快速增长，用地规模不断扩大等因素影响，湿地被大规模围垦和改造，无论是在面积上还是在深度上，湿地都在不断地受到挤压，湿地的"块头"在不断的减小，呈现"萎缩"的症状。20 世纪 50 年代以来，全国湿地开垦面积达 1000 万公顷，全国沿海滩涂面积已削减过半，长江三角洲、珠江三角洲以及江淮平原、成都平原的大面积水稻田变成了城市、高速公路；东北大批风景优美的湿地变成了耕地；沿海很多地方则直接把海边的小山或者高地炸平，将土石填到向海洋过渡的滩涂湿地上，使很多宽阔的滩涂湿地也永久性地消失，现在全国各类大小湖泊消失了上千个，约 1/3 的天然湿地正经历着被改变与丧失的危险。

In a rapidly growing economy such as China's, where population growth is also an important factor, the need for new land has resulted in massive reclamation pressure on many of the wetlands. Large-scale reclamation projects are transforming wetlands into smaller and smaller pockets of habitat. Since the 1950s, China has reclaimed 10 million hectares of its wetlands, and as a result, the total area of coastal wetlands has dropped by 50%. Large areas of agricultural rice fields in the Yangtze River Delta, the Pearl River Delta, the Jianghuai Plain, and the Chengdu Plain have been converted to urban land or for highway development. In Northeast China, a great number of beautiful wetlands have been converted into large-scale agricultural land; and, many coastal areas have eliminated wetlands using land fill techniques to create more land, a practice that has permanently eliminated large areas of coastal wetland. More than 1,000 small lakes have been lost across the country, and about one-third of all the currently available natural wetlands are facing the danger of being changed or lost.

以北京市为例，新中国成立初期，北京市湿地面积占全市总面积的 15%，有大小河流 200 余条，大中小型水库 84 座，大小湖泊 30 余个，至 2014 年北京市湿地面积已降至全市陆地面积的 3.13%，只剩 50000 多公顷。而更加令人担忧的是，由于对湿地的重要性认识不够，一些地方政府部门还对湿地的开垦和占用持鼓励态度，甚至给予经济补偿。

Take Beijing as an example. Shortly after the founding of the People's Republic of China, the city's wetlands accounted for 15% of its total area, and there were over 200 small and large rivers, 84 reservoirs of various sizes, and over 30 lakes. By 2014, its wetland area, which now stands at a little over 50,000 hectares, is equivalent to a mere 3.13% of its land area. The more worrying fact is that due to a lack of awareness of the importance of wetlands, some local governments even encouraged land reclamation in wetlands and promoting their use by providing economic compensation.

以上仅是湿地众多危机中的几项，湿地还面临着许多已知及未知的其他危机的威胁，亟待人们的重视与救治。所谓"亡羊补牢，未为晚矣"，人类是时候采取适当的措施去保护她了。

The wetland is of course afflicted with other ailments in addition to the aforementioned ones. It is imperative that people attach greater importance to wetland protection. Man should take appropriate measures to protect the wetlands "by mending the fold after some sheep have been stolen" before each and every one of them is permanently lost.

拓展阅读
Extra Reading Material

中国湿地退化的原因
Reasons That China's Wetlands Are Deteriorating

自然变化如全球变化、暴雨洪水、干旱和风浪侵袭等对湿地带来的生态影响往往是巨大和不可逆转的。人为因素主要发生于人类对湿地过度的开发和利用过程中，如湿地的无序开垦和改造、污水乱排、生物资源过度开发和水资源的不合理利用等。随着科学技术的进步，人类改变自然的能力越来越强，相应对自然的影响也越来越大。对于中国湿地而言，退化和损失的主要原因是全球变化、湿地围垦、资源无序利用、污染物排放和水资源不合理配置等。

The ecological impact made on wetlands by natural events like global change, torrential rain, floods, drought, and invasion by stormy waves is often huge and irreversible. Human activity also contributes to the deterioration of wetlands, particularly when man exploits them to excess, like reclaiming land from them or transforming them in a disorderly manner, discharging sewage into them freely, and exploiting their biological and water resources excessively. As science and technology progress, man's ability to change nature grows stronger and stronger, exerting an increasing influence on it in the process. As far as China's wetlands are concerned, the reasons that they deteriorate and get lost include global change, land reclamation on wetlands, disorderly use of resources, pollutant discharges, and irrational allocation of water resources.

我国湿地退化影响因素、发生区域、表现方式及退化趋势
Factors That Contribute to Wetland Deterioration, Regions Where It Takes Place, Symptoms Affected Regions Display, and Associated Trends

影响要素 Factors	主要发生区域 Major regions where wetland deterioration takes place	表现方式 Symptoms affected regions display
湿地围垦和资源无序利用 Land reclamation and disorderly use of resources	人口密集的沿海、沿湖地区，主要集中在长江中下游平原，珠江三角洲地区与东南沿海地区 Densely populated coastal and laky regions, most of which are situated in the plains along the middle and lower reaches of the Yangtze River, the Pearl River Delta, and the coastal regions in southeastern China	湿地生物多样性降低，生态服务功能下降，栖息地破碎化 The wetlands' biodiversity drops, their ecological service function drops, and the habitats they host become more segmented
污染物排放 Pollutant discharges	以中国东部湿地分布区为主，特别是环渤海地区，长江下游和珠江三角洲等经济发达地区 Wetland regions in eastern China, particularly those in the Bohai Economic Rim, the lower reaches of the Yangtze River, the Pearl River Delta, and other economically developed regions	湿地水质恶化，自净功能丧失，生物多样性降低 The wetland ecosystem's water quality deteriorates, and so do its self-cleaning function and biodiversity
湿地水资源配置失衡和水利工程建设不合理 Unbalanced distribution of water resources within a wetland ecosystem and irrational irrigational works	西北和华北地区 Northwest China and North China	流域下游湿地水源减少甚至枯竭，植被退化、面积减少，生境破碎化，湿地功能下降 The water sources feeding the wetland areas downstream of the wetland ecosystem in question are dropping in number and in water supply capability; the vegetation deteriorates and shrinks, the habitats it hosts become more segmented, and the wetland function deteriorates

续表

影响要素 Factors	主要发生区域 Major regions where wetland deterioration takes place	表现方式 Symptoms affected regions display
全球变化 Global Change	以沿海地区和青藏高原高寒湿地分布区为主 Mostly in coastal regions and elevated cold wetlands in the Tibetan Plateau	湿地面积减少，湿地水资源调蓄功能降低，沿海滩涂湿地退化，生物多样性受损 The wetland ecosystem decreases in area, and its function of storing and regulating water resources deteriorates; in case of a coastal wetland ecosystem, its mudflats deteriorate, and so does its biodiversity

古代先民的生态理念
Chinese's Ecological Views in Ancient Times

　　中国古代的先民，对于自然有着其独到的见解，不管是老子的"人法地，地法天，天法道，道法自然"一说，还是儒家的"天人合一"主张，都时时告诫着后人，只有依循了世间万物的自然属性，遵守了这世事发展的客观规律，才能达到合一，即为真正的和谐。以此为始，让我们看看古人之于自然生态的先见：

In ancient times the Chinese people held its unique set of views on how man should interact with nature. Although different individuals and groups endorsed different views, from the one held by Lao-tzu that "Man should submit to the earth, the earth to heaven, and heaven to The Way, so man and nature could coexist with each other peacefully" to the Confucian view that "Man is an integral part of nature," all of them point to the ultimate truth that only by not running against the nature of everything under heaven and by complying with the laws governing how they behave can complete unity as the ultimate form of harmony be achieved.

Now, let's take a look at the remarkable foresight our ancestors showed when contemplating the relationship between man and nature:

图 3.20　先民的生态观点（改绘自昵图网）
Picture 3.20　Ancient Chinese's Ecological Views (The Illustration Adapted from nipic.com)

　　宋李衡在《周易义海撮要》卷七中写道，"凡所行事，皆范模于天地阴阳之端，至如树木以时伐，禽兽以时杀，春夏则生育之，秋冬则肃杀之，使物遂其性，民安其所，是范围天地之道（参照天地运转的规律）而无过越也"。这实际上是一种对天地万物生灭的平衡法则，也就是今天所说的生态平衡论。而这又与孟子在《梁惠王上》中所言同理，其谓"数罟不入洿池"而"斧斤以时入山林"，即网罟须四寸之目、鱼不满尺，而采伐则须待草木零落、斧斤始入。

As Li Heng of the Song Dynasty wrote in Volume 7 of the book "*Zhou Yi Yi Hai Cuo Yao,*" "Man must do everything by complying with the laws they follow. Trees should be felled in the right season; domestic animals should be handled according to the season, meaning they should be allowed to breed their young and grow in spring and summer and that they should be slaughtered in autumn and winter; other things should be done similarly by choosing the right time, the right place, and the right way. This is how everything under heaven should be done." This view in fact explains how everything under heaven comes into being and dies out, and can be viewed as an ancient version of what we now refer to as the theory of the balance of nature. Similar views are also reflected by famous figures in other literature, like those expressed by Mencius in the book "*Liang Hui Wang Shang.*"

　　唐朝诗人陆龟蒙在《南泾渔父》中说，他在南泾遇到的一位渔父告诉他一个道理："孜孜告吾属，天物不可暴（糟蹋、损害）。大小参（检验、验证）去留，候其孳养（养育、蓄育）报。终朝获鱼利，鱼亦未尝耗。同覆天地中，违仁辜覆焘（通"帱"，施恩，加惠）。"（《全唐诗》卷619)。中国古代先民早有自然界物产消耗殆尽的危机意识及其对策。如唐人舒元舆在《坊州按狱》中说："山秃愈高采，水穷益深捞。龟鱼既绝迹，鹿兔无遗毛"（《全唐诗》卷489)，诗人描述山秃、水涸，龟鱼鹿兔消失殆尽的画面，表述着对生态环境被破坏的不尽忧虑。

 Lu Guimeng, a famous poet who lived during the Tang Dynasty, mentioned in his poem "*Nan Jing Yu Fu*" (or the Old Fisherman in Nanjing, which can be found in Volume 619 of the *Complete Anthology of Tang Dynasty Poetry*) that an old fisherman told him the following truth: "It is a crime against humanity to show a lack of respect for what nature has to offer us. Man needs to treat his environment and all animals and plants in it well so that he and nature can coexist harmoniously." In China, our ancestors began to show a strong sense of crisis when they worried about what to do if a particular natural resource was completely depleted and to find ways to cope with such crises when they did occur. As Shu Yuanyu, a scholar who lived during the Tang Dynasty, put it in the poem "*Fang Zhou An Yu*" (which can be found in Volume 489 of the *Complete Anthology of Tang Dynasty Poetry*) in a bid to express his concern about the prevalent destruction of the ecological environment back then, "Ruthless exploitation proceeds nonstop even when the mountain becomes bald at low altitudes, nor does aggressive fishing stop even when the fishery resources become severely depleted; until fishes or turtles or deer or rabbits are nowhere to be found."

　　中国古代这一整套"天人合一"的学说和"天地之道"的理论，构成了古代先民生态观的基础，并被古代先民奉为一种神圣的精神，贯穿于自己安身立命的生活理念

图 3.21 古代先民的生态意识（改绘自昵图网）
Picture 3.21　Ancient Chinese's Ecological Awareness (The Illustration Adapted from www.nipic.com)

之中，形成了对自然界生灵的一种"遂性"观念，即让生灵万物各按其本性自由自在地去生存、发展。一方面推崇生灵遂性发展，另一方面对自然资源作有限制的索取，这是中国古代较完整的一种生态平衡意识观，并被历朝历代贯彻于法令之中。例如唐朝便规定"凡采捕畋（打猎、耕种）猎必以其时，冬春之交，水虫孕育，捕鱼之器，不施川泽；春夏之交，陆禽孕育，馁兽之药不入原野；夏苗之盛，不得蹂籍；秋实之登，不得焚燎。"对于这套传统的保护生态的四时之禁，到了后来更为丰富具体。如到了明代，据《明史·职官志》的记载："虞衡典山泽采捕、陶冶之事。凡鸟兽之肉皮革骨角羽毛，可以供祭祀、宾客膳羞之需，礼器军实之用，岁下诸司采捕：水课禽十八，兽十二；陆课兽十八，禽十二，皆以其时。冬春之交，网罟不施川泽；春夏之交，毒药不施原野；苗盛禁蹂躏，谷登禁焚燎……"这表明，直到明清时期，仍在继承着夏周以来的保护生态的律令和政策。由此看到，中国古代几千年来，一直有着保护生态、平衡生态发展的优良传统（引《光明日报》，作者乜小红）。

The full set of views and theories that emerged in ancient China, including the view that "Man is an integral part of nature" and the one that "Man must respect nature's laws," formed the basis for the ecological mindset of ancient Chinese, and was held in high esteem as a sacred spirit by them; these views and theories ran through the philosophy they stuck to in life, thus helping create the idea of treating every living being under heaven with great respect and care and letting each develop and grow according to its unique way. On the one hand, special emphasis was placed on letting wildlife develop and grow in its wide variety of ways; on the other, controls were imposed to ensure the restrained taking of the bounties of nature, which reflects the existence in ancient China of a fairly complete set of views and theories revolving around the balance of nature. This set of views and theories was indeed applied to laws and regulations during the past dynasties. For example, during the Tang Dynasty, the imperial court stipulated that "All hunting and farming activities should be done in their respective appropriate seasons so that between late winter and early spring, when fishes and aquatic animals breed, no fishing tools are used in lakes or rivers; that between late spring and early summer, when land animals breed, no poisons are used in open country; that no trampling is allowed on farmlands when seedlings grow robustly in summer; and that no farmland waste is burned during or after harvest in autumn." Primitive as it was, this rule about what was not allowed to be done in each of the four seasons, aiming at protecting ecology, became richer and more specific over time. During the Ming Dynasty, according to the book "*Ming Dynasty Historical Record · Officials*" "Yu Heng, the official title of an official charged with all matters related to hunting and farming, performed his duties by ordering various agencies under his leadership to organize hunting and harvesting activities to ensure that the hide, meat, bones, and feathers of wild animals and birds were collected for use as sacrifices, at feasts and banquets, and for various other purposes. He ordered that all these agencies make sure that those activities took place in their respective appropriate seasons, so that between late winter and early spring, when fishes and aquatic animals bred, no fishing tools were used in lakes or rivers; that between late spring and early summer, when land animals bred, no poisons were used in open country; that no trampling was allowed on farmlands when seedlings grew robustly in summer; and that no farmland waste was burned during or after harvest in autumn." which is a worthy testament to the fact that the laws and regulations installed since the Xia and Zhou Dynasties were kept alive even during the Ming and Qing Dynasties. It is obvious that for thousands of years China has maintained the tradition of protecting ecology and promoting balanced ecological development (quoted from an article published in Guangming Daily by Mie Xiaohong).

红树林之碑
The Stone Tablet of Mangroves

《奉官立禁》碑刻："山良中树木……如盗大树罚钱三千文拿者赏钱三千文外人赏罚加倍……"它规定：山良中的树木不论生枯大小多少，凡私自偷盗者都要罚钱，而积极捉拿偷盗者的村民可得赏钱，如果发现是外人来偷盗则罚款加倍，外人帮忙抓拿偷盗者的赏钱加倍。而它所约定保护的树木，正是红树林，且据专家推断，这种以制定法规和立保护碑的形式来禁止人们砍伐、破坏的方式，是光绪十四年（公元1888年），朝廷为了保护红树林这一稀有的具有防风消浪、促淤保滩、固岸护堤、净化海水和空气功能的木本胎生植物而施行。

It is inscribed on the stone tablet titled "Feng Guan Li Jin," a piece of stone bearing the text of an official order, that "As for any trees on these mountain, anyone from this locality who steals large trees will be fined 3,000 coins, anyone from any area other than this locality who steals large trees will be fined twice that sum, anyone from this locality who succeeds in capturing such thieves will receive a reward, and anyone from any area other than this locality who succeeds in capturing such thieves will receive a double reward." And it was mangroves that the order was intended to protect. According to experts, this approach to the prevention of unrestrained felling and destruction involving drawing up legislation and erecting stone tablets was adopted in 1888 AD (or the 14th year of the reign of Emperor Guangxu of Qing) with the aim of protecting mangroves, a rare sort of ligneous viviparous tree that can perform a wide variety of functions, including guarding against winds, waves, protecting beaches and marshlands, purifying seawater and air.

这块经历了 120 多年风霜的石碑，证明了以红树林为代表的人类的生态保护意识乃是自古有之。石碑高不到 1 米，宽 40 厘米左右，现位于海南省文昌市文城镇头苑村委会下村二队的云氏公庙内，碑面清晰，被予以很好的保护，只有那记述着历史的繁体碑文中才泄露着岁月的痕迹。

This stone tablet has withstood over 120 years of tough weather and born witness to the existence of man's awareness of ecological protection since ancient times. Less than 1 meter high and about 40 centimeters wide, the tablet sits now inside Yun Family Public Temple in Team 2, Xia Village, Touyuan Village Committee, Wencheng Town, Wenchang City, Hainan Province. What is written in traditional Chinese characters on the tablet testifies to its long history, though it has a smooth, clear surface and is in good condition.

据碑文所载，聚集在这片村子繁衍生息的村民，由于属于滨海田园地带，觅食安居总赖门前的海山良。后来"人心日变户口日繁而偷取无不日甚"，所以该村云昌振

(李幸璜摄)
图 3.22 "奉官立禁"
Picture 3.22 "Feng Guan Li Jin" (Photo by Li Xinghuang of *Hainan Daily*)

等有名望的乡绅父老就于光绪十三年联合众人立下村规民约保护村前的海山良，定下了让今人受教的禁山良定行例条。除前述内容外，具体条文还包括：红树林枯木不能私自折，只能每年的正月初十折一次；乱取私折枯木罚一千文；不管好自家的牛踏坏了红树林小苗罚五百文；正在生长的红树林被刀斧损失罚得最重两千文；每家出两人巡逻，发现"顽夫""有污心棍徒"，要"鸣鼓而攻"等多项细致内容。也正是因为上述陈列了百多年的限行条例，你才可以看到如今立碑之地依旧郁郁葱葱扎根此处，日日逗水戏浪蔓延入海的红树林。

According to the tablet text, "The villagers who lived and multiplied in this village, which was on a costal area, at the time built houses and did many other activities in front of the mountain, but they became more and more greedy over time and resorted to theft frequently." To curb this social ill, Yun Changzhen, a man of standing in the village, joined hands with other villagers of standing in issuing in the 13th year of the reign of Emperor Guangxu of Qing an order, whose text was later transferred to the tablet, to protect the aforementioned, the order stipulated that without authorization no dead mangroves should be allowed to be cut at any time but on January 10 each year according to the traditional Chinese calendar; that anyone who was caught cutting dead trees without authorization be fined 1,000 coins; that anyone whose cattle trampled mangrove seedlings be fined 500 coins; that anyone who damaged or felled mangrove trees with a cutting tool be fined up to 2,000 coins; that each family send out two persons on patrol to spot anyone who violated the order in any way and, if any such person was spotted, capture or help capture them. It is because of this century-old order that you can still see around where the stone tablet sits miles of mangrove wood extending to the sea.

想一想
Give This Some Thought

除课文中提到的"疾患"外, 湿地还有其他"疾患"吗?

Are there any other ailments in addition to those mentioned as afflicting wetlands in the text?

试一试
Give This A Try

试着找出身边"患病"的湿地，并找出它"患病"的主要原因?

Try to find "diseased wetlands" around your area and figure out why each of them is "sick"?

参考文献
References

[1] 安娜 , 高乃云 , 刘长娥 . 中国湿地的退化原因、评价及保护 [J]. 生态学杂志 , 2008, 27(5): 821–829.

[1] An, N., Gao, N.Y., Liu, C.G., 2008. Wetland Degradation in China: Causes, Evaluation, and Protection Measures. Chinese Journal of Ecology, 27(5): 821–829.

[2] 陈克林 , 张小红 , 吕咏 . 气候变化与湿地 [J]. 湿地科学 , 2003, 1(1): 73–77.

[2] Chen,K.L., Zhang, X.H., Lv, Y., 2003. Climate Change and Wetlands. Wetland Science, 1(1): 73–77.

[3] 崔丽娟 . 湿地价值评价研究 [M]. 北京 : 科学出版社 , 2001.

[3] Cui,L.J.,2001. Assessment on Wetland Value. Beijing : China Architecture & Building Press.

[4] 高念东 , 文剑平 . 建设健康湿地对北京市水环境的影响 [J]. 北京水利 , 2004, (2): 40–41.

[4] Gao,N.D.,Wen,J.P.,2004.Impacts on Water Environment of Beijing for Healthy Wetland Building. Journal of Beijing Water Conservation. (2): 40–41.

[5] 国家林业局湿地办 , 中国湖泊的变迁 .

[5] Wetland Office, State Forestry Administration of China. Changes in Chinese Lakes.

[6] 孔红梅 , 姬兰柱 . 生态系统健康评价方法初探 . 应用生态学报 , 2002, 13(4): 486–490.

[6] Kong, H.M., Ji, L.Z., 2002. Methods of Ecosystem Health Assessment. Chinese Journal of Applied Ecology. 13(4): 486–490.

[7] 来红州 , 莫多闻 , 苏成 . 洞庭湖演变趋势探讨 [J]. 地理研究 , 2004, 23(1): 78–85.

[7] Lai, H.Z., Mo, D.W., Su, C., 2004. Discussion on the Evolutionary Trend of Dongting Lake. Geographical Research, 23(1): 78–85.

[8] 李鹏 . 中国湿地 , 走向干涸 [N]. 北京科技报 ,2011.

[8] Li, P., 2011.Chinese Wetlands Go Drying Up. Beijing Science & Technology Newspaper.

[9] 陆琴燕 , 刘永 , 李纯厚 , 等 . 海洋外来物种入侵对南海生态系统的影响及防控对策 [J]. 生态学杂志 , 2013, 32(8): 2186–2193.

[9] Lu, Q.Y., Liu, Y., Li, CH.H.,2013.Impacts of Alien Species Invasion on the South China Sea Ecosystem and Related Control Strategies. Chinese Journal of Ecology, 32(8): 2186–2193.

[10] 罗跃初 , 周忠轩 , 孙轶 , 等 . 流域生态系统健康评价方法 [J]. 生态学报 , 2003, 23(8): 1606–1614.

[10] Luo,Y.CH., Zhou,Z.U., Sun,T., etc., 2003. Assessment Methods of Watershed Ecosystem Health. Acta Ecologica Sinica. 23(8):1606–1614.

[11] 乜小红 . 我国古代先民的生态保护意识 [N]. 光明日报 , 2008.

[11] Nie, X.H., 2008. Ecological Protection Awareness of Chinese Ancestors. Guangming Daily.

[12] 濮培民 . 健康水生生态系统的退化及其修复——理论、技术及应用 [J]. 湖泊科学 , 2001,13(3):193–203.

[12] Pu, P.M.,,Degradation and Restoration of Healthy Aquatic Ecosystems—Theory, Technology & Application. Journal of Lake Sciences. 2001， 13(3): 193–203.

[13] 上官修敏 , 韩美 , 王海静 , 等 . 中国湿地生态健康评价研究进展 [J]. 山东师范大学学报 (自然科学版), 2013, 28(2): 77–82.

[13] Shangguan, X.M., Han, M., Wang, H.J., etc. Progress in China Wetland Ecosystem Health Assessment. Journal of Shandong Normal University (Natural Science). 2013，28(2): 77–82.

[14] 王苏民 , 窦鸿身 . 中国湖泊志 [M]. 北京 : 科学出版社 , 1998.

[14] Wang, S.M., Dou, H.SH., 1998. China Lake Chi. Beijing: Science Press.

[15] 吴赘 . "农进渔退"：20 世纪下半叶鄱阳湖区生态环境之恶化 [J]. 江汉论坛 , 2013, (10): 42–47.

[15] Wu, ZH., Farming Made Fishery Shrink: Poyang Lake District Deterioration of the Ecological Environment of the Second Half of the 20th Century. Journal of Jianghan Forum.2013 (10): 42–47.

[16] 徐海根 , 王建民 , 强胜 , 等 .《生物多样性公约》热点研究 : 外来物种入侵生物安全遗传资源 [M]. 北京 : 科学出版社 , 2004.

[16] Xu, H.G., Wang, J.M., Qiang, SH., etc. Hotspot Research on Convention on Biological Diversity: Invasive Alien Species Biosafety Genetic Resources. Beijing: Science Press 2004.

[17] 尹发能 . 洪湖自然环境演变研究 [J]. 人民长江 , 2008, 39(5): 19–22.

[17] Yin, F.N.,Research on Hong Lake Evolution of the Natural Environment. YANGTZE RIVER, 2008，39(5): 19–22.

[18] 俞立中 , 许羽 , 蔡述明 , 等 .GIS 技术在洪湖环境演变研究中的应用 [J]. 湖泊科学 , 1993, 5(4): 350–357.

[18] Yu, L.ZH., Xu, Y., Cai, SH.M., etc. A GIS Based Study on Recent Environmental Change in Hong Lake. Journal of Lake Sciences,1993， 5(4): 351－358.

[19] 赵淑清 , 方精云 , 唐志尧 , 等 . 洪湖湖区土地利用 / 土地覆盖时空格局研究 [J]. 应用生态学报 ,2001,12(5):721–725.

[19] Zhao, SH.Q., Fang, J.Y., Tang, ZH.Y., etc., Spatio－temporal Patterns of Land Use and Land Cover Changes in Hong Lake Region, Hubei Province, China. Chinese Journal of Applied Ecology, 2001 , 12(5): 721－725.

[20] 郑北鹰 . 湿地的呼喊 [N]. 光明日报 , 2009.

[20] Zheng, B.Y., 2009.Shouting of Wetlands, Guangming Daily.

[21] 2013 年中国环境状况公报 [R]. 北京 : 中华人民共和国环境保护部 .

[21] Report on the State of Environment in China 2013. Beijing：Ministry of Environmental Protection of the People's Republic of China.

第四章 保护湿地：我们在行动
Chapter 4 Wetland Protection: We Are in Action

　　湿地是人类及许多野生动植物赖以生存的基础，对维护生态平衡、保护生物多样性具有特殊的意义。但是，多年来随着全球化进程的加快，全球湿地不断遭到破坏，使得保护湿地成为一个世界性的问题，国际上也陆续加强了湿地的保护与管理。

Wetlands are the foundation on which human beings and many wild animals and plants rely for survival, and hence of special significance to maintaining ecological equilibrium and protecting biodiversity. However, with the acceleration of globalization over the years, wetlands across the world are constantly subject to destruction, which has made wetland protection a global issue. As a result, the international community has successively strengthened the protection and management of wetlands.

第一节 湿地保护公约及相关内容
Section I International Conventions on Wetland Protection and Related Information

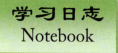

　　你知道哪些与湿地保护相关的公约与组织呢？先在日志中写出你的答案，然后通过下面的学习，把你的答案补充完整吧！

What conventions and organizations do you know about wetland protection? Write down your answer in the notebook first, and improve it after reading the text below.

一、《湿地公约》

I. *The Ramsar Convention on Wetlands*

1971年2月2日，来自18个国家的代表在伊朗南部海滨小城拉姆萨尔签署了《关于特别是作为水禽栖息地的国际重要湿地公约》（*Convention on Wetlands of International Importance Especially as Waterfowl Habitat*），也称作《拉姆萨尔公约》，简称《湿地公约》。其秘书处设在瑞士的格兰特，是由缔约方（Contracting Parties）、缔约方大会（Meetings of Contracting Parties,COPs）、常务委员会（Standing Committee）、科技评估委员会（Scientific & Technical Review Panel,STRP）及湿地公约局/秘书处（Ramsar Bureau/Secretariat）共同运作的。同时，还有《湿地公约手册》（The Ramsar Convention Manual）用于指导各缔约方合理地履约。

On February 2, 1971, representatives from 18 countries entered into the *Convention on Wetlands of International Importance Especially as Waterfowl Habitat* (hereinafter referred to as the Ramsar *Convention on Wetlands*, or the *Ramsar Convention*) in Ramsar, a coastal city in the south of Iran. Its Secretariat established in Grant of Switzerland. The *Ramsar Convention on Wetlands* is operated jointly by the Contracting Parties, Meetings of Contracting Parties ("COPs"), the Standing Committee, the Scientific & Technical Review Panel ("STRP"), and the Ramsar Bureau/Secretariat. Meanwhile, the *Ramsar Convention Manual* is used to guide the Contracting Parties on the proper performance of the convention.

该公约于1975年12月21日正式生效，到2014年，共有168个缔约成员，2187块湿地被列入国际重要湿地名录，总面积为208608257公顷。它旨在通过各成员国之间的合作加强对世界湿地资源的保护及合理利用，以实现生态系统的持续发展。

The *Ramsar Convention on Wetlands* formally came into force on December 21, 1975. By 2014, it has had 168 signatories in total, and 2,187 wetlands on the "List of Wetlands of International Importance", and have a total area of 208,608,257 hectares, It aims to strengthen the protection and reasonable utilization of the world's wetland resources through collaboration among member states to realize sustainable development of the ecosystem.

中国于1992年1月3日批准加入《湿地公约》，1992年3月31日递交加入书，1992年7月31日《湿地公约》正式对中国生效。2005年11月14日，中国在乌干达首都坎帕拉举行的第九届《湿地公约》缔约方大会全体会议上当选为新一届常务委员会理事国，这是中国首次当选该常务委员会理事国。

China was approved to access the *Ramsar Convention on Wetlands* on January 3, 1992, and submitted its instrument of accession on March 31, 1992, with the convention formally taking effect for China on July 31, 1992. China was elected as a member of the Standing Committee at a plenary session of the ninth Meeting of the Contracting Parties for *the Ramsar Convention on Wetlands* held on November 14, 2005 in Kampala, capital of Uganda. It was the first time China was elected to the Standing Committee.

CONVENTION ON WETLANDS

(Ramsar, Iran, 1971)

图 4.1 《湿地公约》标志
Picture4.1   Logo of *the Ramsar Convention on Wetlands*

《湿地公约》的标志于 1998 年确定，由蓝绿色的背景、两条象征河流的白色波浪形线条和一个白色的加拉蒙字体的 "Ramsar"（拉姆萨尔）构成。

The logo of the *Ramsar Convention on Wetlands*, finalized in 1998, consists of a bluish green background, two white wavy lines representing rivers, and a white "Ramsar" in Garamond font.

《湿地公约》发展历程
Development History of *the Ramsar Convention on Wetlands*

年份 Year	内容 Content
1960 年 1960	霍夫曼（Luc Hoffmann）先生启动了一个项目叫 MAR (from "MARshes"，"MAR ê cages"，"MARismas")，当时国际自然与自然资源保护联盟（现更名为国际保护联盟，International Union for Conservation of Nature, IUCN）、国际水鸟与湿地研究局（International Waterfowl and Wetlands Research Bureau, IWRB，即现在的湿地国际，Wetlands International）、国际保护鸟类理事会（International Council for Bird Preservation, ICBP，即现在的国际鸟类联盟，BirdLife International）也参与项目活动 Mr. Luc Hoffman launched a program called MAR (from "MARshes", "MARécages", "MARismas"). Then the International Union for Conservation of Nature and Natural Resources (predecessor of the now International Union for Conservation of Nature ("IUCN")), the International Waterfowl and Wetlands Research Bureau ("IWRB", predecessor of Wetlands International), and the International Council for Bird Preservation ("ICBP", predecessor of BirdLife International) also took part in the program
1962 年 11 月 November 1962	在法国开会，研究了保护湿地的问题 A meeting was held in France to study the issue of wetland protection
1971 年 2 月 February 1971	经过 8 年的多次会议协商，起草了《湿地公约》的文本，其核心内容是保护水禽，并且 18 个国家在公约上签字 After eight years of negotiations at several meetings, the text of the Ramsar Convention on Wetlands was drafted, whose main content centered on waterfowl protection; and it was signed by 18 countries
1980 年 11 月 November 1980	在意大利卡利亚里（Cagliari）召开了第一届《湿地公约》缔约方大会（COP1），规定了国际重要湿地标准 The first Meeting of the Contracting Parties (COP1) to the Ramsar Convention on Wetlands was held in Cagliari of Italy, during which the criteria for Wetlands of International Importance were stipulated

年份 Year	内容 Content
1982 年 12 月 December 1982	在法国巴黎联合国教科文组织（United Nations Educational, Scientific and Cultural Organization, UNESCO）总部召开了缔约方特别大会，通过了对公约文本的修正，即巴黎议定书（1986 年 10 月生效） A special COP was held in the headquarters of the United Nations Educational, Scientific and Cultural Organization ("UNESCO") in France, during which the amendment to the text of the convention was approved, i.e. Paris Protocol (which took effect in October 1986)
1984 年 5 月 May 1984	在荷兰格罗宁根（Groningen）召开了第二届《湿地公约》缔约方大会（COP2），制定了公约实施框架 The second Meeting of the Contracting Parties (COP2) was held in Groningen of the Netherlands and the implementation framework for the convention was formulated
1987 年 5~6 月 May-June 1987	在加拿大里贾纳(Regina)召开了缔约方特别大会以及第三届《湿地公约》缔约方大会(COP3)，规定了缔约方大会的权力、建立常委会、预算和常设执行局（或称秘书处）。但此项修正条款直到 1994 年 5 月 1 日才生效，因为在 1987 年通过的决议（III.4）中规定了自愿原则。大会还修改了国际重要湿地标准和建立湿地合理利用工作组 A special COP and the third Meeting of the Contracting Parties (COP3) were held in Regina of Canada, during which the powers of the COPs were prescribed, and the Standing Committee and the Budget and Permanent Executive Bureau (also known as the Secretariat) were established. But this amendment didn't take effect until May 1, 1994, for the resolution (III.4) passed in 1987 contained a principle of voluntariness. Also at COP3, the criteria for wetlands of international importance were revised and a working group for the rational use of wetlands was set up
1988 年 1 月 January 1988	第 1 任公约秘书长纳维德（Dan Navid）上任 Dan Navid, the 1st Secretary General of the Ramsar Convention on Wetlands took office
1989 年 7 月 July 1989	公约有了自己的会标。在瑞士蒙特勒市（Montreux）召开了第四届《湿地公约》缔约方大会（COP4）。大会再次修改国际重要湿地标准，决定建立蒙特勒档案（Montreux Record），设立湿地保护基金（后来更名为湿地公约湿地保护与合理利用小额赠款基金），决定把西班牙文作为公约的 3 种工作语言之一，其他 2 种工作语言是英文和法文 The convention had its own logo. The fourth Meeting of the Contracting Parties (COP4) was held in Montreux of Switzerland, during which the criteria for wetlands of international importance were revised again; a Montreux Record was resolved to be established; a wetland protection fund (renamed later to the wetland protection and reasonable utilization small grants fund for the Ramsar Convention on Wetlands) was set up; Spanish was resolved to become one of the three working languages of the convention, with the other two being English and French
1991 年 12 月 December 1991	在巴基斯坦卡拉奇（Karachi）召开《湿地公约》第一次亚洲区域会议 The 1st Asia Regional Meeting of the Ramsar Convention on Wetlands was held in Karachi of Pakistan
1993 年 6 月 June 1993	在日本钏路（kushiro）召开第五届《湿地公约》缔约方大会（COP5），发表了钏路声明，决定要建立科技审评组 The fifth Meeting of the Contracting Parties (COP5) was held in Kushiro of Japan, during which the Kushiro Statement was issued, and it was resolved to set up a scientific & technical review team
1996 年 3 月 March 1996	在澳大利亚布里斯班（Brisbane）召开了第六届《湿地公约》缔约方大会（COP6）。大会通过了 1997—2002 年战略计划 The sixth Meeting of the Contracting Parties (COP6) was held in Brisbane of Australia, during which the 1997-2002 strategic plan was approved

续表

年份 Year	内容 Content
1996 年 10 月 October 1996	常委会通过决议，宣布每年 2 月 2 日为世界湿地日 The Standing Committee passed a resolution and announced February 2 of each year to be the World Wetlands Day
1998 年 10 月 October 1998	常委会决定更换会标 The Standing Committee decided to change the logo of the convention
1999 年 5 月 May 1999	在哥斯达黎加（Costa rica）召开了第七届《湿地公约》缔约方大会（COP7） The seventh Meeting of the Contracting Parties (COP7) was held in Costa Rica
2002 年 2002	在西班牙（Spain）召开第八届《湿地公约》缔约方大会（COP8） The eighth Meeting of the Contracting Parties (COP8) was held in Spain
2005 年 11 月 November 2005	第九届缔约方大会（COP9）在乌干达（Uganda）举行，中国第一次当选为公约常委会成员国 The ninth Meeting of the Contracting Parties (COP9) was held in Uganda, and China was elected as a member of the Standing Committee for the first time
2008 年 10 月 October 2008	第十届缔约方大会（COP10）在韩国昌原（Changwon）开幕，大会的主题是"健康的湿地，健康的人类"。来自五大洲的 100 多个国家和地区以及几十个国际自然资源保护组织的一千多名政府和非政府组织代表参加了会议 The tenth Meeting of the Contracting Parties (COP10) was opened in Changwon of South Korea, under the theme of "Healthy Wetlands, Healthy People". Over 1,000 representatives of government and non-government organizations from more than 100 countries and regions across the five continents and dozens of international organizations for the protection of natural resources attended the meeting
2011 年 11 月 14~18 日 November 14 – November 18, 2011	第十一届《湿地公约》缔约国大会亚洲区域协调会（Ramsar Pre-COP11 Asia Regional Meeting）在印度尼西亚首都雅加达（Jakarta）召开，会议就亚洲各缔约国"《湿地公约》2009—2015 战略计划"执行情况、亚洲湿地区域动议报告、当前履约面临的主要问题等方面进行了深入而广泛的磋商和交流，预选了 2013—2015 年亚洲区域常委会成员 The Ramsar Pre-COP11 Asia Regional Meeting was held in Jakarta, capital of Indonesia, during which in-depth and extensive discussions and exchanges were carried out on the implementation condition of the "2009—2015 Strategic Plan" by the Contracting Parties in Asia, regional initiative report on the wetlands in Asia, and existing major issues about the performance of the convention; and members of the Asia regional standing committee for 2013—2015 were pre-elected
2012 年 2012	在罗马尼亚（Romania）召开了《湿地公约》第十一届缔约方大会（COP11） The eleventh Meeting of the Contracting Parties (COP11) was held in Romania
2014 年 9 月 8~10 日 September 8 – September 10, 2014	《湿地公约》科技评估委员会（STRP）2013~2015 年的第二次会议在瑞士格兰特（Grant）《湿地公约》总部秘书处召开 The second meeting of the Scientific & Technical Review Panel (STRP) for 2013-2015 was held at the Secretariat of the headquarters of the Ramsar Convention on Wetlands in Grant of Switzerland
2015 年 6 月 1~9 日 June 1 – June 9, 2015	第十二次缔约方会议（COP12）将在乌拉圭（Uruguay）举行 The twelfth Meeting of the Contracting Parties (COP12) was held in Uruguay

二、其他与生态环境保护相关的国际公约
II. Other Related International Conventions on Ecological Environmental Protection

1.《保护世界文化和自然遗产公约》
1. *Convention Concerning the Protection of the World Cultural and Natural Heritage*

该公约简称《世界遗产公约》，于 1972 年 11 月 16 日正式通过。该公约中有全球有特殊文化或生态意义的地点的列表，在公约上签字的国家保证该列表中的其领土范围内的各地点得到保护。

Also known as the *World Heritage Convention*, it was duly passed on November 16, 1972. It contains the list of places with special cultural or ecological significance worldwide, and the contracting nations thereto pledged to protect the places on the list within their respective territories.

图 4.2 《世界遗产公约》标志
Picture 4.2　Logo of *World Heritage Convention*

中国于 1985 年 12 月 12 日加入该公约，成为缔约方。1999 年 10 月 29 日，中国当选为世界遗产委员会成员，并于 1986 年开始向联合国教科文组织申报世界遗产项目。自 1987 年至 2014 年 7 月，中国先后被批准列入《世界遗产名录》的世界遗产已达 46 处。其中中国的九寨沟、黄龙、云南三江并流、西湖、大运河等多处世界遗产就属于湿地。

China joined this convention and became a contracting party on December 12, 1985; and it was elected as a member of the World Heritage Committee on October 29, 1999; and it began to apply for world heritage projects to the UNESCO in 1986. From 1987 to July 2014, 46 heritage sites in China were approved to be added to the World Heritage List. Among them, Jiuzhaigou, Huanglong, Three Parallel Rivers of Yunnan, West Lake and the Grand Canal are wetlands.

2.《濒危野生动植物物种国际贸易公约》
2. *Convention on International Trade in Endangered Species of Wild Fauna and Flora*, CITES

1973 年 3 月 3 日 21 个国家在华盛顿签署了 CITES，又称《华盛顿公约》，该公约于 1975 年 7 月 1 日生效。CITES 制定了一个濒危物种名录，通过许可证制度控制这些物种及其产品的国际贸易，由此而使 CITES 成为打击非法贸易、限制过度利用的有效手段。CITES 在保护野生动植物资源方面取得的成就及享有的权威和影响举世公认，已成为当今世界上最具影响力、最有成效的环境公约之一。1981 年 1 月 8 日，中国政

府向该公约保存国瑞士政府交存加入书。同年 4 月 8 日，该公约对我国生效。

On March 3, 1973, 21 countries entered into CITES in Washington, also known as the Washington Convention, which came into force on July 1, 1975. CITES has developed a list of endangered species and controlled the international trade in such species and their products through a licensing system, which has made CITES an effective means to crack down

图 4.3　CITES 标志
Picture 4.3　Logo of CITES

on illegal trade and curb excessive utilization. CITES is universally recognized for its achievement in the conservation of wild fauna and flora resources, as well as its authority and influence, and has become one of the world's most influential and effective environmental conventions. On January 8, 1981, the Chinese government submitted the instrument of accession to the convention's depositary government of Switzerland. On April 8 of that year, the convention entered into force for China.

3.《保护野生动物迁徙物种公约》

3. *Convention on the Conservation of Migratory Species of Wild Animals*, CMS

1979 年 6 月 23 日，该公约签订于德国波恩，因此又名《波恩公约》，于 1983 年 12 月 1 日生效，其秘书处设在波恩，中国于 1986 年成为缔约国。CMS 旨在保护所有陆上的、水中的和空中的迁徙生物，是保护跨境迁徙野生物种的最重要国际公约。立约的目的是通过严格执行保护工作和签订国际公约，保护迁徙物种及其生境。

图 4.4　《波恩公约》标志
Picture 4.4　Logo of CMS

On June 23, 1979, this convention was signed in Bonn, thereby also known as the *Bonn Convention*, and entered into force on December 1, 1983, with its secretariat established in the city of Bonn, Germany. China became a contracting nation in 1986. CMS aims to protect all the migratory species on the land, in the water and in the sky, and is the most important international convention on the conservation of cross-border migratory wild species. The purpose of this convention is to protect migratory species and their habitats with relentless protection efforts and the conclusion of global convention.

4.《生物多样性公约》

4. *Convention on Biological Diversity*, CBD

CBD 是一项保护地球生物资源的国际性公约，它于 1992 年 6 月 1 日在内罗毕由联合国环境规划署发起的政府间谈判委员会第七次会议中通过，并于 1992 年 6 月 5 日，在巴西里约热内卢举行的联合国环境与发展大会上签署。公约于 1993 年 12 月 29 日

图 4.5 《生物多样性公约》标志
Picture 4.5 Logo of CBD

正式生效。常设秘书处设在加拿大的蒙特利尔。联合国《生物多样性公约》缔约国大会是全球履行该公约的最高决策机构，一切有关履行 CBD 的重大决定都要经过缔约国大会通过。

As an international convention on the conservation of the world's biological resources, CBD was approved at the 7th meeting of the inter-governmental negotiating committee initiated by the United Nations Environment Programme ("UNEP") in Nairobi on June 1, 1992, and signed by the contracting nations on June 5, 1992 at the United Nations Conference on Environment and Development held in Rio de Janeiro of Brazil. CBD formally took effect on December 29, 1993 and its permanent secretariat is established in Montreal of Canada. The Meetings of the Contracting Parties are the supreme decision-making body of CBD, and all the major decisions about the performance thereof shall be approved at such meetings.

该公约是一项有法律约束力的公约，旨在保护濒临灭绝的植物和动物，最大限度地保护地球上的多种多样的生物资源，以造福于当代和子孙后代。中国于 1992 年 6 月 11 日签署该公约，1992 年 11 月 7 日批准，1993 年 1 月 5 日交存加入书。

CBD is a legally binding convention aimed to protect endangered plants and animals and maximally conserve varieties of biological resources on the earth for the benefit of ourselves and future generations. China signed this convention on June 11, 1992, obtained the approval on November 7, 1992, and submitted the instrument of accession on January 5, 1993.

三、湿地保护的相关国际组织
III. International Organizations for Wetland Protection

与湿地保护密切相关的国际组织主要有湿地国际、世界自然基金会、全球环境基金、国际鹤类基金会、世界自然保护联盟、国际鸟类联盟等。

International organizations closely related to wetland protection include Wetlands International, World Wide Fund For Nature, Global Environment Facility, International Crane Foundation, International Union for Conservation of Nature and Natural Resources, and BirdLife International.

1. 湿地国际

1. Wetlands International, WI

湿地国际创建于 1995 年，由亚洲湿地局（Asian Wetlands Bureau, AWB）、国际水禽和湿地研究局（International Waterfowl and Wetlands Research Bureau, IWRB）和美洲湿地组织（Wetlands for the Americas, WA）3 个国际组织合并组成。它是全球性非营利、非政府组织，总部设在荷兰，在 18 个国家设立办事处，致力于湿地保护和可持续管理，其宗旨是：通过在全球范围内开展研究、信息交流和保护活动，维持和恢复湿地，保护湿地资源和生物多样性，造福子孙后代。湿地国际中国办事处于 1996 年 9

图 4.6 湿地国际标志
Picture 4.6 Logo of Wetlands International

月 26 日在北京成立，其成立的目的是通过引进技术和资金，提供人员培训和技术支持，开展信息交流来促进中国和东北亚的湿地保护与合理利用。

Established in 1995, WI consists of three international organizations merged - Asian Wetlands Bureau ("AWB"), International Waterfowl and Wetlands Research Bureau ("IWRB") and Wetlands for the Americas ("WA"). As a global non-profit and non-governmental organization, WI is committed to wetland protection and sustainability management, and aims to maintain and restore wetlands by carrying out research, exchanges of information and conservation efforts worldwide, and conserve wetland resources and biological diversity for the benefit of future generations. WI's headquarters is set up in the Netherlands, with offices in 18 countries. Its Chinese office, established in Beijing on September 26, 1996, serves to promote the conservation and reasonable utilization of wetlands in China and Northeast Asia by introducing technology and capital, providing personnel training and technical support, and carrying out exchanges of information.

2. 世界自然基金会

2. World Wide Fund For Nature, WWF

WWF 自 1961 年成立至今 50 余年以来，投资超过 13000 个项目。1996 年，WWF 正式成立北京办事处，此后陆续在全国 9 个城市建立了办公室。至 2014 年，WWF 在中国共资助开展了 100 多个重大项目，项目领域由最初的大熊猫保护扩大到物种保护、淡水和海洋生态系统保护与可持续利用等领域。

图 4.7 世界自然基金会标志
Picture 4.7 Logo of WWF

Since its establishment in 1961 up to now, WWF has invested in more than 13,000 projects, involving funds of around USD10 billion. In 1996, WWF's Beijing office was formally set up, followed by another 8 offices in different cities in China. By 2014, WWF financed over 100 major projects in the country, concerning areas ranging from protection of giant pandas, to conservation of species, protection and sustainable utilization of freshwater and marine ecosystems.

WWF 的使命是遏制地球自然环境的恶化，创造人类与自然和谐相处的美好未来。

致力于保护世界生物多样性；确保可再生自然资源的可持续利用；推动减少污染和浪费性消费的行为。WWF 已在全球 50 多个流域开展湿地与淡水保护及流域综合管理示范工作。

The mission of WWF is to arrest the deterioration of the natural environment on the earth, and create a beautiful future where mankind and nature co-exist harmoniously. It is committed to: protect the world's biological diversity; ensure the sustainable utilization of renewable natural resources; and promote the initiative to reduce pollution and wasteful consumption. WWF carries out wetland and freshwater conservation, and integrated river basin management pilot programs in more than 50 river basins worldwide.

3. 全球环境基金
3. Global Environment Facility, GEF

在 1989 年法国提出建立一种全球性的基金用以鼓励发展中国家开展对全球有益的环境保护活动。1990 年 11 月，25 个国家达成共识建立全球环境基金（GEF），由世界银行、联合国开发计划署（United Nations Development Programme, UNDP）和联合国环境开发署（United Nations Environment Programme, UNEP）共同管理，基金捐款国定期向基金捐款。

图 4.8 全球环境基金标志
Picture 4.8 Logo of GEF

At the annual meeting of the Development Committees of the International Monetary Fund ("IMF") and the World Bank in 1989, France proposed establishing an international fund to encourage developing countries to carry out environmental protection activities for the good of the whole world. In November 1990, 25 countries agreed to set up GEF, co-managed by the World Bank, the United Nations Development Programme ("UNDP") and United Nations Environment Programme ("UNEP"), with donor countries contributing to the facility on a regular basis.

作为一个国际资金机制，GEF 主要是以赠款或其他形式的优惠资助，为受援国（包括发展中国家和部分经济转轨国家）提供关于气候变化、生物多样性、国际水域和臭氧层损耗 4 个领域以及与这些领域相关的土地退化方面项目的资金支持，以取得全球环境效益，促进受援国环境的可持续发展。

As an international facility, GEF provides funding support to recipient countries (including developing countries and some countries during economic transition) in the four areas of climate change, biological diversity, international waters and ozone layer depletion as well as land degradation projects associated with these areas, mainly by means of donations or other forms of preferential assistance, so as to reap global environmental benefits, and promote environment-friendly and sustainable development of the recipient countries.

4. 国际鹤类基金会

4.International Crane Foundation, ICF

ICF 是非营利性的民间自然保护组织，1973 年由美国人让·索伊和乔治·阿其博创建，其宗旨是：通过提供关于鹤类的经验、知识，激发人们的兴趣，致力于挽救世界范围内的鹤类及其栖息环境。

ICF is a non-profit private nature conservation organization and was founded in 1973 by Ron Sauey and George Archibald from the Unites States. It aims to inspire people's interest by providing experiences and knowledge about cranes, and save cranes and their habitats around the world.

图 4.9　国际鹤类基金会标志
Picture 4.9　Logo of ICF

ICF 的主要工作包括环境教育、科学研究、生境恢复和保护、饲养繁殖、鹤类再引入，尤其在鹤类的饲养繁殖方面，ICF 作出了巨大贡献。ICF 在全世界参与许多项目，如在美国实施建立美洲鹤（*Grus americana*）东部迁徙种群的行动；在塞内加尔、埃塞俄比亚等非洲 20 多个国家为黑冠鹤（*Balearica pavonina*）及其栖息地的自然保护制定了行动计划；在越南帮助保护濒危赤颈鹤（*Ardea antigone*）的越冬地及其他湿地稀有鸟类等。

ICF principally engages in environmental education, scientific research, habitat restoration and protection, breeding and reintroduction, and has made great contributions to the breeding of rare and endangered crane species in particular. ICF has taken part in many projects worldwide, including implementing the initiative to establish a migratory species of *Grus americana* in the east of America; formulating action plans for natural conservation of *Balearica pavonina* and their habitats in over 20 African countries, including Senegal and Ethiopia; and, helping protect the wintering grounds of the endangered *Ardea antigone* and other wetland rare birds in Vietnam. They have also been assisting Chinese scientists for several decades on the conservation and captive breeding of many of China's crane species.

5. 世界自然保护联盟

5.International Union for Conservation of Nature and Natural Resources, IUCN

IUCN 创立于 1948 年，是目前世界上最久也是最大的全球性环保组织，旨在为全球最紧要的环境与发展挑战寻求系统化解决方案。IUCN 是由 200 多个国家和政府机构会员、1000 多个非政府组织会员，和来自 181 个国家超过 11000 名科学委员会会员和分布在 50 多个国家的 1000 多名秘书处员工组成的独特的世界性联盟，它是自然和自然资源、特别是生物多样性保护的国际组织，在国际环境公约和政策等方面拥有重要影响力。

图 4.10　世界自然保护联盟标志
Picture 4.10　Logo of IUCN

Founded in 1948, IUCN is now the world's oldest and biggest international organization for environmental protection, and aims to seek systemized solutions to the most urgent challenges from environment and development worldwide. It is a unique international union composed of over 200 countries and government organizations, over 1,000 non-governmental organizations, more than 11,000 scientific commission members from 181 countries, and over 1,000 secretariat employees distributed across over 50 countries. IUCN is an international organization for the conservation of nature and natural resources, especially biological diversity, and wields great influence in international environmental conventions and policies.

IUCN 的工作重心在于评估和保护自然，确保对自然有效而公平的管理利用，并为应对气候、粮食和发展等全球挑战提供以自然为本的解决方案。愿景是实现一个尊重与保护自然的公平世界。IUCN 的使命是影响、鼓励、协助全社会保护自然的完整性和多样性，并确保任何自然资源的使用都是公平的、在生态学意义上是可持续的。

IUCN mainly engages in evaluating and conserving nature to ensure efficient and fair management and utilization of nature, and provides nature-based solutions to global challenges concerning climate, food and development. Its vision is to realize a fair world that respects and protects nature, while its mission is to influence, encourage and assist society to protect the integrity and diversity of nature, and ensure that any use of natural resources is fair and sustainable ecologically.

6. 国际鸟类联盟

6. BirdLife International

成立于 1922 年，创办者为吉尔勃特·皮尔森（Gilbert Pearson）与尚提奥多德拉库尔（Jean Theodore Delacour），它是一个国际生态保护联盟。其拥有全球的伙伴组织组成的网络，包括英国皇家鸟类保护协会、直布罗陀鸟类学暨自然史学会、奥杜邦学会、孟买自然史学会、澳洲鸟会、中华鸟会、香港观鸟会等多个组织。在世界自然保护联盟与物种存续委员会合著出版的世界自然保护联盟濒危物种红色名录中，鸟类的部分保护工作由国际鸟类联盟负责。

Founded in 1922 by Gilbert Pearson and Jean Theodore Delacour, BirdLife International is an international ecological conservation union. It has a network composed of global partner organizations, including the Royal Society for the Protection of Birds, the Gibraltar Ornithological & Natural History Society, National Audubon Society, Bombay Natural History Society, BirdLife Australia, Chinese Wild Bird Federation, and Hong Kong Bird Watching Society. BirdLife International is responsible for the protection of birds in the IUCN Red List of Threatened Species co-authored and published by IUCN and its Species Survival Commission.

图 4.11　国际鸟类联盟标志
Picture 4.11　Logo of BirdLife International

四、有关湿地的特殊日期
IV. Special Dates about Wetlands

1. 世界湿地日
1.World Wetlands Day

1971 年 2 月 2 日，《湿地公约》在伊朗拉姆萨尔签署，为了纪念这一重要事件，1996 年 10 月《湿地公约》常务委员会第 19 次会议决定，每年的 2 月 2 日定为"世界湿地日"，并且每年都确定一个不同的主题，以便开展各种活动来提高公众对湿地的认识，促进湿地保护。从 1997 年开始，世界各国在这一天都举行不同形式的活动，来宣传保护湿地资源和生态环境，政府组织和公民采取各种各样活动来提高公众对湿地价值和效益的认识，从而更好地保护湿地。

On February 2, 1971, the *Ramsar Convention on Wetlands* was signed in Ramsar of Iran. To mark this significant event, the 19th meeting of the Standing Committee of the convention decided in October 1996 that February 2 of each year should be the "World Wetlands Day", and a different theme be set each year so as to carry out various kinds of activities to raise the public's awareness of wetlands and promote wetland protection. Starting from 1997, different forms of activities are staged on this day all across the world to publicize the conservation of wetland resources and ecological environment. Government organizations and citizens take various measures to enhance the public's awareness of the value and benefits of wetlands so as to better protect them.

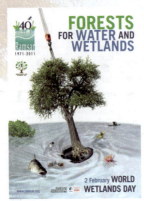   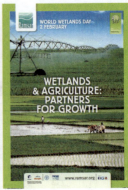

图 4.12 湿地日宣传画
Picture 4.12   Posters about World Wetlands Day

历年"世界湿地日"主题
Themes of "World wetlands Day"in Previons Years

年份 Year	历年主题 Themes of Previous Years
1997	"湿地是生命之源" Wetlands: a Source of Life
1998	"湿地之水，水之湿地" Water for wetlands, wetlands for water
1999	"人与湿地，息息相关" People and Wetlands: the Vital Link
2000	"珍惜我们共有的国际重要湿地" Celebrating Our Wetlands of International Importance
2001	"湿地世界——一个有待探索的世界" Wetlands World - A World to Discover
2002	"湿地：水、生命和文化" Wetlands: Water, Life, and Culture
2003	"没有湿地就没有水" No Wetlands - No Water!
2004	"从高山到大海，湿地在为人类服务" From the Mountains to the Sea, Wetlands at Work for Us!
2005	"湿地文化多样性与生物多样性" There's Wealth in Wetland Diversity - Don't Lose It!
2006	"湿地与减贫" Wetland as a Tool in Poverty Alleviation
2007	"为了明日的鱼类" Fish for tomorrow?
2008	"健康的湿地，健康的人类" Healthy Wetlands, Healthy People

续表

2009	"上游、下游：湿地连接你和我" Upstream-Downstream: Wetlands Connect Us All
2010	"湿地、生物多样性与气候变化：携手保护湿地，应对气候变化" Wetlands, Biodiversity and Climate Change
2011	"湿地与森林：森林与湿地和水息息相关" Wetlands and Forests: Forests For Water and Wetlands
2012	"湿地旅游：一种美妙的体验" Wetland Tourism: A Great Experience
2013	"湿地与水资源管理：湿地守护水资源" Wetland and Water Resource Management: Wetlands Take Care of Water
2014	"湿地与农业：共同成长的伙伴" Wetlands and Agriculture: Partners for Growth
2015	"湿地，我们的未来" Wetlands for our future

2. 国际生物多样性日

2.International Day For Biological Diversity

联合国大会决定，从 1995 年起，将每年的 12 月 29 日定为"国际生物多样性日"。从 2001 年开始，根据第 55 届联合国大会第 201 号决议，国际生物多样性日由原来的每年 12 月 29 日改为 5 月 22 日。

The United Nations General Assembly ("UNGA") decided that starting from 1995, December 29 of each year should be the "International Day For Biological Diversity". Then according to Resolution No. 201 of the 55th UNGA, the "International Day For Biological Diversity" should be changed from December 29 to May 22 of each year, with effect from 2001.

图 4.13 国际生物多样性日标志
Picture 4.13 Logo of International Day for Biological Diversity

历年"国际生物多样性日"主题
Themes of "Intemational Day For Biological Diuersity"in Previons Years

年份 Year	历年主题 Themes of Previous Years
2001	"生物多样性与外来入侵物种管理" Biodiversity and Management of Invasive Alien Species
2002	"林业生物多样性" Dedicated to Forest Biodiversity
2003	"生物多样性和减贫——对可持续发展的挑战" Biodiversity and Poverty Alleviation - Challenges for Sustainable Development
2004	"生物多样性：全人类食物、水和健康的保障" Biodiversity:Food, Water and Health for all
2005	"生物多样性——变化世界的生命保障" Biodiversity: Life Insurance for Our Changing World
2006	"保护干旱地区的生物多样性" Protect Biodiversity in Drylands
2007	"生物多样性与气候变化" Biodiversity and Climate Change
2008	"生物多样性与农业" Biodiversity and Agriculture
2009	"外来入侵物种" Invasive Alien Species
2010	"生物多样性就是生命，生物多样性也是我们的生命" Biodiversity, Development and Poverty Alleviation
2011	"森林生物多样性" Forest Biodiversity
2012	"海洋生物多样性" Marine Biodiversity
2013	"水和生物多样性" Water and Biodiversity
2014	"岛屿生物多样性" Island Biodiversity
2015	"生物多样性助推可持续发展" Biodiversity for Sustainable Development

3. 世界水日
3.World Water Day

1977 年联合国召开水会议，向全世界发出警告：水不久将成为一个严重的社会危机，继石油危机之后的下一个危机便是水。1993 年联合国大会通过决议，将每年的 3

月 22 日定为"世界水日"，用以开展广泛的宣传教育，提高公众对开发和保护水资源的认识。

In 1977, the United Nations Water Conference was held, with a stern warning issued to the whole world: Water would soon become a profound social crisis, just following the oil crisis. In 1993, the UNGA passed a resolution to set March 22 of each year as the "World Water Day" so as to carry out extensive promotion and education, and raise the public's awareness of the development and protection of water resources.

1988 年《中华人民共和国水法》颁布实施，并确定每年 7 月第一周为"水法宣传周"。以后结合世界水日，把每年的 3 月 22 日所在的一周，定为"中国水周"，每年有特定的宣传主题。

In 1988, the *Water Law of the People's Republic of China* was issued and entered into force, which prescribes that the first week of July each year should be the "Publicity Week for the Water Law". Later based on the World Water Day, it is decided that the week containing March 22 of each year be the "China Water Week", with specific publicity themes set for each year.

图 4.14　世界水日宣传标志
Picture 4.14　Logo of World Water Day

历年"世界水日"主题
Themes of "World Water Day" in Previous Years

年份 Year	历年主题 Themes of Previous Years
1994	"关心水资源是每个人的责任" Caring for Our Water Resources is Everyone's Business
1995	"女性和水" Women and Water

1996	"为干渴的城市供水" Water for Thirsty Cities
1997	"水的短缺" Water Scarce
1998	"地下水——正在不知不觉衰减的资源" Groundwater —The Invisible Resource
1999	"我们（人类）永远生活在缺水状态之中" Everyone Lives Downstream
2000	"21 世纪的水" Water for the 21st Century
2001	"卫生用水" Water and Health-Taking Charge
2002	"水与发展" Water for Development
2003	"水——人类的未来" Water for the Future
2004	"水与灾害" Water and Disaster
2005	"生命之水" Water for Life
2006	"水与文化" Water and Culture
2007	"应对水短缺" Water Scarcity
2008	"涉水卫生" International Year of Sanitation
2009	"跨界水——共享的水、共享的机遇" Transboundary Water— Shared Opportunities
2010	"水质量" Water Quality
2011	"城市水资源管理" Water for Cities
2012	"水与粮食安全" Water and Food Security
2013	"水合作" Water Cooperation
2014	"水与能源" Water and Energy
2015	"水与可持续发展" Water and Sustainable Development

4. 世界地球日

4. World Earth Day

世界地球日起源于美国，1970 年 4 月 22 日为世界上第一个"地球日"。这一天，美国哈佛大学法学院学生丹尼斯·海斯发动并组织的保护环境活动，这是人类有史以来第一次规模宏大的群众性环境保护运动，它得到了美国环境保护工作者和社会名流的支持。此后，联合国将 4 月 22 日确定为"地球日"，并逐渐发展成为全球性的活动。每年的世界地球日设有国际统一的特定主题，它的总主题始终是"只有一个地球"。我国从 1990 年开始，每年都进行"地球日"的纪念宣传活动。

Originating in the United States, April 22, 1970 was declared the world's first "Earth Day". On that day, Dennis Hayes, a student from Harvard Law School, initiated and organized an environmental protection activity, which was the first large-scale mass movement of its kind in human history, and obtained the support of environmentalists and social celebrities in the United States. Later, the United Nations set April 22 as "Earth Day", and it has gradually developed into a globally recognized day. There is no universally uniform theme for Earth Day each year, but its general theme has always been "Only One Earth". China has carried out various activities to mark and publicize the day each year since 1990.

图 4.15 世界地球日宣传画
Picture 4.15 Poster of World Earth Day

5. 世界环境日

5. World Environment Day

1972 年 6 月 5 日至 16 日，在瑞典斯德哥尔摩举行的联合国人类环境会议上，各国建议将联合国人类环境会议开幕日即 6 月 5 日定为"世界环境日"。同年，第二十七届联合国大会接受并通过这项建议。

From June 5 to June 16, 1972, at the United Nations Conference on the Human Environment ("UNHEC") held at Stockholm of Sweden, member states proposed setting the opening day of UNHEC, i.e. June 5, as the "World Environment Day". In the same year, the 27th UNGA accepted and approved the proposal.

制定"世界环境日"的意义在于提醒全世界注意全球环境状况的变化，以及人类活动对环境造成的危害，要求联合国系统和世界各国政府在每年的这一天开展各种活动，以强调保护和改善人类环境的重要性和迫切性。联合国环境规划署也将在每年的世界环境日发表环境现状的年度报告书，以及确定该年"世界环境日"的主题。

The setting of a "World Environment Day" aims to remind people all over the world to heed changes in global environmental conditions and the harm done by human activities to the environment, and require the UN system and governments worldwide to carry out various activities on this day each year to emphasize the importance and urgency of protecting and improving the human environment. UNEP also issues an annual report on the present environmental status on this day and determines the yearly theme of the day each year.

图 4.16 联合国环境规划署标志
Picture 4.16 Logo of UNEP

在世界环境日当天，各国政府和人民都要举行各种形式的纪念活动，宣传环境保护的重要性，呼吁人们为维护、改善人类环境而不懈努力。

On the World Environment Day each year, governments and people all over the world stage various forms of activities, publicize the importance of environmental protection, and call on all the people to make unrelenting efforts to maintain and improve the human environment.

拓展阅读
Extra Reading Material

北京湿地日
Beijing Wetland Day

《北京市湿地保护条例》于 2013 年 5 月 1 日正式施行，根据该条例规定，每年 9 月的第三个星期日设为"北京湿地日"，北京成为中国首个设立湿地纪念日的城市。

The *Regulations of Beijing Municipality on Wetland Protection* formally entered into force on May 1, 2013, pursuant to which, the third Sunday of September each year is set as the "Beijing Wetland Day". Beijing has hence become the first city in China that has set a wetlands day.

2013 年 9 月 15 日是北京市第一个"北京湿地日"，主题为"依法保护湿地、建设美丽北京"，"北京湿地日"宣传活动在房山区长沟湿地公园举办，共有社会各界人士 600 余人参加此次活动。

September 15, 2013 was the first "Beijing Wetland Day", with a campaign under the themes of "protecting wetlands in accordance with law and building a beautiful Beijing" and "Beijing

Wetland Day" staged in Changgou Wetland Park, Fangshan District of Beijing. More than 600 people from all walks of society attended the event.

此次"北京湿地日"宣传活动中，由学生代表向全体北京市民发出保护湿地倡议，并公布了湿地摄影和征文获奖名单并颁奖，开展了"保护湿地大签名"活动，活动现场还举办了野生动物图片展以及黑鹳等湿地动物的标本展，使游客近距离接触湿地野生动物。

During the campaign, student representatives launched a wetland protection initiative to all the citizens of Beijing; the list of winners of photo and essay contests about wetlands was announced and prizes were presented; a "wetland protection signature" activity was carried out. Also at the venue of the campaign, a photo exhibition about wild animals and a specimens show about wetland animals including black stocks were staged to enable tourists to have close contact with wetland wild animals.

（孙宝娣摄）

图 4.17 北京湿地日宣传报
Picture 4.17 Poster of Beijing Wetland Day
(Photo by Sun Baodi)

图 4.18 北京湿地专用标志
Picture 4.18 Logo of Beijing Wetland Day

想一想
Give This Some Thought

1. 我们每个人都有义务保护湿地，那么，同学们还知道哪些保护湿地的措施呢？请同学们根据个人生活经验为保护湿地提出一点建议吧！

1. All of us have the obligation to protect wetlands. So what other wetland protection measures do you know? Please offer your suggestion on wetland protection based on your personal life experience.

2. 你还能说出哪些与湿地有关的特殊节日？

2. Can you spell out other special days about wetlands?

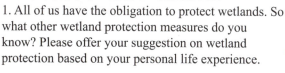

试一试

Give This A Try

1. 请你为明年的世界湿地日制定一个主题吧！
1. Please set a theme for next year's World Wetlands Day.

2. 请你为明年的世界湿地日策划一场活动吧！
2. Please make an activity plan for next year's World Wetlands Day.

第二节　湿地保护措施
Section II　Measures for Wetland Protection

　　我国根据第二次湿地资源调查结果显示，相比 2003 年首次湿地资源调查湿地保护面积增加了 525.94 万公顷，湿地保护率由 30.49% 提高到 43.51%。新增国际重要湿地 25 块，新建湿地自然保护区 279 个，新建湿地公园 468 个，初步形成了较为完善的湿地保护体系。截止 2013 年底，已建立各种类型湿地保护区 577 处，这些保护区的建立对保护湿地资源有着重要作用。湿地自然保护区主要保护珍稀水禽、动植物资源以及湿地环境和湿地生物多样性等，建立各种湿地类型的自然保护区是保护湿地生态系统和湿地资源的有效措施之一。

The second national wetland resource survey showed that the area of wetland protected areas in China had increased by 5,259,400 hectares since 2003 when China conducted its first national wetland survey. Accordingly, China's wetland protection rate increased from 30.49% to 43.51%. With the inclusion of 25 designated wetlands of international importance (Ramsar sites); 279 wetlands within the National Protected Areas network; and, 468 newly-developed National Wetland Parks, a comprehensive wetland protected areas system is started to take shape in China. As of the end of 2013, China had 577 wetland protected areas of various types. Such protected areas have played a very important role in protecting wetland resources. Wetland nature reserves are dedicated to protecting rare aquatic animals, animal and plant resources, the wetland environment and wetland biodiversity, etc. Strengthening wetland nature reserves and protected areas is one of the most effective measures in protecting wetland ecosystems and wetland resources in China.

学习日志
Notebook

通过上面的学习，我们已经知道湿地公园与湿地自然保护区的建立都是湿地保护的有效措施，那么，根据你的理解说出湿地公园与湿地自然保护区的区别有哪些？并且试着在你的学习日志中写出两者的异同吧！

We have known, from knowledge mentioned above, that both wetland parks and wetland nature reserves are effective measures for wetland protection. Could you write down in the notebook the similarities and differences of wetland park and wetland nature reserve based on your understanding?

学海拾贝
Pearls of Knowledge

自然保护区是指对有代表性或者有重要保护价值的自然生态系统、珍稀濒危野生动植物物种的天然集中分布区、有特殊意义的自然遗迹等保护对象所在的陆地、陆地水体或者海域，依法划出一定范围予以特殊保护和管理的区域。中国湿地自然保护区分为国家级、省区级、地市级和县级。虽然中国自然保护区制度并不仅仅针对湿地保护，但有相当规模的湿地划入到自然保护区范围，并且"内陆湿地"被明确为自然保护区的一个类型，因此自然保护区方式对于中国湿地保护发挥了相当重要的作用，下面介绍几个独具特色的湿地自然保护区。

Wetland nature reserve refers to legitimately designated land, land area water body or sea area under special protection and management for typical or significant natural ecological system of high protection value, naturally concentrated area of rare and endangered wild life, and natural relic of special value. Wetland nature reserve in China can be divided into wetland nature reserve of national, provincial, municipal and country level. Though China's nature reserve system is not only targeted at wetland protection, it has had a large scale of wetlands included under its coverage. Inland wetland has been clearly designated as one type of nature reserve. Therefore, wetland natural reserve has played a significant role in the protection of wetlands in China. Now, we would like to introduce you several fantastic wetland nature reserves.

1. 黑龙江扎龙国家级自然保护区

1. Heilongjiang Zhalong National Nature Reserve

"扎龙"为蒙古语，是"扎兰"之音转，意为饲养牛羊的圈。相传这里是一片盐碱地，方圆百里内只有一个几十户人家的小村落。一日，疾风顿起，乌云蔽空随着阵阵哀鸣，一个庞然怪物从天而降，人们惊慌不已，大胆壮汉赶去察看发现一条巨龙在干涸的地上。巨龙的龙爪深深地抠进干裂的土中，双目垂泪挣扎，欲飞不能。一位长者告诉大家："龙是水性天神，能为人间行雨造福，大家赶紧搭棚浇水，救它脱凡归天。"人们搭了巨大的凉棚，还从远处担来清水浇在龙的身上。可是天气燥热，巨龙身上鳞片开始脱落。此时天上的"百鸟仙子"被人们感动，派丹顶鹤率领众鹤及众多小鸟飞到人间，为巨龙遮日蔽荫，呼风唤雨。不久暴雨狂泻、洪水猛涨，巨龙得水后，一跃腾入高空，飞走之后，人们发现在巨龙飞起的地方，形成巨大的大泡子，泡中鱼虾丰盛，荷花、菱角花芳艳诱人，周围被龙尾扫过的地方还长出了茂密的芦苇。从此，这里成为风调雨顺、地产丰富的宝地，丹顶鹤便留下定居了。因此，扎龙成了鹤的故乡。

In Mongolia language, "Zhalong" is the transliteration of "Zhalan", with the meaning of lair and sheepfold. A beautiful legend is spread wide about Zhalong and cranes in ancient time when Zhalong was only a stretch of saline-alkali soil accommodating a small village of dozens of families. One day, against sudden gust and black clouds, a howling monster of super-size slumped to ground unexpectedly. Amid terrified people, the bold guys rush to have a close look for what was happening. A giant dragon was seen lying at the dried up land motionlessly. As surrounded by astonished onlookers, the dragon, with tears in his eyes and claws deeply inserted into dried soil, was struggling hopelessly for his deprived ability of fly. Upon seeing the scene, one senior explained to others: "dragon is the celestial power for water. It can bring us blessing of rainfall. Let's build a shelter for him immediately and give him badly-needed water to help him go back to heaven. " Following the suggestions of the resourceful man, locals built a huge shelter over the dragon and sprayed water fetched from far away over his body. Even so, scales on the dragon started to drop due to scorching hot. Moved by the savage below, the Deity for Birds ordered grus japonensis to lead his followers like white crane, grus monacha, grus vipio, grus grus, anthropoides virgo, whooper swan as well as numerous small birds to come to the rescue of the dying dragon. Sheltered by the bodies of such birds and fed with flood conjured up by celestial spirits, the thirsty huge dragon finally came back to his life and suddenly soared to sky, disappearing. With delightful astonishment, locals found that the place where the huge dragon had lied turned out to be a huge water pond with booming water lily, water chestnut, and swimming fish and shrimps. Dense reeds also grew in places swept by the dragon tail. Afterwards, the place became a blessed place with agreeable climate and Grus japonensis was also attracted to settle here permanently. So Zhalong became the hometown of cranes.

保护区被誉为鸟和水禽的"天然乐园"。主要保护对象是丹顶鹤（*Grus japonensis*）、白枕鹤（*Grus vipio*）等珍禽及其湿地生态。其中，白鹤（*Grus leucogeranus*）数量为世界之最，丹顶鹤为国内外罕见。这里还有丰富的水生植物和鱼类资源，是丹顶鹤等水禽栖息的理想场所，是我国最大的以丹顶鹤等鹤类及大型水禽为主体的珍稀鸟类和湿地生态类型的国家级自然保护区。除此之外，保护区还是中国目前面积最大的芦苇沼泽湿地，在丰茂密实、层层叠叠如墙的芦苇丛的保护下，该区生息繁衍着鱼类、鸟类以及昆虫类等多种动物，是一个自由而喧闹的动物乐园。

Reserve is known as "natural paradise" for birds and aquatic creatures. he nature reserve is committed to the protection of wildlife, with rare animals like Grus japonensis and Grus vipio as well as their wetland ecology as key protected subjects. In fact, no place in the world has as much as more Grus leucogeranus like the nature reserve has. The great population of Grus japonensis available here is also a rare scene in the world. Abundant with rich aquatic plant and fish resources, the national-level nature reserve is the biggest wetland eco-friendly one in the nation with large aquatic birds like Grus japonensis and rare birds as major protected subjects. Besides, as the biggest reed marsh wetland of China, under the shelter of wall-like dense reed bushes live freely many animals such us fish, birds and insects. It was a huge and bustle "Animal Paradise".

（崔丽娟摄）

图 4.19 动植物和谐共存
Picture 4.19 The Coexistence of Animals and Plants (Photo by Cui Lijuan)

2. 北京汉石桥湿地自然保护区
2. Hanshiqiao Wetland Nature Reserve

这是一片位于京东平原地带的美丽湿地，是北京市唯一现存的大型芦苇沼泽湿地，苇蒲丛生，莲藕满塘，水面清澈，水鸟鸣啼，蕴含着纯洁恬静的自然之美，有着"京东白洋淀"之称。大面积生长的芦苇（*Grus japonensis*）是这里的标志，人们在此可以领略到京郊平原独有的荒野景观。夏天的保护区内有 2 米多高的芦苇，微风吹拂，芦苇此起彼伏，犹如浩瀚的"绿海"，景色颇为壮观。行船进入湿地植物园，还可见到多姿多彩的湿地植物，俯仰碧波之上的鱼跃鸟飞，有一种置身白洋淀的感觉。

Spreading out across the plains to the east of Beijing, this beautiful wetland is the only large-scale reed marsh wetland within Beijing. The wetlands support dense stands of *Cortaderia selloana* and lotus, and echo with the sounds of water birds. The natural wetlands of Hanshiqiao have been called the east Beijing version of Baiyang Lake. Wide expanses of *Phragmites communis* create a striking scene within the nature reserve, and Beijing residents can appreciate the unique beauty of a wilderness area within the Beijing suburbs. In summer, a vast "sea of green" unfolds in front of you, as the 2 meter tall reeds sways gently in the breeze. Take a boat ride, and you will be greeted by colorful wetland plants inside the wetland garden, so beautiful is the scenery that you would be forgiven for thinking that you were touring the famed Baiyangdian wetlands.

保护区内共有鸟类 150 多种，接近北京市鸟类种数的一半。其中，除国家一级保护鸟类黑鹳（*Ciconia nigra*）和金雕（*Aquila chrysaetos*）外，还有国家二级保护鸟类 17 种，北京市Ⅰ级重点保护鸟类 10 种，以及北京市Ⅱ级重点保护鸟类 54 种，无论是鸟类的绝对数量还是单位面积的物种数量在北京地区都极为少见。除此之外，作为鸟类迁徙途中的重要驿站，汉石桥湿地还吸引了大量的旅鸟。

More than 150 species, or about half of bird species available in Beijing, are hosted in the nature reserve. In addition to birds under first-grade state protection like Ciconia nigra and Aquila chrysaetos, the nature reserve is also home to 17 species of birds under second-grade state protection, 10 species of birds under I-grade protection in Beijing, 54 species of birds under II-grade protection in Beijing. The nature reserve is rare phenomenon in Beijing no matter in absolute bird quantity or bird species sheltered per unit area. What's more, as one significant stop for migratory birds, Hanshiqiao wetland has attracted a great deal of migratory birds.

（李国新摄）

图 4.20　汉石桥
Picture 4.20　Hanshiqiao (Photo by Li Guoxin)

（王成摄）

图 4.21　秋之恋
Picture 4.21　Love in Autumn (Photo by Wang Cheng)

3. 海南东寨港国家级自然保护区

3. Hainan Dongzhaigang National Nature Reserve

该保护区是以保护红树林生态系统和鸟类为主的自然保护区。保护区于 1980 年 1 月经广东省人民政府批准建立，1986 年 7 月晋升为国家级，是我国第一个红树林类型的湿地自然保护区，1992 年被列入《湿地公约》中的国际重要湿地名录。

Dongzhaigang National Nature Reserve is dedicated to protecting the inter-tidal mangrove ecosystem and the birds and other biodiversity it supports. Established with the approval of the People's Government of Guangdong Province in January 1980, and recognized as national nature reserve in July 1986, Hainan Dongzhaigang was the first wetland nature reserve in China established to protect mangroves, and was listed on the Ramsar List of *Wetlands of International Importance* in 1992.

（张曼胤摄）

图 4.22 自然保护区美景
Picture 4.22 Scenery of Hainan Dongzhaigang National Nature Reserve (Photo by Zhang Manyin)

红树林素有"护岸卫士、造陆先锋、鸟类天堂、鱼虾粮仓"的美誉，是不可多得的湿地生态系统。该保护区是我国连片面积最大的红树林保护区，也是我国红树林资源最多，树种最丰富的自然保护区，对保护当地生态环境起着重要作用。

Acclaimed as "guardian for river bank, pioneer for land formation, paradise for birds, granary for fish and shrimps", mangrove is very precious wetland ecological system. The nature reserve, with the richest mangrove species never seen in its counterparts, is also the biggest mangrove nature reserve in the nation in terms of area. The nature reserve has played a very important role in protection of local ecological environment.

红树林的生境多样性为鸟类提供了很好的觅食、栖息、繁殖的场所。它已成为许多迁徙水禽的重要停歇地，也是连接不同生物区界鸟类的重要环节。在亚洲，从南到北或从北到南的大部分迁徙候鸟要在东寨港稍作停留以补充营养并继续飞行。另外，红树植物大量的凋落物，为鱼、虾、蟹等提供了丰富的食物，星罗棋布的小沟，形态多样、纵横交错的根系，也为它们提供了良好的生长发育的环境。

The biodiversity of mangrove has provided excellent environment for the forage, rest and reproduction of birds. The nature reserve has become the important stop for many migrating aquatic birds and the important habitat linking birds from different biosphere together. The majority of migratory birds which travel among north-south route in Asia will stop at the nature reserve for food replenishment before resuming their journey again. In addition, the withered parts of mangrove provide sufficient foods for fish, shrimps and crabs. The densely-woven trenches, and stagger roots of mangrove also make for excellent growth environment for such creatures.

4. 青海湖国家级自然保护区

4. Qinghai Lake National Nature Reserve —Niaodao ("Bird Island")

保护区位于青藏高原东北部，祁连山系南麓。其范围包括东自环青海湖东路，南自 109 国道、西自环湖西路北自青藏铁路以内的整个青海湖水体、湖中岛屿及湖周沼泽滩涂湿地。该区是以保护青海湖湿地以及鸟类资源及其栖息地为宗旨，集资源保护、科学研究、生态旅游于一体，属于湿地生态系统和野生动物类型的自然保护区。始建于 1975 年，是我国最早被列入《湿地公约》国际重要湿地名录的保护区，同时又是全国八大鸟类自然保护区。

Qinghai Lake sits at the foot of the Qilian Mountains, northeast of the Tibetan Plateau. The Qinghai Lake National Nature Reserve is well connected to several roads and railways and relatively easily accessible for such a remote part of China. Qinghai Lake National Nature Reserve is adjacent to Circle-Qingdao Lake East Road to the east, National 109 Road to the south, Circle-Qingdao Lake West Road to the west, and Qingdao-Tibet Railway to the north. The Nature Reserve was established in 1975 to protect the entire lake ecosystem, including the internal islands, and the peripheral marshes and wetlands, as well as the birds and their associated habitats. The Nature Reserve supports a rich biodiversity and was the first Nature reserve in China to be included on the Ramsar List of Wetlands of International Importance. Also, it has been designated as one of the eight most important bird nature reserves in the country.

保护区属于内陆性盐湖湿地，主要由鸟岛、鸬鹚岛、沙岛、海心山、三块石等岛屿和水域及环湖沿岸的水域、湖岸、泥滩、沼泽草地以及河口等组成。由于巨大的水体及其周边水系流域的存在，在这个我国最大的内陆咸水湖泊流域内，造就和孕育了面积广袤、类型独特的高原内陆湿地生态系统，为众多野生动物提供了理想的繁衍生息的场所。对于丰富青藏高原生物多样性、调节西北地区气候、保持水源、维护生态平衡起到不可替代的巨大作用。

Falling into the category of inland salt lake wetland, the nature reserve is mainly comprised by islands like bird island, cormorant island, sand island, mid-lake island, stone zone, as well as water area, bank, mud, marsh grassland and estuary along lake bank. Under the influence of huge water body and nearby water system, the biggest inland salt water lake basin in China has given birth to a vast and distinctive plateau inland wetland ecological system, and provided an ideal breeding venue and habitat for numerous wild creatures. It has played an irreplaceable role in enriching the biodiversity of Tibetan Plateau, adjusting climate in northwest region, maintaining water resource and ecological balance.

（俞肖剑摄）

图 4.23 湿地风光
Picture 4.23 Wetland Landscape (Photo by Yu Xiaojian)

想一想
Give This Some Thought

湿地自然保护区的建立对于湿地的保护起着重要作用，你能说出它的建立可以在哪些具体方面起到保护作用吗？

What role does wetland nature reserve play in protecting wetland? Can you tell us what specific roles it plays in wetland protection?

试一试
Give This A Try

请你拿起望远镜和照相机到家或学校附近的湿地自然保护区观察一下，找一找湿地公园中的美丽景色，并且比对一下与其他类型的公园有什么不同吧。

Take your telescope and camera along with you to wetland nature reserve near your home or school for a close observation, and find out beautiful sceneries in such wetland nature reserve and compare them with those you find in other types of parks.

第三节　中学生：我为湿地添光彩

Section III　Middle School Students: Let's Make Due Contributions to Wetland Protection

随着经济的发展，湿地的破坏越来越严重，湿地保护迫在眉睫。但是，湿地保护是一件任重而道远的事情，增强人们的湿地保护意识至关重要。湿地学校的建立以及环境教育活动对增强同学们湿地保护意识、增加湿地知识是十分必要的。

Damages to wetlands are getting worse as economy grows, highlighting the urgent need for wetland conservation. However, wetland conservation is a long-term, arduous task and the key lies in strengthening people's awareness of protection. Wetland schools and environmental education campaigns are crucial to increasing the awareness of wetland conservation and knowledge of wetlands among secondary school students.

一、湿地学校

I. Wetland Schools

湿地学校是以自然湿地生态为师，以志愿者为载体的、面向大众进行科普教育的场所，为动植物提供良好的生境，为学生提供环保知识，增强保护湿地意识，为环保志愿者、学生提供完善的科研、科考环境。

Wetland schools are natural wetland sites that serve as the bases for popular science education with the help of volunteers. These sites offer favorable habitats for animals and plants, environmental protection knowledge for students, ideal research grounds for environmental volunteers and university students, and boost awareness of wetland conservation.

2005 年 3 月，由湿地国际中国办事处命名的全国第一所"湿地实验学校"在麋鹿故乡江苏省盐城大丰市挂牌成立；2005 年 8 月 1 日，齐齐哈尔扎龙中学挂上了"湿地实验学校"的牌子，成为了我国的第二所湿地实验学校；2005 年 9 月 8 日，浙江绍兴新区"镜湖国家城市湿地学校"成立；2006 年 7 月，兰州市水车园湿地学校举行挂牌仪式，并迎来中日韩青少年湿地保护交流活动的师生；2007 年 3 月 3 日，广东首个"湿地教育基地"在华南师范大学附属中学挂牌；2012 年 8 月 16 日，"湿地自然学校"在苏州太湖湿地公园正式成立；2013 年 5 月 14 日，江苏省姜堰中学在中国溱湖湿地科普馆挂牌"溱湖湿地实践基地"；2014 年 1 月 12 日，深圳市首个自然学校——华侨城湿地自然学校正式挂牌。

The first Wetland Experimental School in China is located in Dafeng, a county-level city in Yancheng City, Jiangsu Province, which is known for elk. The School got its title from

Wetlands International-China in March 2005. Soon afterwards on August 1, 2005, Zhalong Middle School in Qiqihar became the second of its kind in China. On September 8, 2005, Mirror Lake National City Wetland School was founded in Shaoxing New District, Zhejiang. In July 2006, the inauguration of Water Mill Park Wetland School in Lanzhou was celebrated with teachers and students from China, Japan and South Korea participating in wetland conservation exchanges. On March 3, 2007, the first Wetland Education Base in Guangdong was born in the Affiliated High School of South China Normal University. On August 16, 2012, a Wetland Nature School was announced open in Lake Tai Wetland Park in Suzhou. On May 14, 2013, Jiangsu Jiangyan Middle School set up its Qin Lake Wetland Training Base in the China Qin Lake Wetland Science Museum. On January 12, 2014, Shenzhen's first nature school, Overseas Chinese Town Wetland Nature School, was erected.

二、湿地环境教育活动
II. Wetland Education Campaign

事件一：2012 年 4 月 22 日，中国林业科学研究院湿地所在颐和园举办湿地及生物多样性科普宣传活动。工作人员用生动形象的语言为学生们详细介绍了展板中的湿地知识，并在内容的讲解中渗透了提高湿地保护意识，保护湿地资源的理念。

Example 1: On April 22, 2012, the Institute of Wetland Research, Chinese Academy of Forestry, launched a campaign to popularize knowledge of wetlands and biodiversity in the Summer Palace. Organizers spoke about our knowledge of wetlands, as shown on display panels at the event, and communicated the concept of wetland conservation to students participating in the event.

（张曼胤摄）

图 4.24 颐和园科普宣传活动
Picture 4.24 A Campaign Promoting Wetland Science in Summer Palace (Photo by Zhang Manyin)

事件二：2012 年 9 月 5 日，中国林业科学研究院湿地研究所在北京市野生动物救护中心开展宣教活动，活动包括讲座、参观园区两部分。首先，湿地专家为北京人大附中的同学们进行了湿地基本知识的讲解，然后带领同学们参观了净化污水的人工湿地，在参观的过程中随时随地传授湿地知识，回答同学们提出的问题，使同学们在认识湿地植物、动物的同时，增强了湿地保护意识。

Example 2: On September 5, 2012, the Institute of Wetland Research, Chinese Academy of Forestry, organized an educational campaign that included a talk on wetlands and a tour around the constructed wetlands in the Beijing Wildlife Rescue & Rehabilitation Center. After explaining basic knowledge of wetlands to students from the High School affiliated to Renmin University, wetland experts led the students in a tour around the constructed wetlands used for wastewater purification. During the tour, information about wetlands was shared, and questions were raised and answered. Students learnt to identify some of the wetland plants and animals, and awareness of wetland conservation was built for the future.

(张曼胤摄)

图 4.25　北京市野生动物救护中心宣教活动
Picture 4.25　Educational Campaign in Beijing Wildlife Rescue & Rehabilitation Center (Photo by Zhang Manyin)

事件三：2013 年 9 月 15 日，在首个"北京湿地日"宣传活动中，学生代表发出保护湿地倡议，同时，中国林业科学研究院湿地研究所、北京市野生动物保护协会、北京市野生动物救护中心等单位组织的专业技术人员和志愿者，现场向学生、游客和市民开展湿地保护知识咨询。

Example 3: On September 15, 2013, a student representative called for actions to protect wetlands during a campaign promoting the first Beijing Wetland Day. Professionals and volunteers organized by the Institute of Wetland Research, Chinese Academy of Forestry, Beijing Wildlife Conservation Association, Beijing Wildlife Rescue & Rehabilitation Center and other organizations shared knowledge about wetland conservation to students, tourists and citizens during the event.

事件四：2014 年 3 月 2 日，北京市园林绿化局、顺义区园林绿化局、湿地保护协会共同在北京汉石桥湿地自然保护区举办以"加强野生动物保护，建设鸟语花香美丽北京"为主题的宣传活动，其中牛栏山一中百余名学生参加了此次活动。

Example 4: On March 2, 2014, a campaign with the theme of "Promoting Wildlife Conservation, Building a Beautiful Beijing", was organized by the Beijing Municipal Bureau of Landscape and Forestry; the Shunyi District Bureau of Landscape and Forestry and the, Shunyi District Wetland Conservation Association. The venue for the campaign was the Hanshiqiao Wetland Nature Reserve, Beijing, and over 100 students from Niulanshan First Secondary School participated in the event.

（孙宝娣摄）

图 4.26 北京湿地日房山湿地活动
Picture 4.26 Wetland Campaign in Fangshan on Beijing Wetland Day (Photo by Sun Baodi)

拓展阅读
Extra Reading Material

活动感受：
What We Learnt:

　　这次活动的意义一方面在于让我们认识湿地。湿地作为三大生态系统之一，在我们生活中起着不可或缺的作用。讲座中，老师给我们讲了湿地的八大用途，可见其重要，其用途不仅仅是净化水，净化水只是一个新兴的用途。另一方面，我们知道一个野生动物保护基地是如何运转的。除此之外，就是让我们知道科研院所中的人们是如何把理论应用到实践中，并证明其效果的。我们将来如果要做研究，这种能力是必需的。

Firstly, we've learnt about basic knowledge concerning wetlands. As one of the three major ecosystems, wetlands play an indispensable role in our lives. Its importance can be reflected through the eight functions explained by the teacher during the lecture, and water purification is just an emerging application. Secondly, we've learnt about how a wildlife protection center is operated. At last, we've learnt about how professionals at research institutions apply theories to practices and prove their effects. Such ability is nec essary if we want to become researchers in the future.

人民大学附属中学早培班学生
Students from Experimental Class, High School
Affiliated to Renmin University

2012 年 9 月 5 日
September 5, 2012

（引自：新浪微博 —— 雨打小树）
(Quoted from Sina Microblog — Yudaxiaoshu)

参观北京顺义区人工处理湿地有感
Some Deliberation after a Tour of Constructed Wetlands in Shunyi, Beijing

我们在北京顺义区野生动物救护中心听了一个简短的讲座，林业科学研究院湿地研究所的老师为我们讲关于湿地的基本知识。老师说，湿地有三要素，首先是要有水，其次是底部要有泥土，第三是里面要有生物。在此基础上，我们提出了一个问题叫做"加了土，里面有人的游泳池算湿地吗？如果不算，如何去证明？"其实这个问题并不白痴，它反映了科学的严谨性。真正的湿地中不是要有生物，而是要有比陆生植物更多的水生植物，因此人是肯定不符合条件的。

At Shunyi District Wildlife Rescue & Rehabilitation Center, we listened to a brief lecture on basic knowledge of wetlands given by a teacher from the Institute of Wetland Research, Chinese Academy of Forestry. We learnt that wetlands have three basic elements: water, soil underneath and living organisms. In this regard, we posed the question "does a swimming pool with soil and people in it count as the wetland? If no, why?" This is not a stupid question, because it reflects the rigor of science. Actually, what wetland necessitates is not simply living organisms, but more aquatic plants than terrestrial plants, so "people" do not qualify as the living organisms of wetlands.

之后，我们在人工处理湿地中参观，观察如何通过湿地生态系统来净化水。老师拿了两个烧杯，在人工湿地净化系统的入口处接了一杯水，非常的浑浊；在出口处，老师又接了一杯水，已经是非常的清澈了。在此要说一点，这里不是像污水处理厂那样一层层过滤，而是完全通过湿地的植物、动物、微生物来对污水进行净化的。

After the lecture, we toured around the constructed wetlands and observed how wetland ecosystems worked to purify water. The teacher brought two beakers, filled one beaker with water at the inlet of the purification system, which was pretty turbid, and then filled the other beaker with water at the outlet, which was rather clear. It is necessary to point out that sewage water here is not purified as in a water treatment plant through layers of filtration, but rather cleaned by the plants, animals and microorganisms in wetlands.

图 4.27 老师讲解人工湿地净化原理
Picture 4.27 Teacher explaining the purification process by constructed wetlands

图 4.28 两个烧杯的水清浊度对比明显
Picture 4.28 Comparison between water in two beakers

参与此净化过程的除了水葫芦（*Eichhornia crassipe*）、槐叶萍（*Salvinia natans*）、浮萍（*Lemna minor*）、香蒲（*Typha orientalis*）、芦苇（*Phragmites communis*）等水生植物，还有不计其数的微生物也参加了此过程。

Besides such aquatic plants as *Eichhornia crassipe*, *Salvinia natans*, *Lemna minor*, *Typha orientalis* and *Phragmites communis*, numerous microorganisms also contribute to the purification process.

致北京市中小学同学们的一封信
A Letter to Primary and Secondary School Students of Beijing

《丑小鸭》的故事，大家一定都耳熟能详，可是，在不久的将来，这也许会变成天方夜谭。这不是在开玩笑。

You might be quite familiar with the story "The Ugly Duckling", but what happened in the story may never happen again in the near future. And I mean it.

"湿地"这个词也许好多同学没听过。我可以告诉大家，《沙家浜》的故事就发生在湿地，沙家浜是白天鹅、丹顶鹤的家。电影《铁道游击队》中的微山湖也是湿地。

Many of you may not have heard the word "wetlands", but that's exactly where the story of "Shajiabang" took place. Shajiabang is home to white swans and red-crowned cranes. Weishan Lake in the film "Railway Guerrillas" is also a wetland site.

多么美妙，多么神奇的世界，而如今却面临着灭顶之灾！

Those once pearl-like sites are now facing catastrophic threats!

众多的湿地被无情的破坏着，这也是我写这封信的原因。

Too many wetlands are being wrecked ruthlessly, and that's why I wrote this letter.

你可曾见过北京干涸的河床？也许你不知道，那里永远都不会再有水了；也许你不知道，那里曾经是丹顶鹤的家！同学们，你们可见过大量死亡的鸟类？它们死亡，正是因为找不到回家的路了，因为，家已经被毁了，干了，没了！

Have you ever seen dried-out river beds around Beijing? You may not know that these rivers will never be filled up again; you may not know that these rivers were once home to red-crowned cranes! Have you ever seen large flocks of dead birds? They died because they couldn't find their way home, because their home is destroyed, drained and lost!

想一想，如果白鹭已经灭绝了，老师在教学生诗句"一行白鹭上青天"的时候，有同学要问"白鹭"是什么，同学们，如果你是那个见过白鹭的老师，你的心里会是怎么样？会有几多酸楚？

Picture this: if white egrets went extinct, how would a teacher explaining the verse "a row of white egrets are ascending the blue sky" feel when asked by the students what "white egrets" looked like? If you were the teacher who had seen white egrets, would you be immersed in sorrow and grief?

你也许不知道，在被保护的鸟类中，有一半以上是湿地鸟类！像天鹅、丹顶鹤，没有了湿地，它们都将会灭亡。

You may not know that over half of the protected birds, including swans and red-crowned cranes, belong to wetlands and will die out as wetlands vanish.

如果不停止破坏湿地，将会有无数干涸的河床和湖泊，就会有大量死亡的鸟、鱼，许多鸟类和鱼类都将失去它们的家园。

Huge amounts of birds and fishes will die or lose their homes as a result of dried-out rivers and lakes if wetland destruction can't be halted.

湿地自远古以来就有，而且是地球不可缺少的一部分，但它却在短短的百年之内被蹂躏得如此不堪……

Wetlands have been in existence since remote antiquity and are integral to our planet. However, it takes only a hundred years to wreck them into such a disgraceful scene…

　　同学们，我们要保护湿地，而且呼吁全社会去保护湿地——虽然我们的力量很微小，但是只要我们齐心协力，一定会有成果的！

Therefore, we need to organise ourselves to protect our wetlands and appeal for the whole society to join us — insignificant though we may seem, together we can make a difference if we are united!

　　为了不让《丑小鸭》中美丽的天鹅消失，同学们，让我们行动起来吧！保护湿地，就是保护我们人类自己。

Let's get started and begin to protect our wetlands so that the beautiful swans in "The Ugly Duckling" can stay with us, and so that our home planet can survive.

　　我们生活在首都北京，北京是我们的家园，所以，我们要一起努力，把北京变成一个鸟儿自由飞翔、鱼儿欢乐游泳的美丽城市，让湿地为北京增光添彩！

We live in the capital city of Beijing. This is our homeland. We should endeavor to protect wetlands in Beijing to make Beijing an environment-friendly city and live in harmony with nature!

　　我倡议：

I propose to:

　　了解湿地，关注湿地，保护北京湿地，不让湿地再减少，不让湿地再遭到破坏！

Learn about wetlands, care about wetlands and protect wetlands in Beijing to prevent further decrease and destruction!

牛栏山一中实验学校初一年级（16）班
Class 16, Grade 1, Niulanshan First Secondary School

王昔非
Wang Xifei

2010 年 2 月 2 日
February 2, 2010

保护湿地由我做起
Let's Get Started to Protect Wetlands!

1 珍惜并循环使用水，例如使用淘米水灌溉植物。
Save and recycle water. For example, irrigate plants with water left after washing rice.

2 洗手、刷牙、洗衣服和蔬菜时，不要持续开启水龙头。
Turn off the tap to keep water from running when washing hands, brushing teeth, and washing clothes and vegetables.

3 集中清洗衣服，减少洗衣次数。
Wash more clothes at once to reduce the frequency of laundry.

4 淋浴时应用低流量的喷头。
Use low-flow spray for shower.

5 使用能够分档调节出水量大小的节水龙头。
Use water-saving taps that can adjust water flow.

6 向亲友说明湿地的重要性。
Explain the importance of wetlands to relatives and friends.

7 不向河道、湖泊里扔垃圾，不乱仍废旧电池，防止对自然造成污染。
Do not drop waste into rivers or lakes or leave waste battery around to prevent pollution to nature.

8 外出时，自带水杯或容量小的瓶装水，减少对剩余瓶装水的浪费。
Take water bottles or low-volume bottled water for outgoings to prevent waste of leftover bottled water.

9 自行车清洁时，不用水冲，改用湿布擦脏的地方，也宜用洗衣物后的余水冲洗。
Use wet cloth for stains or water left after washing clothes to clean bicycles.

10 关注水资源运用和环境保护的话题，并积极发表意见。
Pay attention to issues concerning water use and environment protection and share your opinions.

参考文献
References

[1] *Wetlands Ecology and Management*：http://link.springer.com/journal/11273

[2] *Wetlands*：http://www.sws.org/Publications/wetlands-journal.html

[3] 保护野生动物迁徙物种公约：http://www.cms.int/

[4] 北京湿地中心：http://www.shidi.org/sf_F8EE320D9F3045E1AA54EDA4A993B6C7_151_ bjsd.html

[5] 北京湿地专用标志：http://www.bjrd.gov.cn/zt/jjsdbhtl/sdzs/201304/t20130418_116368. html

[6] 北京市人民代表大会常务委员会网址：http://www.bjrd.gov.cn/zt/jjsdbhtl/sdzs/201304/ t20130418_116368. html

[7] 崔丽娟 . 认识湿地 [M]. 北京 : 高等教育出版社 ,2012.

[7] Cui,L.J.,2012.Knowing Wetlands. Beijing: Higher Education Press

[8] 国际鹤类基金会：http://www.savingcranes.org/

[9] 国际鸟类联盟：http://www.birdlife.org/worldwide/partnership/about-birdlife

[10] 国家林业局湿地保护管理中心：http://sdzg.forestry.gov.cn/portal/sdzg/s/2962/ content-441957.html

[11] 海南东寨港国家级自然保护区：http://www.mangroves.org.cn/

[12] 汉石桥湿地自然保护区：http://www.hsq.bjshy.gov.cn/about.asp?pid=59

[13] 黑龙江扎龙国家级自然保护区管理局：http://www.chinazhalong.gov.cn/main.asp

[14] 联合国教育科学及文化组织：http://whc.unesco.org/

[15] 青海湖国家级自然保护区：http://www.qinghailake.cn/jj/bhqjj/1012.html

[16] 全球环境基金：http://www.thegef.org/gef/

[17] 生物多样性公约：https://www.cbd.int/

[18] 湿地公约：http://www.ramsar.org/cda/en/ramsar-about-about-ramsar/main/ramsar/1- 36%5E7687_4000_0__

[19] 湿地公约标志：http://www.ramsar.org/cda/en/ramsar-media-logo/main/ ramsar/1-25-402_4000_0__

[20] 湿地国际：http://www.wetwonder.org/en/page.asp?cid=4

[21] 湿地科学：http://wetlands.neigae.ac.cn/CN/column/column79.shtml

[22] 湿地科学与管理：http://lkgl.chinajournal.net.cn/WKC2/WebPublication/wkTextContent.as px?navigationContentID=487fde44-deb1-4a91-946b-5465c2a6c8be&mid=lkgl

[23] 湿地中国：http://www.shidi.org/

附录 1
Appendix 1

中国的国际重要湿地名录
Wetlands in China of International Importance

时间 Date	名称 Name	省份 Province	面积 (公顷) Area (hectare)	地理区位 Geographic location
1992.03.31	湖南东洞庭湖国家级自然保护区 Hunan East Dongting Lake National Nature Reserve	湖南 Hunan	190000	29°19′49″N 112°59′00″E
1992.03.31	海南东寨港国家级自然保护区 Hainan Dongzhaigang National Nature Reserve	海南 Hainan	5400	19°59′N 110°35′E
1992.03.31	青海湖国家级自然鸟岛 保护区 Qinghai Lake National Nature Reserve -Niaodao ("Bird Island")	青海 Qinghai	53600	36°50′N 100°10′E
1992.03.31	江西鄱阳湖国家级自然保护区 Jiangxi Poyang Lake National Nature Reserve	江西 Jiangxi	22400	29°10′N 115°59′E
1992.03.31	吉林向海国家级自然保护区 Jilin Xianghai National Nature Reserve	吉林 Jilin	105467	44°02′N 122°41′E
1992.03.31	黑龙江扎龙国家级自然保护区 Heilongjiang Zhalong National Nature Reserve	黑龙江 Heilongjiang	210000	47°12′N 124°12′E
1995.09.04	香港米埔—后海湾湿地 Mai Po Marshes and Inner Deep Bay Ramsar Site	香港特别行政区 Hong Kong Special Administrative Region	1540	2°29′20″N 114°01′44″E
2002.01.11	上海市崇明东滩鸟类自然保护区 Shanghai Chongming Dongtan Nature Reserve for Birds	上海 Shanghai	32600	31°38′N 121°58′E
2002.01.11	大连斑海豹国家级自然保护区 Dalian National Nature Reserve for Spotted Seal	辽宁 Liaoning	11700	39°15′N 121°15′E
2002.01.11	江苏大丰麋鹿国家级自然保护区 Jiangsu Dafeng National Nature Reserve for Elaphurus Davidianus	江苏 Jiangsu	78000	33°05′N 120°49′E

续表

时间 Date	名称 Name	省份 Province	面积 （公顷） Area (hectare)	地理区位 Geographic location
2002.01.11	内蒙古达赉湖国家级自然保护区 Inner Mongolia Dalai Lake National Nature Reserve	内蒙古自治区 Inner Mongolia Autonomous Region	740000	48°33′N 117°30′E
2002.01.11	内蒙古鄂尔多斯遗鸥国家级自然保护区 Inner Mongolia Ordos National Nature Reserve for Larus Relictus	内蒙古自治区 Inner Mongolia Autonomous Region	7680	39°48′N 109°35′E
2002.01.11	黑龙江洪河国家级自然保护区 Heilongjiang Honghe National Nature Reserve	黑龙江 Heilongjiang	21836	47°49′N 133°40′E
2002.01.11	黑龙江三江国家级自然保护区 Heilongjiang Sanjiang National Nature Reserve	黑龙江 Heilongjiang	164400	47°56′N 134°20′E
2002.01.11	黑龙江兴凯湖国家级自然保护区 Heilongjiang Xingkai Lake National Nature Reserve	黑龙江 Heilongjiang	222488	45°17′N 132°32′E
2002.01.11	广东惠东港口海龟国家级自然保护区 Guangdong Huidong Harbor National Nature Reserve for Sea Turtle	广东 Guangdong	400	22°33′N 114°54′E
2002.01.11	广东湛江红树林国家级自然保护区 Guangdong Zhanjiang Mangrove National Nature Reserve	广东 Guangdong	20279	20°54′N 110°08′E
2002.01.11	湖南南洞庭湖省级自然保护区 Hunan South Dongting Wetland and Waterfowl Nature Reserve	湖南 Hunan	168000	28°50′N 112°40′E
2002.01.11	广西山口红树林国家级自然保护区 Guangxi Shankou Mangrove National Nature Reserve	广西壮族自治区 Guangxi Zhuang Autonomous Region	4000	21°28′N 109°43′E
2002.01.11	湖南汉寿西洞庭湖省级自然保护区 Hunan Hanshou West Dongting Lake (Mupinghu) Nature Reserve	湖南 Hunan	35000	29°01′N 112°05′E

时间 Date	名称 Name	省份 Province	面积 (公顷) Area (hectare)	地理区位 Geographic location
2002.01.11	江苏盐城国家级珍禽自然保护区 Jiangsu Yancheng National Nature Reserve for Rare Birds	江苏 Jiangsu	453000	33°31′N 120°22′E
2004.12.07	云南碧塔海湿地 Yunnan Bitahai Wetland	云南 Yunnan	1985	27°50′33″N 99°59′10″E
2004.12.07	云南省大山包黑颈鹤国家级自然保护区 Yunnan Province Dashanbao National Nature Reserve for Black-necked Crane	云南 Yunnan	5958	27°25′36″N 103°19′33″E
2004.12.07	云南拉什海湿地 Yunnan Lashihai Wetland	云南 Yunnan	3560	26°53′48″N 100°08′06″E
2004.12.07	云南纳帕海湿地 Yunnan Napahai Wetland	云南 Yunnan	2083	27°51′16″N 99°38′44″E
2004.12.07	青海扎陵湖湿地 Qinghai Zhaling Lake Wetland	青海 Qinghai	64920	34°54′43″N 97°16′29″E
2004.12.07	青海鄂陵湖湿地 Qinghai Eling Lake Wetland	青海 Qinghai	65907	34°54′25″N 97°40′48″E
2004.12.07	西藏麦地卡湿地自然保护区 Tibet Maidika Wetland Nature Reserve	西藏自治区 Tibet Autonomous Region	43496	31°11′55″N 92°40′51″E
2004.12.07	西藏玛旁雍错国家级自然保护区 Tibet Mapangyong Cuo National Nature Reserve	西藏自治区 Tibet Autonomous Region	73782	30°44′29″N 81°19′43″E
2004.12.07	辽宁双台河口国家级自然保护区 Liaoning Shuangtai Estuary National Nature Reserve	辽宁 Liaoning	128000	40°54′45″N 121°45′41″E
2008.02.02	福建漳江口红树林国家级自然保护区 Fujian Zhangjiangkou Mangrove National Nature Reserve	福建 Fujian	2358	23°55′N 117°25′E
2008.02.02	广东海丰公平大湖自然保护区 Guangdong Haifeng Gongping Lake Wetland Nature Reserve	广东 Guangdong	11591	22°59′N 115°19′E

续表

时间 Date	名称 Name	省份 Province	面积 （公顷） Area (hectare)	地理区位 Geographic location
2008.02.02	广西北仑河口国家级自然保护区 Guangxi Beilun Estuary National Nature Reserve	广西壮族自治区 Guangxi Zhuang Autonomous Region	3000	21°34′N 108°08′E
2008.02.02	湖北洪湖湿地 Hubei Honghu Wetland	湖北 Hubei	43450	29°50′N 113°19′E
2008.02.02	上海市长江口中华鲟自然保护区 Shanghai Yangtze Estuarine Wetland Nature Reserve for Chinese Sturgeon	上海 Shanghai	3760	31°31′N 122°05′E
2008.02.02	四川若尔盖湿地国家级自然保护区 Sichuan Ruoergai Wetland National Nature Reserve	四川 Sichuan	166570	33°43′N 102°44′E
2009.07.07	浙江杭州西溪国家湿地公园 Hangzhou Xixi National Wetland Park	浙江 Zhejiang	325	30°16′N 120°03′E
2011.09.01	黑龙江南瓮河国家级自然保护区 Heilongjiang Nanweng River National Nature Reserve	黑龙江 Heilongjiang	229523	51°19′14″N 125°22′52″E
2011.09.01	黑龙江省七星河国家级自然保护区 Heilongjiang Qixing River National Nature Reserve	黑龙江 Heilongjiang	20000	46°44′18″N 132°13′53″E
2011.09.01	黑龙江省珍宝岛国家级自然保护区 Heilongjiang Zhenbaodao Wetland National Nature Reserve	黑龙江 Heilongjiang	44364	46°07′40″N 133°38′14″E
2011.09.01	甘肃省尕海则岔自然保护区 Gansu Gahai Wetland Nature Reserve	甘肃 Gansu	247431	34°16′40″N 102°26′53″E

时间 Date	名称 Name	省份 Province	面积 （公顷） Area (hectare)	地理区位 Geographic location
2013.10.16	湖北沉湖湿地自然保护区 Hubei Chenhu Lake Wetland Nature Reserve	湖北 Hubei	11579	30° 20′ 01″ N 113° 49′ 34″ E
2013.10.16	湖北神农架大九湖湿地 Hubei Shennongjia Dajiu Lake Wetland	湖北 Hubei	9320	31° 28′ 14″ N 110° 02′ 51″ E
2013.10.16	黑龙江东方红湿地国家级自然 保护区 Heilongjiang Dongfanghong Wetland National Nature Reserve	黑龙江 Heilongjiang	31538	46° 18′ 34″ N 133° 44′ 57″ E
2013.10.16	吉林莫莫格国家级自然 保护区 Jilin Momoge National Nature Reserve	吉林 Jilin	144000	45° 54′32"N 123° 45′56"E
2013.10.16	山东黄河三角洲国家级 自然保护区 Shandong Yellow River Delta National Wetland Nature Reserve	山东 Shandong	95950	37° 42′ 18″ N 119° 09′ 02″ E
共计 Total	46 处湿地 46 wetlands		4002240	

附录 2
Appendix 2

湿地保护管理规定
Administrative Provisions on Wetland Protection

第一条　为了加强湿地保护管理，履行国际湿地公约，根据法律法规和国务院有关规定，制定本规定。

Article 1　The provision is formulated in accordance with laws, regulations and related provisions of the State Council to consolidate administration over wetland protection, and implement international conventions about wetlands.

第二条　本规定所称湿地，是指常年或者季节性积水地带、水域和低潮时水深不超过 6 米的海域，包括沼泽湿地、湖泊湿地、河流湿地、滨海湿地等自然湿地，以及重点保护野生动物栖息地或者重点保护野生植物的原生地等人工湿地。

Article 2　Wetlands under the provision refer to perennial or seasonal water-logged belt, water area, or sea area with water depth lower than 6 meter at the time of low tide. Wetlands can be divided into natural wetlands including marsh wetlands, lake wetlands, river wetlands, coastal wetlands and constructed wetlands including habitats of wild animal under key protection, and habitats of wild plants under key protection.

第三条　国家对湿地实行保护优先、科学恢复、合理利用、持续发展的方针。

Article 3　Policies giving priority to wetland protection, promoting scientific recovery, rational usage, and consistent development of wetlands will be implemented in the nation.

第四条　国家林业局负责全国湿地保护工作的组织、协调、指导和监督，并组织、协调有关国际湿地公约的履约工作。

Article 4　State Forestry Administration is held responsible for the organization, coordination, instruction, supervision of wetland protection in the nation, and is held accountable for the organization and coordination of implementation of international conventions about wetlands.

县级以上地方人民政府林业主管部门按照有关规定负责本行政区域内的湿地保护管理工作。

Forestry administrative authorities in local people's government above county level are held accountable for the protection and management of wetlands falling into its jurisdiction in accordance with related regulations.

第五条　县级以上人民政府林业主管部门及有关湿地保护管理机构应当加强湿地保护宣传教育和培训，结合世界湿地日、爱鸟周和保护野生动物宣传月等开展宣传教育活动，提高公众湿地保护意识。

Article 5 Forestry administrative authorities in the people's government above county level and related wetland protection regulatory authorities should reinforce mass education and training about wetland protection, conduct publicity and education activities on special occasions like World Wetlands Day, Bird Protection Week, and Wildlife Protection Month so as to enhance social awareness on wetland protection.

县级以上人民政府林业主管部门应当组织开展湿地保护管理的科学研究，应用推广研究成果，提高湿地保护管理水平。

Forestry administrative authorities in the people's government above county level are held accountable to organize scientific research on management over wetland protection, and promote the research results, so as to boost management over wetland protection.

第六条　县级以上地方人民政府林业主管部门应当鼓励、支持公民、法人和其他组织，以志愿服务、捐赠等形式参与湿地保护。

Article 6 Forestry administrative authorities in the people's government above county level should encourage and support citizens, legal person and other organizations to participate in wetland protection in forms like volunteer service and donation, etc.

第七条　国家林业局会同国务院有关部门编制全国和区域性湿地保护规划，报国务院或者其授权的部门批准。

Article 7 State Forestry Administration should cooperate with related departments under the State Council to work out national and regional wetland protection planning and submit them to the State Council or other competent authorities for review and approval.

县级以上地方人民政府林业主管部门应当会同同级人民政府有关部门，按照有关规定编制本行政区域内的湿地保护规划，报同级人民政府或者其授权的部门批准。

Forestry administrative authorities in local people's government above county level should, in collaboration with related department of the people's government of the same level, work out wetland protection planning for administrative region under their jurisdiction in accordance with related regulations, and submit it to the people's government or department under its authorization for review and approval.

第八条　湿地保护规划应当包括下列内容：湿地资源分布情况、类型及特点、水资源、野生生物资源状况；保护和利用的指导思想、原则、目标和任务；湿地生态保护重点建设项目与建设布局；投资估算和效益分析；保障措施。

Article 8　Wetland protection planning should cover the following contents: the distribution, type and feature of wetland resources, the status quo of water resources and wildlife resources; the guiding ideas, principle, aim and task of wetland protection and usage; key projects for wetland ecological protection and related supporting construction and deployment projects; investment estimation and benefit analysis, and supporting measures.

第九条　经批准的湿地保护规划必须严格执行；未经原批准机关批准，不得调整或者修改。

Article 9　Upon approval, wetland protection planning must be implemented strictly. No adjustment or alteration on wetland protection planning is allowed without the approval of original approval authority.

第十条　国家林业局定期组织开展全国湿地资源调查、监测和评估，按照有关规定向社会公布相关情况。

Article 10　State Forestry Administration should conduct survey, supervision and evaluation on national wetland resources on regular basis and have related survey, supervision and evaluation results publicized to the public in light of related regulations.

湿地资源调查、监测、评估等技术规程，由国家林业局在征求有关部门和单位意见的基础上制定。

The technical regulations governing survey, monitor and evaluation of wetland resources should be made by State Forestry Administration after soliciting opinions from related departments and organizations.

县级以上地方人民政府林业主管部门及有关湿地保护管理机构应当组织开展本行政区域内的湿地资源调查、监测和评估工作，按照有关规定向社会公布相关情况。

Forestry administrative authorities in local people's government above county level and related wetland protection regulatory authorities should organize related departments to survey, monitor and evaluate wetland resources within regions under their jurisdiction and have such survey, monitor and evaluation results publicized to the society in light of related regulations.

第十一条　县级以上人民政府或者林业主管部门可以采取建立湿地自然保护区、湿地公园、湿地保护小区、湿地多用途管理区等方式，健全湿地保护体系，完善湿地保护管理机构，加强湿地保护。

Article 11 The people's government above county level or forestry administrative authority are encouraged to adopt feasible approaches like setting up wetland nature reserve, wetland park, wetland protection community, wetland multipurpose administration area to consolidate wetland protection system, optimize wetland protection regulatory authority and enhance wetland protection.

第十二条 湿地按照其重要程度、生态功能等，分为重要湿地和一般湿地。

Article 12 Wetlands will be divided into significant wetlands and common wetlands in light of their importance and ecological function, etc.

重要湿地包括国家重要湿地和地方重要湿地。

Significant wetlands consist of national and local significant wetlands.

重要湿地以外的湿地为一般湿地。

All wetlands except for significant wetlands are generally termed as common wetlands.

第十三条 国家林业局会同国务院有关部门划定国家重要湿地，向社会公布。

Article 13 State Forestry Administration will, in collaboration with departments under the State Council, designate wetlands of national significance and publicize them to the public.

国家重要湿地的划分标准，由国家林业局会同国务院有关部门制定。

The designation criterion of national significant wetlands should be prescribed by State Forestry Administration together with related departments under the State Council.

第十四条 县级以上地方人民政府林业主管部门会同同级人民政府有关部门划定地方重要湿地，并向社会公布。

Article 14 Forestry administrative authority in the people's government above county level will, in collaboration with related department of the people's government at the same level, designate wetlands of local significance and publicize them to the public.

地方重要湿地和一般湿地的管理办法由省、自治区、直辖市制定。

The management method on local significant wetlands and common wetlands should be prescribed by concerned provinces, autonomous regions and municipalities directly under the central government.

第十五条 符合国际湿地公约国际重要湿地标准的，可以申请指定为国际重要湿地。

Article 15 Wetlands which live up to standards of wetlands of global significance can apply to be recognized as globally important wetlands.

申请指定国际重要湿地的，由国务院有关部门或者湿地所在地省、自治区、直辖市人民政府林业主管部门向国家林业局提出。国家林业局应当组织论证、审核，对符合国际重要湿地条件的，在征得湿地所在地省、自治区、直辖市人民政府和国务院有关部门同意后，报国际湿地公约秘书处核准列入《国际重要湿地名录》。

For wetlands intended to be recognized as globally important wetlands, the related department of State Council or forestry administrative authorities in the people's government of concerned provinces, autonomous regions and municipalities under the central governments where the wetlands are located in, are held responsible to lodge applications on behalf of such wetlands to State Forestry Administration. The latter is responsible to organize demonstration and evaluation efforts on such applications, and after gaining approval from the people's government of the concerned provinces, autonomous regions, and municipalities directly under the central government, report to secretariat of the international wetland convention for including those wetlands, which have been proved up to criterion of globally important wetlands, into *Ramsar List of Wetlands of International Importance* upon verification.

第十六条　国家林业局对国际重要湿地的保护管理工作进行指导和监督，定期对国际重要湿地的生态状况开展检查和评估，并向社会公布结果。

Article 16　State Forestry Administration is responsible to give instruction and supervision over the management of protection of wetlands of global significance, and to regularly review and evaluate the ecological status of wetlands of global significance and have the review and evaluation results publicized to the public.

国际重要湿地所在地的县级以上地方人民政府林业主管部门应当会同同级人民政府有关部门对国际重要湿地保护管理状况进行检查，指导国际重要湿地保护管理机构维持国际重要湿地的生态特征。

Forestry administrative authorities in local people's government above county level and related wetland protection regulatory authorities of the place where globally important wetlands are located in should be, in collaboration with related departments of people's government of the same level, inspect the management over globally important wetlands, and guide the regulatory organizations in charge of globally important wetlands to maintain the ecological characteristics of such wetlands.

第十七条　国际重要湿地保护管理机构应当建立湿地生态预警机制，制定实施管理计划，开展动态监测，建立数据档案。

Article 17　The administrative authorities for protection of wetlands of global significance are responsible to establish wetland ecological early warning mechanism, work out implementation management plan, conduct dynamic supervision and establish data archive.

第十八条　因气候变化、自然灾害等造成国际重要湿地生态特征退化的，省、自治区、直辖市人民政府林业主管部门应当会同同级人民政府有关部门进行调查，指导国际重要湿地保护管理机构制定实施补救方案，并向同级人民政府和国家林业局报告。

Article 18 Forestry administrative authority should, in collaboration with related department of the people's government of the same level, conduct investigation into ecological degeneration of wetlands of global significance as a result of climate change or natural disaster, and guide regulatory authorities for protection of such wetlands to work out and implement rescue planning and report the progress to the people's government of the same level and State Forestry Administration.

因工程建设等造成国际重要湿地生态特征退化甚至消失的，省、自治区、直辖市人民政府林业主管部门应当会同同级人民政府有关部门督促、指导项目建设单位限期恢复，并向同级人民政府和国家林业局报告；对逾期不予恢复或者确实无法恢复的，由国家林业局会商所在地省、自治区、直辖市人民政府和国务院有关部门后，按照有关规定处理。

For globally important wetlands whose ecological characteristics are degraded or even disappeared by engineering construction projects, forestry administrative authorities in people's government of related provinces, autonomous regions and municipalities under the central government should, in collaboration with related departments of people's government of the same level, supervise and guide concerned project owners to restore such ecological characteristics of wetlands within limited time span and report to the people's government of the same level or State Forestry Administration. For those project owners who fail to restore or have no way to restore such ecological characteristics of wetlands over required time span, State Forestry Administration should, after consulting the people's government of related provinces, autonomous regions and municipalities directly under the central government, and related departments of State Council, deal with such cases in light of related regulations.

第十九条　具备自然保护区设立条件的湿地，应当依法建立自然保护区。

Article 19 Wetlands which are qualified as nature reserves should be made into nature reserves in the light of laws and regulations.

自然保护区的设立和管理按照自然保护区管理的有关规定执行。

The establishment and management of nature reserves should be in line with related regulations concerning nature reserves.

第二十条　以保护湿地生态系统、合理利用湿地资源、开展湿地宣传教育和科学研究为目的，并可供开展生态旅游等活动的湿地，可以建立湿地公园。

Article 20　Wetlands, which are constructed for the protection of wetland ecological system, feasible usage of wetland resources, wetland mass education and scientific research and are suitable for eco-tourism, can be made into wetland parks.

湿地公园分为国家湿地公园和地方湿地公园。

Wetland parks could be divided into national wetland parks and local wetland parks.

第二十一条　建立国家湿地公园，应当具备下列条件：一是湿地生态系统在全国或者区域范围内具有典型性；或者区域地位重要；或者湿地主体生态功能具有典型示范性；或者湿地生物多样性丰富；或者生物物种独特。二是具有重要或者特殊科学研究、宣传教育和文化价值。

Article 21　Wetlands qualified to be recognized as national wetland parks are: 1. wetlands with typical national or regional ecological system, or wetlands of great regional significance, or wetlands whose major ecological function is typical and demonstrative, or wetlands with rich biodiversity, or wetlands with unique species. 2. wetlands with significant or unique value in terms of scientific research, mass education and culture domain.

第二十二条　申请建立国家湿地公园的，应当编制国家湿地公园总体规划。

Article 22　Wetlands applying to be recognized as national wetland parks should prepare national wetland park overall planning.

国家湿地公园总体规划是国家湿地公园建设管理、试点验收、批复命名、检查评估的重要依据。

The overall planning for national wetland park is the important basis on which national wetland park would be built, examined for acceptance, approved, denominated, inspected and evaluated.

第二十三条　建立国家湿地公园，由省、自治区、直辖市人民政府林业主管部门向国家林业局提出申请，并提交总体规划等相关材料。

Article 23　Wetlands applying to be recognized national wetland parks should have their applications together with related materials like overall planning submitted to State Forestry Administration by forestry administrative authorities of the people's government at provincial level, autonomous region or municipality directly under the central government level.

国家林业局在收到申请后，对提交的有关材料组织论证审核，对符合条件的，同意其开展试点。

Upon acceptance of application, State Forestry Administration should organize related personnel to demonstrate and verify related materials and give consent to the operation of national trail wetland park which have proved to be qualified upon verification.

试点期限不超过 5 年。对试点期限内具备验收条件的，省、自治区、直辖市人民政府林业主管部门可以向国家林业局提出验收申请，经国家林业局组织验收合格的，予以批复并命名为国家湿地公园。

The operation of trial national wetland parks could not exceed five years. For those which meet acceptance condition within trial operation, forestry administrative authorities in people's government of related provinces, autonomous regions and municipalities under the central government should lodge acceptance application for such national wetland parks under trial operation. Station Forestry Administration is responsible to organize examination for acceptance to such trail national wetland parks and formally recognize them as national wetland parks.

在试点期限内不申请验收或者验收不合格且整改后仍不合格的，国家林业局应当取消其国家湿地公园试点资格。

For those wetlands which fail to apply examination for acceptance or fail to meet acceptance condition as national wetland parks after making verification within trial operation duration, State Forestry Administration will rescind their qualification as trial national wetland parks.

第二十四条　国家林业局组织开展国家湿地公园的检查和评估工作。

Article 24　State Forestry Administration is responsible to have national wetland parks properly reviewed and evaluated.

因管理不善导致国家湿地公园条件丧失的，或者对存在问题拒不整改或者整改不符合要求的，国家林业局应当撤销国家湿地公园的命名，并向社会公布。

For national wetland parks which are disqualified as national wetland parks due to poor management or fail to make required rectification for problems or fail to make satisfactory rectification up to demanded standard, State Forestry Administration is entitled to revoke the title of the wetland as national wetland park and make the decision known to the public.

第二十五条　地方湿地公园的建立和管理，按照地方有关规定办理。

Article 25　Local wetland parks should be established and managed in the light of related local requirements.

第二十六条　县级以上人民政府林业主管部门应当指导国家重要湿地、国际重要湿地、国家湿地公园、国家级湿地自然保护区保护管理机构建立健全管理制度，并按照相关规定制定专门的法规或者规章，加强保护管理。

Article 26 Forestry administrative authorities of the people's government above country level should guide regulatory authorities for wetlands of national or global significance, national wetland parks, national wetland nature reserve to consolidate administrative regime, work out specialized regulations or rules, and enhance administration over wetland protection accordingly.

第二十七条　因保护湿地给湿地所有者或者经营者合法权益造成损失的，应当按照有关规定予以补偿。

Article 27 Wetland owners or operators whose legitimate rights are compromised for the protection of wetlands should be compensated accordingly.

第二十八条　县级以上地方人民政府林业主管部门及有关湿地保护管理机构应当组织开展退化湿地恢复工作，恢复湿地功能或者扩大湿地面积。

Article 28 Forestry administrative authorities of people's government above county level and related regulatory authorities for wetland protection should organize related departments to have degraded wetlands recovered with function restored or area expanded.

第二十九条　县级以上地方人民政府林业主管部门及有关湿地保护管理机构应当开展湿地动态监测，并在湿地资源调查和监测的基础上，建立和更新湿地资源档案。

Article 29 Forestry administrative authorities of people's government above county level and related regulatory authorities for wetland protection should conduct wetland dynamic monitoring, establish and renew wetland resource archive based on wetland resource investigation and survey results.

第三十条　县级以上人民政府林业主管部门应当对开展生态旅游等利用湿地资源的活动进行指导和监督。

Article 30 Forestry administrative authorities of people's government above county level should guide or supervise ecological tourism activities conducted on wetlands.

第三十一条　除法律法规有特别规定的以外，在湿地内禁止从事下列活动：

Article 31 Except for those specially prescribed by laws and regulations, the following activities are also forbidden on wetlands:

（一）开（围）垦湿地，放牧、捕捞；

(1) reclaim (cultivate) wetlands, graze, and catch aquatic animals;

（二）填埋、排干湿地或者擅自改变湿地用途；

(2) bury waste under wetlands and drain water from wetlands or other activities which might change the nature of wetlands;

（三）取用或者截断湿地水源；

(3) take or cut off wetland water resources;

（四）挖砂、取土、开矿；

(4) dig sand, earth and mineral;

（五）排放生活污水、工业废水；

(5) discharge domestic sewage, and industrial effluents;

（六）破坏野生动物栖息地、鱼类洄游通道，采挖野生植物或者猎捕野生动物；

(6) damage wildlife habitat and fish migration route, dig wild plants or hunt wild animals;

（七）引进外来物种；

(7) introduce foreign species;

（八）其他破坏湿地及其生态功能的活动。

(8) other activities which might destroy the ecological functions of wetlands.

第三十二条 工程建设应当不占或者少占湿地。确需征收或者占用的，用地单位应当依法办理相关手续，并给予补偿。

Article 32 Engineering construction projects could not encroach upon, or at least should occupy as less wetlands as possible. In case that expropriation and occupation of wetlands are not avoidable, the organization which demands expropriation and occupation of wetlands should transact related formalities and make related compensation.

临时占用湿地的，期限不得超过 2 年；临时占用期限届满，占用单位应当对所占湿地进行生态修复。

The temporary occupation of wetlands could not exceed 2 years. Upon expiry, the organization which occupies the wetland is held responsible for ecological restoration of the concerned wetland.

第三十三条 县级以上地方人民政府林业主管部门应当会同同级人民政府有关部门，在同级人民政府的组织下建立湿地生态补水协调机制，保障湿地生态用水需求。

Article 33 Forestry administrative authorities of local people's government above county level should, in collaboration with related department of the people's government of same level, build wetland ecological water compensation mechanism under the organization of the people's government of the same level, so as to safeguard the water consumption demand of the wetland.

第三十四条 县级以上人民政府林业主管部门应当会同同级人民政府有关部门协调、组织、开展湿地有害生物防治工作；湿地保护管理机构应当按照有关规定承担湿地有害生物防治的具体工作。

Article 34 Forestry administrative authorities of people's government above county level should, in collaboration with related department of the people's government of same level, coordinate, organize and implement wetland pest control work; wetland protection regulatory organization is held accountable for detailed implementation of wetland pest control work in light of related regulations.

第三十五条 县级以上人民政府林业主管部门应当会同同级人民政府有关部门开展湿地保护执法活动，对破坏湿地的违法行为依法予以处理。

Article 35 Forestry administrative authorities of people's government above county level should, in collaboration with related department of the people's government of same level, coordinate, and carry out law enforcing activities for wetland protection, so as to put damaging activities against wetlands under penalty.

第三十六条 本规定所称国际湿地公约，是指《关于特别是作为水禽栖息地的国际重要湿地公约》。

Article 36 The international wetland convention as prescribed in this provision refers to *Convention on Wetlands of International Importance Especially as Waterfowl Habitat.*

第三十七条 本规定自 2013 年 5 月 1 日起施行。

Article 37 This Provision will be put into effect from May 1, 2013.

附录 3
Appendix 3

相关期刊
Related Journals

1.《湿地科学》

1. *Wetland Science*

　　《湿地科学》是中国科学院主管、中国科学院东北地理与农业生态研究所主办、科学出版社出版的湿地学科综合学术期刊。《湿地科学》定位于同国际接轨的反映湿地学科前沿的学术类精品期刊，发表国内外有关研究湿地形成与演化规律、湿地发生发展规律、湿地演化过程、湿地环境、湿地生态、湿地保护与管理、湿地开发、湿地工程建设、湿地研究的理论与方法等创新性、前沿性和探索性的学术论文和研究成果。侧重报道国家自然科学基金项目、国家重点实验室基金项目、国家科技攻关项目和国际合作项目的最新研究成果。

Wetland Science is a comprehensive academic journal specializing in wetland science. It is administered by the Chinese Academy of Sciences, sponsored by the Northeast Institute of Geography and Agroecology of the CAS and published by the Science Press. *Wetland Science* strives to keep pace with international development and be a top-notch journal that sheds lights on cutting-edge technology of wetland science. The journal publishes innovative, pioneering and exploratory academic papers and research findings concerning the rules of wetland formation and evolvement, the rules of wetland occurrence and development, the processes of wetland evolvement, wetland environment and ecology, wetland conservation and management, wetland development and engineering construction, as well as theories and methods of wetland research. It prioritizes the reporting of the latest findings made by programs supported by the National Natural Science Foundation and the State Key Laboratory Foundation, as well as by National Key Technology Research & Development Programs and international cooperation programs.

2.《湿地科学与管理》

2. *Wetland Science & Management*

　　《湿地科学与管理》是林业基础性和高科技学术期刊，创刊于 1992 年，国家林业局主管、中国林业科学研究院主办的湿地研究领域的综合性期刊。以宣传国内外湿地保护的政策法规、交流湿地保护的理论与经验、报道湿地科学研究成果或新发现，介绍湿地资源与功能为主要内容。旨在促进我国湿地保护与管理水平的不断提高，推动我国湿地保护与管理的可持续发展。刊载了大量的研究论文，在国内外林业学术交流中起到了重要的作用。

Wetland Science & Management, first issued in 1992, is a forestry-based, high-tech and comprehensive academic journal concerned with wetland research. It is administered by the State Forestry Administration and sponsored by the Chinese Academy of Forestry. The journal is devoted to spreading wetland conservation policies and laws and regulations both home and abroad, communicating wetland conservation theories and experiences, reporting scientific achievements or new findings related to wetland science and introducing wetland resources and functions. Its goal is to boost the level and sustainable development of wetland conservation and management in China. The journal has published a substantial amount of research papers and contributed significantly to academic exchanges in the field of forestry between China and other countries.

3.《湿地》
3. *Wetlands*

《湿地》是一本涉及湿地生物学、生态学、水文学、水化学、土壤和沉积物特征、管理、法律和法规等各个方面的国际期刊。该杂志每年出版 6 期，其目的是为了将一些开创性的湿地工作集中发布，尽管这些工作已经在无数期刊中广泛传播。由于湿地的研究横跨了一系列的学科，所以本刊所发表的文献并不仅只局限于某个特定的学科，而是将所有的相关学科的研究成果都呈现出来。这个范围非常的广泛，已经超越了单纯的自然科学，甚至还包括了一些以管理和监管为焦点的文献。

Wetlands is an international journal concerned with all aspects of wetlands biology, ecology, hydrology, water chemistry, soil and sediment characteristics, management, and laws and regulations. The journal is published 6 times per year, with the goal of centralizing the publication of pioneering wetlands work that has otherwise been spread among a myriad of journals. Because wetland research crosses a range of disciplines, the journal is not restricted to specific subjects but presents manuscripts reporting research results from all relevant disciplines. This broad scope goes beyond the sciences to include articles focusing on management topics and regulatory considerations.

4.《湿地生态与管理》
4. *Wetlands Ecology and Management*

《湿地生态与管理》是一个发布有关淡水、半咸水和海洋海岸湿地生态系统为主题的权威国际期刊。该期刊作为一种多学科和跨学科的杂志，主要解决湿地科学、管理、政策和经济的关键问题。它鼓励环境管理人员、理论和应用的科学家，以及国家和国际机构对湿地科学、政策和生态经济学之间进行信息交流。该杂志独特的湿地管理网站可提供免费的关于湿地管理的问题、方法及影响的文章——为从事资源管理和应用研究的人提供宝贵的资源。

Wetlands Ecology and Management is an international journal that publishes authoritative articles on topics relevant to freshwater, brackish and marine coastal wetland ecosystems. The journal serves as a multi- and interdisciplinary forum for key issues in wetlands science, management, policy and economics. *Wetlands Ecology and Management* encourages the exchange of information between environmental managers, pure and applied scientists, and national and international authorities on wetlands science, policy and ecological economics. The journal's unique Wetlands Management site provides free access to papers on the issues, methods and impacts of wetlands management-a particularly valuable resource for those involved in resource management and applied research.

相关网站
Related Websites

1. 保护野生动物迁徙物种公约：http://www.cms.int/

2. 北京湿地：http://bjsd.shidi.org/

3. 翠湖国家城市湿地公园：http://chsd.bjhd.gov.cn/

4. 国际鹤类基金会：http://www.savingcranes.org/

5. 国际鸟类联盟：http://www.birdlife.org/

6. 国家环境保护湿地生态与植被恢复重点实验室：http://sep.nenu.edu.cn/index.html

7. 国家林业局：http://www.forestry.gov.cn/

8. 汉石桥湿地自然保护区：http://www.hsq.bjshy.gov.cn/

9. 洪泽湖湿地公园：http://www.shhzhsd.com/

10. 联合国环境规划署：http://www.unep.org/

11. 联合国教育科学及文化组织：http://whc.unesco.org/?cid=175

12. 美丽中国——湿地行：http://zmsd.cntv.cn/

13. 全球环境基金：http://www.thegef.org/gef/

14. 生态中国网——湿地：http://shidi.eco.gov.cn/

15. 生物多样性公约：http://www.cbd.int/

16. 湿地公约：http://www.ramsar.org

17. 湿地国际：http://www.wetlands.org

18. 湿地国际中国项目办：http://www.wetwonder.org/

19. 湿地科学：http://wetlands.neigae.ac.cn/CN/volumn/current.shtml

20. 湿地科学家学会（SWS）：http://www.sws.org/

21. 湿地科学与管理：http://lkgl.chinajournal.net.cn

22. 湿地之友：http://www.wowcn.org.cn/

23. 湿地中国：http://www.shidi.org/

24. 湿地中国网微博：http://weibo.com/shidiorg?from=profile&wvr=5&loc=infdomain

25. 世界地球日：http://www.earthday.org/

26. 世界湿地日：http://www.ramsar.org/cda/en/ramsar-activities-wwds/main/ramsar/
    1-63-78_4000_0__

27. 世界水日：http://www.unwater.org/

28. 世界自然保护联盟：http://www.iucn.org/

29. 世界自然基金会：http://www.wwfchina.org/

30. 西溪国家湿地公园：http://www.xixiwetland.com.cn/

31. 香港湿地公园：http://www.wetlandpark.gov.hk/tc/index.asp?

32. 向海国家自然保护区：http://www.xianghai.org/

33. 野鸭湖国家湿地公园：http://www.yeyahu.com/

34. 长江湿地：http://www.cjshidi.org/

35. 中国科学院湿地生态与环境重点实验室：http://klwee.iga.cas.cn/

36. 中国林业科学研究院湿地研究所：http://www.riw.ac.cn/

37. 中国湿地博物馆：http://www.cnwm.org/index.do

38. 中国湿地生态系统定位研究网络：http://cwern.wetlands.cn/index.html

39. 中国湿地：http://www.wetlands.cn

40. 中国湿地植物：http://www.hydrophyte.net/

41. 中国沼泽湿地数据库：http://www.marsh.csdb.cn/

42. 中华人民共和国濒危物种科学委员会：http://www.cites.org.cn/article/list.php?catid=5